ASPECTS OF IRISH ARISTOCRATIC LIFE

*Essays on the FitzGeralds
and Carton House*

Aspects of Irish Aristocratic Life

*Essays on the FitzGeralds
and Carton House*

edited by
PATRICK COSGROVE, TERENCE DOOLEY
AND KAROL MULLANEY-DIGNAM

UNIVERSITY COLLEGE DUBLIN PRESS

PREAS CHOLÁISTE OLLSCOILE
BHAILE ÁTHA CLIATH

FIRST PUBLISHED 2014
by University College Dublin Press
Newman House
86 St Stephen's Green, Dublin 2, Ireland

www.ucdpress.ie
© the editors and contributors, 2014

ISBN 978 1 906359 71 3

Cataloguing in Publication data available
from the British Library

Designed and typeset in England
by Lyn Davies Design
Printed on acid-free paper in England
by Anthony Rowe

Contents

Preface and Acknowledgements

In recent decades, the social, economic, political and cultural histories of the Irish landlord class have attracted the attention of scholars who now seek to explain their complex and changing position in local, national and international contexts. Class, gender, material culture, consumption, country houses as administrative bases for landed estates and the lives of the people who worked in the 'Big House' and on the demesne are just some of the many topics which have gradually established themselves as areas worthy of scholarly research. Such is the case in this collection of essays which more specifically focuses on aspects of Irish aristocratic life and living as seen through the prism of Ireland's premier noble family, the FitzGeralds – earls of Kildare, 1316; marquesses of Kildare, 1761; and dukes of Leinster, 1766.

The FitzGeralds have a claim to be regarded as, possibly, Ireland's most illustrious family over an extended period of almost 800 years – from their arrival with the first wave of Anglo-Norman settlers in 1169, to the break-up of their great estate and the sale of their aristocratic mansion, Carton House, in the first half of the twentieth century. Their pre-eminent economic, political and social status for much of this period and the aristocratic lifestyles they lived at Maynooth Castle as earls of Kildare and later at Carton House as dukes of Leinster, has meant that the family, or individual members, have featured prominently in survey histories and more specialised histories.[1] There is also an expansive (though by no means complete) historiography of Carton House, its material culture and its surrounding landscape: these having attracted the attention of scholars including E. P. Curran, Desmond FitzGerald, David Griffin, Desmond Guinness, Arnold Horner, Edward McParland, Finola O'Kane and Stella Tillyard, all of whose works are cited by various contributors to this volume.

This collection, which attempts to cover the best part of a millennium, makes no claim to fill all of the remaining gaps or to be all encompassing. Instead, it is more appropriate to consider that individually and collectively the chapters add to the existing body of scholarly literature on the aristocracy in Ireland, as well as providing the general reader with a more specific narrative account of the FitzGeralds' long and illustrious history. It is to be hoped that this volume will stimulate further research into the world of the aristocracy in Ireland and encourage others to advance alternative interpretations into the various aspects of aristocratic life and living presented herein.

The opening chapter is intended to provide a broad survey history of the FitzGeralds in Ireland as a means to contextualise the chapters which follow.

The next four chapters look at aspects of the FitzGeralds' early history in Ireland, documenting their rise to ascendancy; examining certain of the exigencies which they faced between the twelfth and sixteenth centuries and describing their fall from power after the Silken Thomas rebellion of 1534.

While the FitzGeralds did not disappear after the rebellion, they were rendered largely anonymous and politically impotent, and both their influence and presence in Ireland were minimal in the interval between the 11th earl, Gerald (1524–1585), and the 19th earl, Robert (1675–1744), a hiatus perhaps best symbolised in the ruinous state of their great castle at Maynooth by the 1680s.[2] This truncation of the family's history and the associated rupture in their archival collections is acknowledged and reflected in this volume; many of the reasons for the FitzGeralds' re-emergence to political and social prominence at the beginning of the eighteenth century remain to be elucidated.

The re-emergence of the FitzGeralds was symbolised by the building and embellishment of the Palladian mansion at Carton, the redevelopment of the surrounding landscape and the planned construction of Maynooth town. The second part of this book focuses on themes relating to the architecture and landscape design, material culture, consumption, entertainment, politics, aristocratic grandeur and socio-economic decline over the two century period from *circa* the 1730s to the 1940s. The volume concludes with an assessment of the FitzGerald (and, indeed, Mallaghan) legacy at Carton; looking beyond the historical, aristocratic world of the FitzGeralds in order to further the debate about the future sustainability of Irish country houses in the much changed economic climate of the twenty-first century.[3]

As noted above, this volume does not pretend to be exhaustive, but in traversing an impressive 800-year chronology the chapters herein testify to the importance of both the FitzGerald family and their Kildare estates in a national context.

This volume of essays emanates from a conference organised by the Centre for the Study of Historic Irish Houses and Estates at the National University of Ireland (NUI) Maynooth and held at Carton House in September 2010. First and foremost, the editors would like to express their gratitude to Lee and Mary and Conor and Alex Mallaghan for their generous support of the event, and to acknowledge their outstanding contribution to the survival of Carton into the twenty-first century. They would also like to thank all of the contributors who gave freely and generously of their time to present at the conference and those who have since contributed to this volume.

There is a widely held belief that in a recessive economic climate, partnerships play a vital role. For the last number of years the Centre for the Study of Historic Irish Houses and Estates at NUI Maynooth has been engaging with both public bodies and the private sector in Ireland (Fáilte Ireland, the Irish Historic Houses Association, the Irish Georgian Society, the Irish Heritage Trust, the Kildare-Wicklow Tourism Initiative, Kildare Fáilte and the Office of Public

Works) in a bid to create greater awareness of the importance of the built heritage and its potential to tourism as an economic stimulator. The editors would like to thank all of these partners for their ongoing support.

The editors would like to say a very special word of thanks to Hon. Desmond Guinness for agreeing to write the foreword to this volume, and to acknowledge, not only the support which he has given to the CSHIHE since its establishment, but also his monumental contribution over many years to the preservation of Ireland's built heritage.

A number of individuals have given generously of their time and knowledge: the editors thank in particular Maurice FitzGerald, 9th Duke of Leinster and his wife, Fiona, for attending the conference; Colette Jordan who in the years in the run-up to the conference worked extremely hard and successfully to encourage the Leinsters to visit their ancestral home; Professor Patrick Duffy for sharing papers in his private possession; likewise the late Mrs Anne Hamilton; and a special thanks to Catherine Murphy for her patience and diligence in the final edit of the manuscript. Thanks also to Sarah Gearty for the cartography in chapter 2.

Gratitude is due also to Professor Marian Lyons, Head of History Department at NUI Maynooth, for her support and encouragement, and to colleagues within the department who contributed to the conference or who have helped in other ways.

Finally, the editors extend their profound thanks to Noelle Moran and the staff of UCD Press for their professionalism, unfailing courtesy and, at times, great patience in bringing this work to fruition.

NOTES

1   See for example, V. P. Carey, *Surviving the Tudors: The 'Wizard Earl' of Kildare and English Rule in Ireland, 1537–1586* (Dublin, 2002); S. G. Ellis, 'Bastard Feudalism and the Kildare Rebellion, 1534–35: the character of rebel support', in William Nolan and Thomas McGrath (eds), *Kildare: History and Society* (Dublin, 2006), pp, 213–32; Colm Lennon 'The FitzGeralds of Kildare and the building of a dynastic image, 1500–1630', in Nolan and McGrath (eds), *Kildare: History and Society*, pp 195–212; Mary Ann Lyons, *Church and Society in County Kildare* c. *1470–1547* (Dublin, 2000); idem., *Gearóid Óg, the Ninth Earl of Kildare* (Dundalk, 1998); Laurence McCorristine, *The Revolt of Silken Thomas: A Challenger to Henry VIII* (Dublin, 1987).

2   See Terence Dooley's chapter in this volume, 'The FitzGeralds: A survey history, 1169–2013' in which he points out that there was a temporary recovery of fortunes as a result of the marriage of the 16th earl of Kildare to the daughter of Richard Boyle, Earl of Cork.

3   For further discussion see Christopher Ridgway, 'Making and meaning in the country house: new perspectives in England, Ireland and Scotland', in Terence Dooley and Christopher Ridgway (eds), *The Irish Country House: Its Past, Present and Future* (Dublin, 2011), pp 203–43.

Foreword

Hon. Desmond Guinness

When, in 1971, William Ryan and I published *Irish Houses & Castles*, one of the important houses we decided to include was Carton, the ancestral home of the FitzGerald family who had first settled in Maynooth at the end of the twelfth century. There they constructed their great medieval castle and built up huge landed estates in Kildare and elsewhere. For much of the eighteenth and nineteenth centuries, Carton was the only ducal residence in Ireland and displayed all the splendour of the same in its architectural design, interior embellishment and grand eighteenth-century landscape, the latter designed largely by James, 1st Duke of Leinster, and his wife, Emily, who at the tender age of sixteen had an instinctive passion for the informal landscape.

By 1971 Carton and its demesne had become the home of Hon. David and Mrs Nall-Cain. David's father, Lord Brocket, had purchased Carton in the late 1940s. In *Irish Houses & Castles* William Ryan and I reflected on Carton's history as a ducal residence with all the trappings of aristocratic living: its architectural evolution from the handsome Dutch-Palladian facade seen in the painting by Van der Hagen (entitled 'Carton before 1738') to the Palladian remodelling by Richard Castle in 1739 and further remodelling in the early nineteenth century by Richard Morrison. We alluded to the magnificence of the Gold Saloon created by the Lafranchini – probably still Ireland's most important and intact eighteenth-century room – and the significance of the Chinese bedroom largely created by Emily.

When we published our book, the rising costs of maintenance at Carton were becoming burdensome for David Nall-Cain. David had opened the house to the public during weekends in summer to try to meet some of these costs, but this was never going to be enough to keep it sustainable and inevitably he was forced to sell it to Powerscreen Ltd and shortly after it passed into the ownership of one of its directors, Mr Lee Mallaghan and his family.

I have very many fond memories of Carton and the short time I spent there with my first wife, Mariga, who I met at Oxford where we married in 1954. After I had spent about a year after our marriage learning how to farm at Cirencester, we began to look for a farm in Ireland where my parents lived. (They were divorced long-since, my father living in Dublin and my mother in Galway.) When we arrived back to Ireland we made contact with Gerald FitzGerald, then Marquis of Kildare and later 8th Duke of Leinster, who lived at Kilkea Castle, Athy, Co. Kildare. Our family brewery was, of course, in Dublin, and one of the brewers was a friend of Gerald's. Gerald offered me a job as a sort of farm manager, while my wife helped Gerald's wife with the shopping and coping with their small children. During that first year, the Kildares took off for London – the marchioness needed a bowler bun for the hunting season, unobtainable in Ireland – leaving me to cope with the harvest. However, it was a great experience and I learned a lot.

How we came to be at Carton by this time – the late 1950s – was very simply as follows: one evening Mariga and I were asked to supper there by the aforementioned Lord Brocket. Knowing that we were in search of a home, he offered to sell us his ravishing pile but, of course, it was well beyond our financial reach. The forestry and farmland covered a thousand acres surrounded by the demesne wall, here and there punctuated by gate lodges. The park was bisected by the Rye Water and its man-made lake. It was simply Paradise beyond our means.

When we told him we could never afford to buy it, David then offered us a bedroom or two, and the run of the house with a butler, cook and maid and naturally we jumped at the offer with gratitude. Our two children, Patrick and Marina, were born there. One social event sticks in my mind: one day Gerald FitzGerald and his wife invited themselves to lunch at Carton, and the wonderful butler, who I believe had been born there, was in a frenzy of excitement at the thought of the family returning, albeit on a short visit. I shall never forget his reaction when he met the marquis and his wife; it was very moving.

During our long stay at Carton, Mariga and I began getting to know Ireland, and in particular Dublin, where streets of Georgian houses were being torn down and replaced by ugly office blocks. It was at Carton that we decided to establish the Irish Georgian Society (IGS) in 1958, exactly 50 years to the day after the founding of the Georgian Society by Provost Pentland Mahaffy of Trinity College. I retired from the IGS's Board of Directors at the end of 2008, but I am now delighted that my son, Patrick, has taken a place on the Board as its president. It was a hectic 50 years for a dedicated conservationist trying desperately to awaken an interest in Ireland's heritage of Georgian architecture and to encourage the development of its tourism potential. I witnessed many defeats (unfortunately, the politically corrupt reasons for some of these have only recently been exposed in tribunals), a few victories and never a dull moment on which to look back.

One of the IGS's greatest triumphs came with the saving of Castletown, Co. Kildare, which I bought in 1967. It has just about the finest staircase (with its brass banisters) in Ireland, and Lafranchini plaster decoration of the type also found at Carton. Both houses were, of course, linked in the eighteenth century by the fact that the Lennox sisters, Emily at Carton and Louisa at Castletown, were chatelaines of their respective homes. Castletown became the first country house in the province of Leinster to open to the public. The house is now in state care, administered by the Office of Public Works.

Carton has, of course, since become a hotel and its landscape has been developed into two golf courses. Its history has been forced to meet the sustainability issues of the twenty-first century in a different way to Castletown. Over almost 800 years the FitzGeralds met many challenges and Carton will undoubtedly continue to meet its own challenges in the years ahead. However, what is most important is that Carton has survived and one has to take great comfort from this fact, and, indeed, to acknowledge the important role of the Mallaghan family in its survival.

This book is another tribute to the work of the Centre for the Study of Historic Irish Houses and Estates (CSHIHE) at NUI Maynooth. I am delighted to have been associated with the CSHIHE since its establishment in 2004. Over the years I have enjoyed tremendously many of the events organised by NUI Maynooth in the magnificent college chapel and in Pugin's wonderful dining hall, as well as the CSHIHE's annual conferences and its winter lecture series at Castletown. Indeed, I am very pleased to say that I played a part in the CSHIHE's choice of logo. When Terry Dooley approached me and told me that he wanted to use a gateway as a metaphoric symbol for a path to future research on the country house I suggested a design based on the wonderful Syon Gates designed by Robert Adam (which may have inspired the gates of Glananea.) The CSHIHE has certainly opened that path to knowledge and I wish it every success in the future and, of course, with this wonderfully enlightening collection of essays on the FitzGerald family and their lives at Carton.

HON. DESMOND GUINNESS
Leixlip Castle
September 2013

List of Plates

Notes on Contributors

CORMAC BEGADON completed a PhD at NUI Maynooth in 2009 on Catholic religious culture in the archdiocese of Dublin *c.* 1780–1830. His interests include Catholic education, devotional literature, and public devotion

LIAM CHAMBERS is Senior Lecturer and Head of the Department of History at Mary Immaculate College, University of Limerick. His publications on late eighteenth-century Irish history include *Rebellion in Kildare, 1790–1803* (1998). He is currently working on a history of Irish colleges, students and priests in Paris from the sixteenth to twentieth centuries.

PATRICK COSGROVE received his PhD in History from NUI Maynooth where he subsequently held a postdoctoral research fellowship. He has lectured and published on various facets of the Irish land question and is the author of *The Ranch War in Riverstown, Co. Sligo, 1908* (2012) as well as articles in leading academic journals including *Irish Historical Studies* and the *Historical Journal*.

TERENCE DOOLEY is Associate Professor of History and Director of the Centre for the Study of Historic Irish Houses and Landed Estates at NUI Maynooth. He is the author of several books relating to Irish country houses and landed estates including *The decline of the big house in Ireland* (2001) and *'The land for the people': the land question in independent Ireland* (2007).

ALISON FITZGERALD lectures in the Department of History at NUI, Maynooth. Her research interests include Irish design history and material culture, in particular the history of goldsmiths, jewelers and allied traders. Her monograph on silver in Georgian Dublin will be published by Ashgate in 2014.

RAYMOND GILLESPIE teaches in the Department of History, NUI Maynooth. He has written extensively on the local experience in early modern Ireland and is editor of the *Journal of the County Kildare Archaeological Society*.

ELIZABETH HEGGS completed her PhD at NUI Maynooth in 2009. Her thesis focused on the responses of Waterford's liberal Protestants to nineteenth-century politics and political thought. Her publications include an analysis of liberal Catholicism in pre-Famine Ireland.

ARNOLD HORNER has written extensively on the geography of Ireland and on the mapping of Ireland past and present. Several articles on the making of Carton demesne and on its maps were among his early publications during the 1970s. In 1995, he was author of the contribution on Maynooth in the Irish Historic Towns Atlas series published by the Royal Irish Academy. His recent work has included books on the early maps of Offaly, Meath and Sligo. Dr Horner formerly taught geography at University College Dublin.

WILLIAM LAFFAN is co-author of *Thomas Roberts, Landscape and Patronage in Eighteenth Century Ireland.*

COLM LENNON is Professor Emeritus of History at NUI Maynooth. His works include *Sixteenth-century Ireland: the incomplete conquest* (1994 and 2005) and *Dublin, 1610–1756: the making of the early modern city* (2009).

MARY ANN LYONS is Head of the Department of History, NUI Maynooth. Professor Lyons has published extensively on Franco-Irish relations and on Irish migration to continental Europe in the early modern period, as well as on various aspects of Irish history. She is co-author with Dr Thomas O'Connor, Department of History, NUI Maynooth of *Strangers to Citizens: The Irish in Europe, 1600–1800* (2008). A fellow of the Royal Historical Society, Professor Lyons has served as joint editor of *Irish Historical Studies*, general editor of the Maynooth Research Guides for Irish Local History Series, chairperson of the Royal Irish Academy National Committee for Historical Sciences, and conference secretary of the Catholic Historical Society of Ireland.

KAROL MULLANEY-DIGNAM holds a PhD from NUI Maynooth where she has lectured on several aspects of Irish society, culture and heritage. Formerly an Irish Research Council Postdoctoral Fellow, she is the author of *Music and Dancing at Castletown, Co. Kildare, 1759–1821* (2011) as well as articles in academic journals, edited volumes, and the *Encyclopaedia of Music in Ireland* (2013).

THOMAS NELSON completed his PhD at NUI Maynooth on the history of Kildare County Council in 2007. He is a secondary school teacher in Coláiste Chiaráin, Leixlip.

CAROL O'CONNOR completed her PhD thesis at NUI Maynooth in 2008 titled 'The "Kildare women", family life, marriage and politics in the early modern period'. Since then she has held positions in NUI Maynooth and the Kildare Town Heritage Company for the Kildare Library Service. She joined Public Affairs Ireland in 2012, where she is now Head of the Education and Training department.

CIARÁN REILLY is a research fellow at the Centre for the Study of Historic Irish Houses and Estates, Department of History, NUI Maynooth. He is author of *John Plunket Joly and the Great Famine in King's County* (2012) and has also contributed to the *Atlas of the Great Irish Famine* (2012).

CHRISTOPHER RIDGWAY is curator at Castle Howard. He is also Chair of the Yorkshire Country House Partnership, a collaborative research project between the University of York and the country houses of Yorkshire. He is Adjunct Professor attached to the Department of History at the NUI Maynooth. His most recent publications are: *The Irish Country House: Its Past, Present and Future* (2011), co-edited with Terence Dooley, *Castle Howard and Brideshead, Fact, Fiction and In-Between* (2011) and *The Morpeth Roll, Ireland Identified in 1841* (2013).

BRENDAN ROONEY is Curator of Irish Art at the National Gallery of Ireland and co-author of *Thomas Roberts, Landscape and Patronage in Eighteenth Century Ireland*.

CHAPTER 1

The FitzGeralds
A Survey History, 1169–2013

Terence Dooley

'It is not, then, greed for monetary rewards or the "blind craving for gold" that has brought us to these parts, but a gift of lands and cities in perpetuity to us and to our children'.[1] These, allegedly, were the words of Robert FitzStephen as he mused upon the ambitions of the first Anglo-Normans to arrive in Ireland in 1169 – an army of just 30 knights, 60 men-at-arms and 300 archers – at the invitation of Diarmait Mac Murchada, the displaced king of Leinster. Vast estates and urban properties were to be the financial bedrocks upon which the economic, social and political power of his descendants would be built in the generations ahead. Robert's own story has, however, been largely consigned to oblivion for it was his half-brother, Maurice FitzGerald (d. 1176), who became the founding father of the Irish Geraldines. It is with the Kildare branch of the FitzGerald dynasty (earls of Kildare after 1316 and dukes of Leinster after 1766) that this work is concerned.

Maurice FitzGerald was described by his kinsman, Giraldus Cambrensis (1146–1223), the medieval chronicler of the Anglo-Norman invasion of Ireland as: 'a man of dignified aspect and modest bearing, of a ruddy good complexion and good features ... of the middle height, neither tall nor short.'[2] This flattering description of Maurice's dignified disposition may have been used merely to highlight the uncivilised character of the native Irish but as Colm Lennon argues (chapter 5), Cambrensis's strong polemical writings began the process of crafting the place of the FitzGeralds in Irish history from their very arrival. Later chroniclers simply continued the myth-building process, including in the late nineteenth century Charles William FitzGerald (1819–87), Marquis of Kildare and later 4th Duke of Leinster, who, in 1857, published his *The Earls of Kildare and their Ancestors*.[3] Indeed, as various chapters in this book show, the FitzGeralds' use of history became a key component in their ability to survive for as long as they did.

First, though, the FitzGeralds had to build up their power and authority, and this could only be achieved with the acquisition of vast landed estates which brought significant wealth as well as social and political status. Thus, Raymond Gillespie (chapter 2) deals with the creation of the original FitzGerald manor in the late twelfth century when, soon after their arrival, Maurice was granted large tracts of land around Maynooth in County Kildare by the leader of the Anglo-Norman expedition, Richard de Clare, Earl of Pembroke (d. 1176). It was there that the FitzGeralds decided to locate their great castle at the confluence of two streams. The process of acquiring and disposing of estates throughout Leinster and further afield continued for generations depending on the family's economic circumstances and the need for astute alliances.

During the fourteenth and early fifteenth centuries, as the English monarchy was preoccupied with the Hundred Years' War with France (1338–1453) and then the struggle between the rival houses of York and Lancaster (1455–85), the ruling of Ireland increasingly fell to prominent Anglo-Norman families. Mary Ann Lyons (chapter 3) describes how during this time the FitzGeralds became the premier noble family in Ireland by virtue of their political, martial and socio-economic power. They retained a remarkable ability to present themselves as 'Irish' to the Gaelic-Irish – as patrons of Gaelic culture and language they created one of the greatest library collections of its time at Maynooth Castle housing a significant Irish language section – while simultaneously asserting their Englishness to the Anglo-Normans of the Pale.[4] As time passed their astute political and marital alliances meant that it was virtually impossible to suppress them and outsiders could only hope to buy into a share of their power, usually at a price that enhanced the FitzGerald standing. But while the FitzGeralds had judicially balanced their relations with the so-called Old English of Ireland, as well as the Gaelic-Irish and the English royal court, they found themselves increasingly alienated as Tudor policy created a 'new aggressive English colonial elite.'[5]

The Tudor revolution in government, and specifically the centralisation of government in Ireland, threatened the Kildare ascendancy. Insurgency by Silken Thomas (1513–37), the 10th Earl of Kildare, provided the government with the pretext for destroying the power of the FitzGeralds and so, in 1537, King Henry VIII (1491–1547) attempted to wipe out the entire family line by executing the 10th earl and his five uncles at Tyburn. The castle at Maynooth was confiscated, their lands (and those of leading members of the collateral branches of the family) were attainted and their period of ascendancy came to an end. However, the FitzGeralds had spent generations maintaining contacts at the English court, cementing family ties on both sides of the Irish Sea and cultivating relationships on the European continent. As Colm Lennon (chapter 5) points out, the FitzGeralds had been particularly keen, at the height of their ascendancy, to nurture cultural relations with their Italian ancestors, the Gherardini of Florence. After 1537 continental assistance was crucial in the survival of Silken Thomas's half-brother, Gerald FitzGerald (d. 1585), who escaped to mainland Europe after the abortive rebellion.[6]

The FitzGeralds spent more than a century rebuilding their political and social position, eventually re-emerging to prominence in the eighteenth century. As early as 1554, Gerald FitzGerald had been restored as 11th earl of Kildare and he returned to Ireland to operate in a hybrid Gaelic-English world. Carol O'Connor (chapter 4) emphasises the important role of the FitzGerald women in the initial rehabilitation of the family, highlighting that it was not simply the men who were capable of performing public roles. The court connections and marriage alliances of Gerald's sisters, Eleanor and Margaret, along with the 'dignified demeanour' of his mother, Lady Elizabeth Grey (fl. 1497–1548), at the English court, all contributed to the survival of the FitzGeralds in the late Tudor maelstrom (while their Geraldine cousins in Desmond were self-destructing).[7]

Moreover, the FitzGerald defiance of the Tudor regime would stand them in good stead in future generations when they would be eulogised as being typical of those families who became 'more Irish than the Irish themselves'. It mattered little to later nationalist historians that Silken Thomas rose in revolt for a complexity of reasons; these were simplified in nationalist historiography and lore as a rebuttal to English attempts at colonisation.

More immediately, Silken Thomas's rebellion had resulted in large areas of Kildare being laid to waste, so becoming worthless to the king's exchequer; it therefore became an immediate concern of the Crown that attainted lands should be rented quickly to its supporters in order to generate income.[8] The Maynooth estate was initially leased to one of the king's retinue, and thereafter to William Talbot (d. 1633), a Catholic lawyer and politician who was granted a lease in 1603.[9]

By the middle of the sixteenth century, the castle at Maynooth, which for a time was the favourite residence of lord deputies in Ireland, had been restored to the FitzGeralds by Edward VI.[10] While they do not seem to have re-occupied it, leaving it to fall into decay, the family did begin to recover their position by purchasing estates in Kildare; in 1558, for example, they bought lands at Kilgraney for £1,600.[11] However, the succession of two minors in a short period of time temporarily halted their rehabilitation and by the time of the death of the 14th earl in 1612 the castle had become dilapidated. In 1620, the 15th earl died young and was succeeded by his seventeen-year-old cousin, George (1612–60), who was then the last surviving FitzGerald of the Kildare line. It was at this time that the extraordinarily wealthy Earl of Cork, Richard Boyle (1566–1643), an Elizabethan adventurer-colonist who made his fortune from the plantation of Munster, cast his eye on the FitzGeralds in the knowledge that association with the prestige of the family would further his own plans for familial aggrandisement and link him into the older network of the Old English nobility.[12] He, therefore, sought the wardship of George, the 16th Earl of Kildare, which he purchased in 1629 for the impressive sum of £6,600. In the same year, he

21

arranged the marriage of George to his daughter, Joan; the alliance would allow Cork to 'bask in the reflected glory of the distinguished Kildare line'.[13]

Boyle was also determined to restore the castle at Maynooth to its former glory so that it would stand as a legacy to his ambitions.[14] In April 1632, he agreed with the stone-cutter, Edward Tingham of Chapelizod, to 'pull down all the rotten, decayed, disproportioned un-useful old buildings' and 'to rebuild three ranges of the square court in a fair and uniform manner, according to a model and articles now in making, and to re-edify the decayed church'.[15] By 1635, the work was completed at a cost of around £2,000 and an inscription over the main gate gave witness that 'this ancient manor house of Maynooth, being totally ruined and ready to fall, was new built and enlarged by the Right Honourable Richard Boyle.'[16] As Arnold Horner, who contributes two chapters to this volume, has contended elsewhere: 'the spirit of the late Renaissance [was] the dominant element in the earl of Cork's rebuilding.'[17]

It should not be overlooked that, from the FitzGeralds' perspective, the alliance with the earl of Cork had a major advantage: an injection of 'new money' that aided their financial recovery so that the 16th earl could now aspire to something of his ancestors' former status. But optimism was misplaced. There followed the Confederate Wars of the 1640s. By descent George belonged to the Old English, but as a Protestant brought up in the English court, he was more sympathetically disposed towards the New English in Ireland. Maynooth Castle was seized in January 1642 by a group of local rebels led by Lawrence Walsh (possibly a priest) of Moortown. Shortly afterwards, another group, ironically led by other local scions of the FitzGeralds, overran the castle, destroying the great library and plundering the contents. Over the next few years it was variously occupied by Royalists, Confederates and Parliamentarians and eventually, in 1647, it was taken by the Catholic Confederate General Owen Roe O'Neill (d. 1649), who had it dismantled.[18] Thereafter, it was uninhabited and the great thirteenth-century symbol of FitzGerald power fell into dereliction. In 1682 it was reported: 'Maynooth, where is to be seen the remains of an ancient pile, venerable in its ruins, and which did partake of the hottest, and felt the fiercest malice of a revengeful enemy in the last rebellion.'[19] (By the mid-nineteenth century a number of houses and other buildings were erected amidst the ruins. In 1848, these were demolished by the then duke of Leinster and the area of the ruins was enclosed and planted in preparation for the visit of Queen Victoria.)

For three generations after 1660, the earls of Kildare continued the FitzGerald family's renewed rise to prominence by securing a variety of political positions: as governors of King's County, Queen's County and Kildare, and members of parliament. As a commissioner for forfeited estates, the 18th earl was undoubtedly in an advantageous position when it came to rebuilding the family estates in Kildare. The political rise of the 19th earl, Robert FitzGerald (1675–

1744), came with his appointment in September 1714 as one of the lords justice for the government of Ireland. He had originally considered restoring the castle at Maynooth as his residence 'but on examination it was found to be too much dilapidated'.[20] Instead, on 21 January 1739, he decided to purchase the reversionary lease on Carton for £8,000.[21] He and his wife, Mary O'Brien, the eldest daughter of the 3rd earl of Inchiquin, then began the process of remodelling Carton (while living at Kilkea Castle) under the direction of Richard Castle. As one eminent historian has put it, the transformation of the original house into a Palladian mansion 'sounded a fanfare for Kildare's re-entry into politics and high society.'[22]

The political career of James FitzGerald (1722–73), 20th Earl of Kildare, began on 17 October 1741 when (as Lord Offaly) he entered the Irish House of Commons as member for Athy. In 1744, the year he succeeded his father, he moved to the Irish House of Lords as the premier earl in the country. He established a reputation when, in 1745, he offered to raise a regiment at his own expense to protect Protestant Ireland against the Jacobite threat. In 1746 he was appointed to the Privy Council and thereafter his political rise continued via his elevation to the English peerage as Viscount Leinster of Taplow, Buckinghamshire, in 1747 and his appointments as lord justice in 1756; master-general of the ordnance (1758–66); major-general (1761) and lieutenant-general (1770). He became marquis of Kildare in 1761 and duke of Leinster in 1766. Some of his appointments offered handsome sinecures that augmented his rental income. He was also one of the most powerful borough patrons, controlling between 12 and 15 MPs, some of whom were his brothers or other more distant relatives, leading opponents of the duke to describe them as mere sycophants and lickspittles. In 1773, for example, it was said of William Burgh of Athy that he was 'a very distant relation of the duke of Leinster by whom he was brought in ...'; and of Walter Hussey that he was 'brought in by the duke of Leinster as he married a distant relation of his'; while Simon Digby was 'brought in by the duke of Leinster and will do whatever he is bid by His Grace.'[23] But it was through such patronage that James maintained his influence on a variety of levels. As an employer of craftsmen, particularly during the building and embellishment of his town house in the 1740s, he also enjoyed the deferential treatment of the freemen of Dublin.[24] His involvement in the regulation of trade, sitting as a trustee of the Linen Board, mixing with the wealthiest merchants and professionals in Dublin society or the Masonic Lodge (of which he was grand master), and his honorary membership of guilds, added to his socio-political standing.[25]

Overall, James enjoyed significant popularity as the leading patriot politician of his generation. In 1753 he presented a memorial to George II (1683–1760) setting out the grievances of Ireland and protesting against the powers of Archbishop George Stone (1708–64) whom he stigmatised as 'a greedy churchman, investing himself with temporal power, and affecting to be a second Wolsey in the State'.[26] It has been argued that in the money bill crisis of 1756, James (then Lord Kildare) was one of the few individuals who emerged with his reputation enhanced, and that his attempts to acquaint the king with Irish grievances 'earned him great popular acclaim, and did something to restore confidence in the aristocracy as champions of Ireland's interest'.[27] At the same time, his marriage to Emily Lennox (1731–1814), a daughter of the 3rd duke of Richmond, was crucial in providing closer access to the English court.

Contemporaries had varying opinions of James. Horace Walpole (1717–97) claimed that 'he was too weak to compose a letter and too obstinate to submit to any correction' but his brother-in-law, Henry Fox (1705–74), declared that he was 'a man of stout honour'.[28] Other contemporaries believed he wanted to be lord lieutenant to restore the historic position of the FitzGeralds' but that 'he lacked flexibility and his career was littered with acts of principle or pique, which were to dog his relationship with successive viceroys.'[29] Only a much-deserved full biography of James will unlock the truth concerning his ability.

In any case, it was imperative that James's residences reflected his rising political and social status. He and his wife, Emily, finished the embellishment of Carton, reshaped the surrounding landscape and began remodelling the village of Maynooth (as well as building a magnificent town house in Dublin). These developments are discussed by Arnold Horner (chapters 6 and 13) who explains how during this 'age of improvement' – a time of increased prosperity and extended internal peace in Ireland – aristocratic families strove to create surroundings of beauty and charm to reflect and enhance that tranquillity. The Kildares, as landlords with social ambition, also invested heavily in the development of Maynooth, illustrating, as Horner has concluded elsewhere, 'the changes a landlord had the power to exert on a given area when he so wished.'[30] The expansion of Maynooth very much depended upon the willingness of larger and more progressive tenants to invest in property development projects; for them, the incentive was long leases with potential long-term lucrative returns (which did not always transpire).

It has been stated that a country estate and a Dublin town house meant that an aristocratic family such as the FitzGeralds could 'devise a social and domestic economy in which country and town houses were integrated.'[31] The 'Household Book' discussed by Terence Dooley (chapter 8) shows the constant movement of servants and goods between Carton and Kildare (later Leinster) House. He focuses on the difficulties in managing an army of staff in the eighteenth century – but effective management was essential if lavish social events were to be catered for. Karol Mullaney-Dignam (chapter 7) contends that outward displays of pomp and ceremony were essential, if not always affordable, as Carton became a hub of entertainment on the outskirts of Dublin; similarly,

Alison FitzGerald (chapter 9) and William Laffan and Brendan Rooney (chapter 10) show how the FitzGeralds, in ostentatious displays of their growing financial strength, commissioned magnificent silver services and collected fine art objects. Interiors were decorated in accordance with the most fashionable contemporary tastes, best exemplified in the adornment of the Gold Saloon, evoking the grandeur of eighteenth-century aristocratic living, and serving as a reminder that during its building and embellishment Carton was a hive of native and foreign craftsmen (most notably the Lafranchini brothers) as the FitzGeralds invested an estimated £21,000.[32]

Yet, even in the eighteenth century, life at Carton was not without its difficulties. In 1798, Lord Edward FitzGerald (1763–98), the younger brother of William Robert (1749–1804), the 2nd Duke of Leinster, turned revolutionary. The complexities of Protestant aristocratic politics in the pre-Union period and the embarrassment caused to the family by Edward's actions are revealed by Liam Chambers (chapter 12). Nevertheless, when Edward became an iconic nationalist hero, presented as a martyr caught up in a dramatic history, later generations of the family were not averse to use his place in Irish social memory to their advantage.[33] Thomas Nelson (chapter 17), in his study of Lord Frederick FitzGerald (1857–1924), the main trustee of the Carton estate following the deaths of the 5th duke and his wife in the 1890s, captures this in his description of the local government elections of April 1899 when Frederick invoked the iconic status of Lord Edward to successfully raise his profile amongst potentially unsympathetic nationalist voters. His election posters even proclaimed: 'Remember the spirit of Lord Edward and 1798.'

Elizabeth Heggs (chapter 14) echoes the point made by Chambers regarding the 2nd duke in making a case for a much more comprehensive biography of Augustus Frederick (1791–1874), the 3rd Duke of Leinster. As one of the most prominent Whig politicians of his era, and possibly one of the most influential men in nineteenth-century Ireland, Heggs notes his longevity – 'his life straddling a most significant and formative period' – taking in such events and movements as Catholic emancipation, Daniel O'Connell's Repeal movement, the Great Famine, the disestablishment of the Irish Church in 1869, the emergence of the land and Home Rule questions in the early 1870s and the introduction of Gladstone's first land act in 1870. Given the duke's centrality to Irish life and politics throughout this period it is bemusing how he has been airbrushed out of Irish history to such an extent that he features only peripherally in any of the major surveys of the nineteenth century. An examination of why this is the case would be highly illuminating, but in the meantime a good starting point for any future biographer might be the tribute paid to Augustus by the *Freeman's Journal* in the late 1830s: 'few men have done more to reconcile the differences and smooth down the asperities that, unfortunately for the well-being of society, exist in this country, than his Grace.'[34]

When Augustus succeeded to the dukedom in 1804, the focus of Irish politics had shifted to Westminster following the passing of the Act of Union in 1800. A Dublin home which functioned as an entertainment venue and a power arena to plot political manoeuvring was no longer necessary. The aristocracy began to abandon the city for the countryside. The number of peers with Dublin residences dropped from 249 before the Union to 34 by 1821; on a slightly wider scope, of 300 MPs with town houses before 1800, only five remained in 1821.[35] Augustus sold Leinster House in 1815 to the Royal Dublin Society for £10,000, and an annual rent of £600 per annum and settled more or less permanently on his Carton estate. From there, it seems, the FitzGeralds played a significant role in shaping the Irish cultural landscape during the nineteenth century. Karol Mullaney-Dignam (chapter 7) reveals, for example, how music was a prominent feature of domestic life at Carton – not least because the duke and his wife were both accomplished musicians with a particular interest in music education.

As a landlord, Augustus was inclined to grant long leases to large farmers. By the early 1870s, his estate was heavily populated by extensive farmers – 'many men of property and great intelligence' – paying rents from £100 to £500 per annum.[36] The benefit of this was that over time it created an estate community of loyal middle-class (predominantly Catholic) farmers who, along with the merchants in the towns of Maynooth and Athy, maintained social control by extending patronage to the social classes below.[37] The local elite traditionally expressed gratitude for the 'bountiful goodness' of the duke in their coming-of-age addresses, in the knowledge that he controlled various channels of power by reserving access to land for dutiful subjects. By the late nineteenth century, as nationalism came to the fore, one unflattering commentator could not help but compare the duke of Leinster to a Russian oligarch who sat in his stately mansion oblivious of the plight of the wider community.[38] Had he examined the situation more closely, he would have found that few outside the demesne walls at Maynooth were complaining.

The 3rd duke's ability to consolidate holdings into large, productive and viable farms had been facilitated to some extent by the impact of the Great Famine (1845–51) on the estate and his use of assisted emigration schemes.[39] Augustus, like most of his fellow landlords, stringently adhered to the prevailing economic philosophies of the time. Ciarán Reilly (chapter 15) questions whether he could have used his private finances to more effect in alleviating suffering on his estate, pointing to the fact that it is difficult to reconcile hardship in the Maynooth area with the lavish celebrations for the arrival of Queen Victoria in 1849. Reilly's chapter, however, is more concerned with another interesting aspect of the Famine: the changing relationship between landlord and middleman tenant.

The last years of Augustus's life were shrouded in a cloud of controversy which had its roots in the introduction of the 1870 Land Act. After decades of relative prosperity and stability on the Leinster estate, Gladstone's attempt to solve the Irish land question brought Augustus into conflict with some of his tenants (primarily in south Kildare, distant from his core estate at Maynooth) when he introduced the so-called 'Leinster lease' which aimed to contract them out of compensation for improvements in the event of their eviction. While Charles William FitzGerald, the 4th duke, persisted with issuing leases, he managed to calm the waters temporarily, until a more serious economic downturn occurred in the late 1870s. Now, the strong farmers and the town traders saw their increased gains threatened; they had no desire to relinquish a generation or so of prosperity, and with a newfound, socio-political confidence they were less apprehensive about confronting an aristocratic landlord such as Leinster – provided they could present a united front. To strengthen this front, they made overtures to the smallholders and labourers who provided the critical mass. In contrast to more impoverished estates in the west of Ireland, the crisis that occurred on the Leinster estate was not so much about survival as about maintaining social status.

The estate also differed to any other in one vital respect: St Patrick's College, the national seminary of the Roman Catholic Church, was located at the opposite end of Maynooth's main street from the main avenue to Carton. Established on FitzGerald land in 1795, St Patrick's College was not only one of Leinster's largest tenants, it was also the very symbol of Catholic Church authority in Ireland. Cormac Begadon (chapter 11) describes how a century before, during equally troubled times, the 2nd duke of Leinster was astute enough to realise that support for the establishment of the national seminary was likely to serve his interests. The dukes who followed were equally astute in continuing close relations – until, that is, the era of the Land War.

By the early 1880s, the face of Irish politics and society had changed radically. The confrontation which occurred on the Leinster estate between Charles William FitzGerald and St Patrick's College over a farm at Laraghbryan symbolised the wider power struggle between landlords and the Catholic Church for control of the people.[40] Although the 4th duke of Leinster asserted his authority by evicting the college from the farm, the college trustees hailed the part played by the Church as a moral victory. In the meantime, the Land War had spread on the estate and relations between the duke, his agent and his tenants were tense, particularly in the Athy and Castledermot areas. The tenants demanded reductions of 25 to 30 per cent on rents; the duke offered reductions of 20 per cent. In the end agreement was reached, with 25 per cent reduction granted to yearly tenants under £50 annual rent, and 15 per cent to those with holdings of 50–100 acres. Leaseholders received some reductions in accordance with the circumstances of each case.[41]

By the time the 1881 Land Act was passed, the loose alliance which had

previously existed between large farmers, smallholders and the labouring class had been broken – the large holders having secured the rent reductions they desired through the fair rent fixing courts adjudicated by the newly-formed Irish Land Commission. (Notably, Gladstone had communicated his ideas to the duke on the proposed legislation.[42]) After 1882, agrarian agitation on the estate never again threatened stability but, from the duke's perspective, the fixing of fair rents had a significant economic impact: an inability to raise capital on the collateral strength of his estates. His agent, Charles Hamilton, wrote to him describing the difficulties that depreciated rental income was creating, and alerting the duke to how difficult it was 'to find money just at present'.[43] When 25 per cent of the estate was sold under the terms of the 1885 Land Act, the bulk of the money went to paying-off family charges and other encumbrances. This sale also coincided with the arrival at Carton of Hermione Duncombe (1864–95), the new bride of Gerald (1851–93), Marquis of Kildare and afterwards 5th Duke of Leinster.

When, in the 1890s, the 5th duke and his wife both died prematurely, the estate passed into trusteeship, their three orphaned children going on to live individually tragic lives.[44] In 1903, under the terms of the Wyndham Land Act, the trustees took the decision to sell what remained of the Leinster estate with the exception of Carton House and its demesne and Kilkea Castle and some of its surrounding lands. The negotiations and outcomes surrounding the sale are described by Patrick Cosgrove (chapter 16). Given the generous sum received, the family might very well have prospered long into the future, but the coincidence of family tragedies and external forces (including the First World War and the ensuing worldwide economic depression), meant that was not to be. Terence Dooley (chapter 18) illustrates how personal tragedy had as much impact on the Leinster estate as any outside forces and examines the events which led to Edward (1892–1976), 7th duke of Leinster, losing control of Carton and its remaining lands to an English financier, Henry Mallaby-Deeley (1863–1937).

In 1948 Mallaby-Deeley's descendants decided to sell Carton – but the asking price was too much for the FitzGerald family. Denis FitzGerald (1911–2003) informed his agent that 'sad though this is I feel that there would not be the remotest chance of [Lord] Kildare [son of the 7th duke] or his successors being able to afford to live at Carton what with taxation and the crippling death duties.'[45] Consequently, Carton was sold to Lord Brocket, an English brewer, for £80,000.[46] He farmed the demesne until the 1970s (using the produce to supply his Irish hotels) until another economic recession and increased taxation forced him, in 1977, to sell to Powerscreen International Ltd, an engineering and manufacturing company set up eleven years previously in Northern Ireland by Lee Mallaghan and a number of partners. Brocket later regretted that 'we had to leave Carton because we could not find those thousands [to maintain the buildings and the parkland], while paying the new taxes.'[47] As for the FitzGeralds, they retained Kilkea Castle on 73 acres of land until 1960 when the 8th Duke of Leinster, Gerald FitzGerald (1914–2004), then Marquis of Kildare, sold it and moved to Oxfordshire where the 9th Duke, Maurice (1948–), continues to reside.[48] Kilkea, the last FitzGerald residence in Ireland, later became a hotel.

Some years after Powerscreen acquired Carton, Lee Mallaghan bought out his partners' share. Christopher Ridgway (chapter 19) brings the story of Carton House, and its surrounding landscape, up to the present day describing its trans-formation into a hotel and leisure complex with two championship golf courses. Ridgway contends that the future sustainability of individual Irish country houses is dependent upon the willingness and need to consider different options for their survival. The evolution of Carton initially attracted negative attention, most particularly from those who adopt what Vincent Comerford has identified as 'a morally charged, uncompromising notion of preservation, or restoration to a supposed pristine state.'[49] One of the most vocal critics of 'ill-considered conversions [of country houses] into spa hotels and golf resorts' has been writer and journalist, Robert O'Byrne.[50] In a book review in the *Irish Times* in 2011, O'Byrne clearly had houses such as Carton in mind when he claimed: 'This is why contentions that an Irish country house has somehow been "saved" when converted into a hotel or golf club are so specious: one might just as easily propose a tree has survived even though all its branches are lopped off.'[51] But this is to lose sight of the fact that a great house such as Carton has long been denuded of the vast estate which sustained it. And while there are, indeed, a few houses such as Ballyfin and Castle Hyde which have been saved through an injection of vast personal resources, alternative options have to be sought in order to sustain other houses. There are times when pragmatism and a com-monsense approach must prevail – sometimes being too dogmatic in terms of restoration and conservation can be just as detrimental as apathy and neglect.[52]

Indeed, the success of the work at Carton has been generally accepted. In 2007 the much-respected conservation architect, James Howley, who, in his own words, had 'long been a strong opponent' of the proposed remodeling of Carton, admitted to a change of attitude in the *Irish Arts Review*. Having set out on his visit to the restored Carton 'with great trepidation', he found himself pleasantly surprised and impressed by the 'sensitive and subtle' nature of the conservation work and praised the fact that: 'Internally there is a very high pro-portion of well-preserved historic fabric that for the most part has been care-fully and sensitively repaired.'[53] Moreover, as Arnold Horner contends in chapter 6, the development of two golf courses, far from being detrimental, has actually done much to restore the eighteenth-century vistas.

Had the Mallaghans not purchased when they did the demesne might have been acquired by a less sympathetic developer, with the ambition to build hundreds of semi-detached houses in the growing university and satellite town of Maynooth. Certainly, in the 1980s, the State and local authorities were not interested in acquiring Carton. In 1986 Bernard Durkan, TD for Kildare, proposed to George Redmond, then assistant Dublin city and county manager, that Kildare and Dublin County Councils should embark on a joint collaborative venture to acquire Carton as a national park. Redmond communicated the proposal to Ray Burke, then chairman of Dublin County Council, whose answer was unambiguous:

> ... the council has expended very considerable sums in recent years in the acquisition and development of regional parks and at the present time it has provided at various localities throughout the county, a total of 2,000 acres ... and 4,500 acres of smaller parks and open spaces. We have no proposal to extend this programme and indeed the cost of development and maintenance of the existing parks is placing an extremely heavy strain on the council's revenues ... It is regrettable I can see no prospect in the present financial climate or in the foreseeable future of the council being in a position to join in a venture of the kind suggested by you.[54]

Just over 20 years later, on 15 October 2008, a decade after the redevelopment of Carton, the former Taoiseach, Dr Garret FitzGerald, at an An Taisce *Heritage in Trust* corporate breakfast, reflected on the general difficulties which had faced his Fine Gael government regarding the protection of the built heritage in the 1980s, and he then referred specifically to Carton and the Mallaghan family:

> I tried in government in the mid-1970s to persuade my colleagues to offer a generous scheme to owners of great houses to restore and maintain them. There is no better way to preserve this part of our built heritage than to draw on and support the extraordinary commitment of the hereditary owners of such houses, or in some cases people who have taken over a commitment to such a dwelling out of a sense of public duty, to save them for future generations. The economic situation in the 1970s and 1980s made this impossible, but some progress has since been made in this direction ... I should have loved to have been able in the 1980s to save the Kildare FitzGeralds' great house at Carton, but this was simply not possible then. I am greatly relieved that this has since been skilfully and sensitively undertaken by a wonderfully committed entrepreneur and his family who has done a better job than the state could ever have done with all the constraints under which it is required to operate.[55]

For those who believe that the historic buildings should be enjoyed by as many as possible, rather than being the preserve of the few, it is notable that at least 250,000 people per annum now visit Carton. The refashioning of Carton has thrown it a lifeline denied far too many other country houses and, moreover, and equally important in the economic climate of the early twenty-first century, it has helped the local tourist economy. Carton offers huge potential as a visitor attraction and if it continues to look to and work with the local community, its public value will be greatly magnified.[56] What Elizabeth Bowen wrote in 1941 when commenting on the challenges facing Irish country houses at that time, might just as easily encapsulate Carton today as it repositions itself in a democratic age: 'The good in the new can add to, not destroy, the good in the old.'[57]

NOTES

1   Quoted in Art Cosgrove (ed.), *A New History of Ireland: Volume II Medieval Ireland 1169–1534* (Oxford, 1993), p. 45.

2   Thomas Wright (ed.), *The Historical Works of Giraldus Cambrensis* (London and New York, 1892), p. 246; Sean Duffy, *Ireland in the Middle Ages* (Dublin, 1997), p. 63.

3   Charles William FitzGerald's *The Earls of Kildare and their Ancestors From 1057 to 1773* was first printed for private circulation in Dublin in 1857 and published in a number of editions thereafter.

4   S. G. Ellis, *Ireland in the Age of the Tudors 1447–1603: English Expression and the End of Gaelic Rule* (London, 1998), p. 106; Colm Lennon, 'The FitzGeralds of Kildare and the building of a dynastic image, 1500–1630', in William Nolan and Thomas McGrath (eds), *Kildare: History and Society* (Dublin, 2006), p. 197.

5   V. P. Carey, 'Collaborator and survivor: Gerald the Eleventh Earl of Kildare and Tudor Ireland', in *History Ireland*, ii:2 (Summer 1994), p. 14.

6   See for example, Vincent Carey, *Surviving the Tudors: The 'Wizard Earl' of Kildare and English Rule in Ireland, 1537–1586* (Dublin, 2002); Steven Ellis, 'Tudor policy and the Kildare ascendancy in the lordship of Ireland, 1496–1534', in *Irish Historical Studies*, xx:79, (1977), pp 235–71; Lennon, 'The FitzGeralds of Kildare'; Mary Ann Lyons, 'Sidelights on the Kildare ascendancy: a survey of Geraldine involvement in the Church, *c.* 1470–*c.* 1520', in *Archivium Hibernicum*, 48 (1994), pp 73–87; idem., 'Revolt and reaction: the Geraldine Rebellion and monastic confiscation in Co Kildare 1535–1540', in *Journal of the County Kildare Archaeological Society* (hereafter *JCKAS*), xviii (1992–3), pp 39–60; Laurence McCorristine, *The Revolt of Silken Thomas: A Challenger to Henry VIII* (Dublin, 1987).

7   Lennon, 'The FitzGeralds of Kildare', pp 205–6.

8   Mary Ann Lyons, 'Revolt and reaction', p. 39.

9   Walter FitzGerald, 'Carton' in *JCKAS*, iv (1903–5), p. 4.

10   Mary Cullen, *Maynooth: A Short Historical Guide* (Maynooth, 1979), p. 25.

11   Document titled 'Manors etc How Acquired', n.d., Public Records of Northern Ireland (herafter PRONI), Leinster Papers, D3078/2/15/23.

12   Raymond Gillespie, *Seventeenth Century Ireland: Making Ireland Modern* (Dublin, 2006), p. 14; Lennon, 'The FitzGeralds of Kildare', p. 207.

13   Ibid.

14   A. B. Grosart (ed.), *The Lismore Papers* (1st series, 5 vols, London, 1886), iv, 45.

15   Ibid., p. 135.

16   Cullen, *Maynooth*, p. 27.

17   Arnold Horner, 'Carton, Co Kildare: a case study of the making of an Irish demesne', in *Quarterly Bulletin of the Irish Georgian Society* (hereafter *QBIGS*), xviii (1975), p. 2.

18   Cullen, *Maynooth*, p. 28.

19   Quoted in ibid., p. 28.

20   FitzGerald, 'Carton', p. 12.

21   Ibid.; Arnold Horner, 'Land transactions and the making of Carton demesne', in *JCKAS*, xv:4 (1974–5), p. 391

22   Toby Barnard, *Making the Grand Figure: Lives and Possessions in Ireland, 1641–1770* (New Haven and London, 2004), p. 69.

23   Pádraig Ó Snodaigh, 'Notes on the politics of Kildare at the End of the eighteenth century', in *JCKAS*, xvii:3 (1981–2), p. 265.

24   Jacqueline Hill, *From Patriots to Unionists: Dublin Civic Politics and Irish Protestant Patriotism, 1660–1840* (Oxford, 1997), p. 132.

25   Ibid., p. 292.

26   Quoted in 'Introduction', *The Irish Georgian Society Records of Eighteenth-Century Domestic Architecture and Decoration in Ireland*, (4 vols, Shannon, 1969 ed.), vol. iv, 48.

27   Hill, *From Patriots to Unionists*, p. 118.

28   Edith Mary Johnson, *Ireland in the Nineteenth Century* (Dublin, 1974), p. 117.

29   Eoin Magennis, 'FitzGerald, James, First Duke of Leinster (1722–1773)', *Oxford Dictionary of National Biography* (hereafter *ODNB*), online edn (http://www.oxforddnb.com/view/article/9565) (accessed 11 Sept. 2011); E. M. Johnson considered him as being 'amongst the politicians who had dominated the reign of George II'; see Johnson, *Ireland in the Nineteenth Century*, p. 129). For more on his popularity see 'Introduction', *The Irish Georgian Society Records*, vol. iv p. 48.

30   Horner, 'Carton, Co Kildare', p. 88.

31   Toby Barnard, 'Mrs Conolly and Castletown 1720–1752' in Nolan and McGrath (eds), *Kildare*, p. 342.

32   FitzGerald, 'Carton', p. 14.

33   See also: Thomas Moore, *The Memoirs of Lord Edward FitzGerald*, ed. Martin Mac Dermott (London, 1897); Stella Tillyard, *Citizen Lord: Edward FitzGerald, 1763–1798* (London, 1997); Liam Chambers, 'FitzGerald, Lord Edward (1763–1798)', *ODNB*, online edn (www.oxforddnb.com/view/article/9546) (accessed 11 Sept. 2011).

34   *Freeman's Journal*, 18 Dec. 1839.

35   Hill, *From Patriots to Unionists*, p. 292.

36   'F. S.' quoted in *The Times*, 9 Dec. 1872.

37   For a study of power, privilege and deference on an Irish estate see Kevin McKenna, 'Power, Resistance, and Ritual: Landlord-Tenant Relations on the Clonbrock Estate 1849–1917' (Unpublished Ph.D. thesis, NUI Maynooth, 2011).

38   *Freeman's Journal*, 20 Mar. 1899. This reference was actually aimed at Lord Frederick FitzGerald (1857–1924), the chief trustee of the Leinster estate on behalf of the 6th Duke, Maurice, who was then still a minor.

39   Finlay Dun, *Landlords and Tenants in Ireland* (London, 1881), p. 21; Karel Kiely, 'Poverty and famine in County Kildare 1820 to 1850', in Nolan and McGrath (eds), *Kildare*, pp 503, 523.

40   *Report of her Majesty's Commissioners of Inquiry into the Working of the Landlord and Tenant (Ireland) Act, 1870 and the Acts Amending the Same*, (Bessborough Commission) (C 2779), HC1881, vol, xviii.

41   Dun, *Landlords and Tenants in Ireland*, p. 23.

42   J. L. Hammond, *Gladstone and the Irish Nation* (London, 1938), p. 189.

43   Charles Hamilton to Leinster, n.d. (*c*.1882) (MS in private possession).

44   Terence Dooley, *The Decline and Fall of the Dukes of Leinster, 1872–1948* (Dublin, forthcoming 2014).

45   Denis FitzGerald to Charles Hamilton, 28 Nov. 1948 (MS in private possession).

46   Michael Estorick, *Heirs and Graces: The Claim to the Dukedom of Leinster* (London, 1981), p. 18.

47   David Nall-Cain to Patrick Duffy, 22 Apr. 1992 (MS in private possession).

48   F. R. Allen to Charles Hamilton, 22 Nov. 1948 (MS in private possession).

49   R. V. Comerford, 'Foreword', in Terence Dooley and Christopher Ridgway (eds), *The Irish Country House: Its Past, Present and Future* (Dublin, 2011), p. 12.

50   Quoted in Robert O'Byrne, *The Last Knight: A Tribute to Desmond FitzGerald, 29th Knight of Glin* (Dublin, 2013), p. 88.

51   Robert O'Byrne, 'Not just glorified villas', *Irish Times*, 16 July 2011.

52   For a brief but erudite discussion on related matters, see R. V. Comerford, 'Foreword' in Dooley and Ridgway (eds), *The Irish Country House*, pp 11–13; also Allen Warren, 'The twilight of the ascendancy and the Big House: a view from the twenty-first century', in ibid., pp 244–56.

53   For the more general decline of Irish country houses, see Terence Dooley, *The Decline of the Big House in Ireland* (Dublin, 2001); idem., 'National patrimony and political perceptions of the Irish Country House in post-Independence Ireland', in Terence Dooley (ed.), *Ireland's Polemical Past: Views of Irish History in Honour of R. V. Comerford* (Dublin, 2010), pp 192–212.; Olwen Purdue, *The Big House in the North of Ireland: Land, Power and Social Elites 1870–1960* (Dublin, 2009).

54   George Redmond to Bernard Durkan, TD, 17 Nov. 1986 (in private possession).

55   Text of speech available at: http://www.antaisce.org/News/AnTaisceRelatedNewsReleases/tabid/1024/articleType/ArticleView/articleId/7/Speech–Given–by–Former–Taoiseach–Dr–Garret–FitzGerald–at–An–Taisce–The–National–Trust–for–Irelands–Heritage–in–Trust–Corporate–Breakfast–15102008.aspx (accessed 18 Jan. 2012).

56   Susan Kellett of Enniscoe, chairperson of the Irish Historic Houses Association, very wisely observed in 2011 that houses have 'to interact with the local community if they want to make a change'; *Irish Times*, 3 Jan. 2011.

57   Elizabeth Bowen, 'The big house' [1941], in Hermione Lee (ed.), *The Mulberry Tree: Writings of Elizabeth Bowen* (London, 1986), p. 30.

CHAPTER 2

The FitzGeralds and the Making
of the Manor of Maynooth

Raymond Gillespie

Such is the iconic status of Carton House and its associated landscape that it requires a considerable effort of the imagination to summon up a picture of that world before the construction of Carton's landscape of pleasure in the middle of the eighteenth century. Yet this dramatic remodelling of the land was only the most recent of a long series of reshapings of the landscape around Maynooth which the FitzGerald family had directed. The earliest connection of the family with the area can be traced in Giraldus Cambrensis's account of the Anglo-Norman settlement of Leinster in the twelfth century. According to Cambrensis, Strongbow, who had been given Leinster by King Henry II (1133–89), granted to the de Hereford family the cantred of the Uí Faéláin territory 'nearest Dublin' while 'he summoned Maurice [FitzGerald] himself back from Wales to Ireland and gave him, to be held under the grant, the middle cantred of Uí Faéláin, which he had formerly held under the king's gift, and with it the castle of Wicklow'.[1] The de Hereford grant comprised the area around Leixlip and also the area to the west of the FitzGerald lands, in the modern barony of Ikethy and Oughtreany.[2] The FitzGerald grant of the lands of Omolrou, Rathmore, Maynooth, Laraghbryan, Tadoe and Trachstrapli was duly confirmed to Maurice's son, Gerald, by Lord John (1166–1216) between 1185 and 1189 as part of a wider scheme to establish effective royal authority over Ireland.[3] At this stage, to judge from the older names used in the grants and the fact that the grant made no mention of manors – the main way in which such a territory was later organised – the FitzGeralds appear to have done little to reshape their lands. Their most notable contribution was probably the construction of an earthwork castle at Maynooth on the site of the present stone castle.[4]

For the early FitzGeralds this territory was of considerable significance. Most importantly it had been a border area before the Anglo-Norman settlement. From the east, Viking influence at Leixlip may have penetrated westwards as far as Maynooth since the boundary of the diocese of Dublin extended this far west. To the north, as Geoffrey Keating noted in the seventeenth century (though drawing on much older evidence), the river known as the Rye Water marked the boundary not only of the Uí Faéláin lordship but also the division between Meath and Leinster.[5] Again, in the saga *Ruis na Rig*, preserved in the eleventh-century *Book of Leinster*, the Ulstermen pushed the defeated Leinstermen as far south as the boundary of the Rye Water marking the edge of Leinster.[6] As such the valley of the Rye was contested territory and had many of the characteristics of a medieval frontier.[7] For instance, it was frequently raided and the high density of churches around Maynooth – including Laraghbryan, Taghadoe, Donaghmore and also the burials at Moneycooly which appear to mark another church site – was also a feature of a frontier world.[8] Over the next 500 years the FitzGeralds, in various ways, reorganised the territory that became the manor of Maynooth. It is the aim of this essay to reconstruct the outlines of this organisation at a number of well-documented points in its history so revealing something of the changing priorities of the family.

The first hundred years of the FitzGeralds' holding of the manor of Maynooth are poorly documented. The death in 1286 of the third Maurice FitzGerald without male heir, saw the family estates divided between his daughters and it was only gradually that the lands were reassembled by the 1st Earl of Kildare, John FitzGerald (d. 1316). He acquired Maynooth from his aunt between 1288 and 1293, and at this point he may have begun remodelling his inheritance.[9] At least part of the manor of Maynooth comes into even clearer focus on the death of John's son, Thomas, in 1328. Since provision had to be made for his widow, this necessitated the compilation of an 'extent' or assessment of the manor of Maynooth and lists of tenants.[10] From this something of the structure of the manor can be examined. The extent clearly shows that the lands, as with most manors, were divided into two types: the lord's demesne and the lands set to tenants. It is clear the demesne landscape was well-settled by the early fourteenth century with a mixture of English names (some with 'field' as a suffix) and Irish names (which are not now traceable), designating particular parts of the lands. At the core lay the Kildare castle complex, which by the early fourteenth century comprised not only the stone castle but a hall and kitchen, a bake house, a barn, cow byre, stable and gardens.[11]

Defining the demesne lands that lie around the castle is difficult. Later surveys, such as that of 1541, make the task easier since they omit the demesne lands and hence the property not listed on these extents probably comprised the demesne. There are still difficulties in equating land units in the later surveys with modern townlands. The definition of the eastern end of the demesne poses particular problems as the creation of the designed landscape in the eighteenth century with Carton at its centre significantly changed the townland boundaries in this area.[12] However, it is possible to hazard a reconstruction of the area of the demesne. Not all the demesne was worked directly as

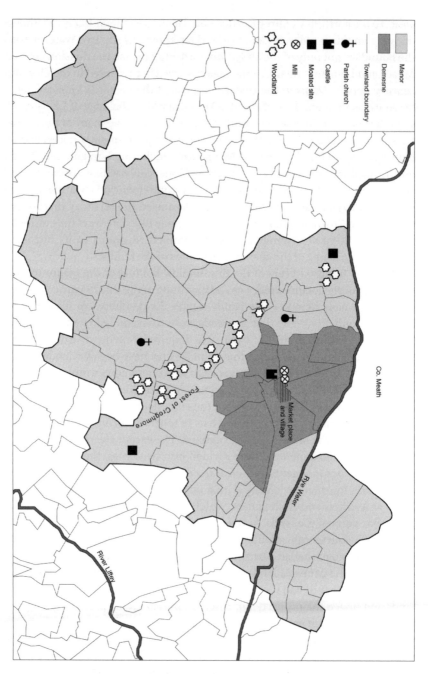

MAP 1 *The Manor of Maynooth in c.1300. Based mainly on Georoid Mac Niocaill (ed.), 'The Red Book of the Earls of Kildare' (Dublin, 1964) pp 119–21, 134 with archeological evidence.*

agricultural land. Parts of it were developed as a village, while a deer park occupied a substantial proportion. However, a very extensive area does seem to have been worked as a home farm. On the evidence of the extents this was divided into three parts of roughly equal size: 90, 97 and 117 acres respectively. It is very tempting to equate these three divisions of the property with the three agricultural divisions on the demesne. In 1328 it was suggested that 72 acres of the demesne was under corn, 66 acres under oats and 63 acres was waste.[13] This is certainly a strong indicator that at least part of the demesne lands was under grain – grown as part of a three-fold crop rotation system in open fields – as may also have been the case in other parts of the Pale. How this land was worked is unclear. None of the fourteenth- or fifteenth-century extents mentions labour services, suggesting that hired labour was used instead. However, the survey of 1540 (discussed below), does record labour services. It is extremely unlikely that these obligations were imposed during a time of falling population in the fifteenth century, and so they may have been present earlier but remained unrecorded for reasons unknown. Much of this grain was most likely processed into flour at the manorial mills recorded in the extent.

Within the manor, the Kildares created the church and the village of Maynooth, all firmly under the lord's control. The church was already well-established in the area. In Glendalough charters dated 1172–6 and 1179, Larghbryan and Tadoe are listed as part of the property of the monastery of Glendalough.[14] The Kildares took that established monastic structure and transformed it. In the late 1240s Maurice FitzGerald had granted the church of Taghadoe to the Augustinian canons of All Hallows near Dublin.[15] In 1248 the archbishop of Dublin, at Maurice FitzGerald's request, constituted Laraghbryan as a prebend of St Patrick's Cathedral in Dublin – although FitzGerald retained the right to present the priest to the living.[16] The original, single-cell church was extended eastwards by about 10 metres (probably after 1248), to reflect its new status as a prebendal church of St Patrick's. Indeed, there are some architectural parallels between the two buildings.[17] By the 1240s, therefore, a territorial parochial system had been established in the Maynooth area to replace an older system whereby individual churches had been associated with a large monastic community. That this creation of territorial parishes was the work of the FitzGeralds is suggested by the fact that the parish boundaries, as they were recorded in the seventeenth-century Civil Survey, are almost identical to the manorial boundaries – a common feature of Anglo-Norman settlements. It seems certain that the FitzGeralds were using the parish as a way of demonstrating family authority. This is suggested by their retention of the right of nomination to the prebend of Maynooth, a right that it was alleged earned the 5th earl a period of imprisonment in 1408 when he refused to cede it to the crown.[18]

The second significant structure on the FitzGerald manor was the village of Maynooth. This had certainly been established by the family by 1311, when a

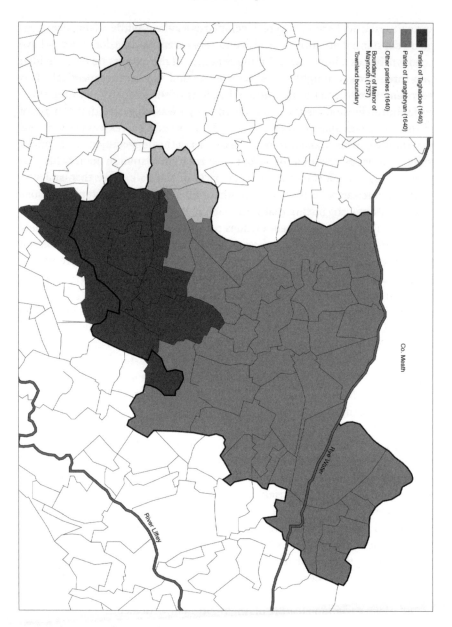

MAP 2 *The Manor of Maynooth and its parishes. The parishes boundaries c.1640 are from R. C. Simington (ed.), 'The Civil Survey: VIII County of Kildare' (Dublin, 1952). The manorial boundary is from John Rocque, A survey of Carton and the manor of Maynooth … 1757' scale 16 Irish perches to an inch. in Department of Geography, NUI, Maynooth.*

market-place at the town was mentioned in a legal action.[19] Grants of the right to hold a market and fair in the village were made in 1286.[20] What this early town looked like is not clear. Archaeological evidence suggests that the village was located roughly on the site of the present one – beside the castle – possibly surrounded by a ditch.[21] What the extents provide is some indication of the range of trades that might be found there, including those most typical of agricultural settlement: smiths, carpenters, tailors and a cobbler. However, a merchant and a 'crossbow man' also appear which suggests production of goods for sale. What is also apparent is that the tenants in the town were from a wide social range; their surnames suggesting they came from both English and Irish backgrounds. At the bottom of the social scale, the cottiers usually paid a rent of only 12d – which points to the fact that their only holding was a house in the town – and it is among this section of the list that most of the surnames associated with trades appear. Twenty farmers paid rents from 36s 3d to 6d suggesting many people lived both in town (for some have trades attached to their names) and on larger holdings in the demesne. Finally, the 'betaghs', who all had native Irish names, could be surprisingly well-off, paying rents from 32s 2d to 1s though none is charged with labour services as would be expected with this group. One holding occupied by them is described as 'the great meadow', and may possibly have been held in common by the betaghs as part of the open field arrangement in the demesne.

Outside the demesne the evidence for the appearance of the landscape is much patchier, and the extents of 1328–9 say little about what it looked like. There was still a substantial wooded area in the manor in the 1290s – named in the 1328 extent, the Forest of Croghmore. The tenants had the right to take houseboot and heyboot (the right to take wood for house building and other farm uses) from this woodland as part of their holdings, forming an important energy source in a world in which turf was scarce.[22] While the Civil Survey of the 1650s recorded shrubby woodland across the manor, good timber was noted in relatively few areas (mainly across the middle of the estate, from Griffinrath in the east to Crinstown in the west), and this may well represent the remains of the Forest of Croghmore.[23] Within this landscape there is very little evidence of secular building to compare with the solid evidence from the churches. Part of a cobbled area with thirteenth-century finds has been located at Crinstown, but its original purpose is uncertain; while on the western edge of the manor there is a possible moated site at Maws, which may have been the residence of a substantial tenant.[24] The social structure associated with this settlement is equally uncertain. The land of the manor described in the extents was divided between a number of different types of tenant, including free tenants and farmers. Since the size or location of their holdings is not given, it is difficult to discern much about the world outside the demesne.

The next point at which the manor of Maynooth comes clearly into view is from a group of documents made in the 1450s. The fate of the FitzGeralds after the death of the 5th earl, Gerald FitzGerald, in 1432, is obscure. The succession of Thomas Fitzmaurice, 7th earl, only took place in the 1450s, with his claim to the property probably not being recognised until 1454. Of Thomas's background nothing is known, but it is possible that he spent his minority under the care of James FitzGerald, 7th Earl of Desmond. Such conjecture is supported by a number of pieces of circumstantial evidence. First, he was married (albeit in an irregular way) to Desmond's daughter, Joan Cam, in the 1450s.[25] Secondly, James was a patron of Irish poets and scribes, as his father Gerald (Gearóid Iarla) had been, and was responsible for an Irish manuscript known as the *Book of the White Earl* which survives in a fragmentary form in the Bodleian Library.[26] If Thomas was raised as part of this learned circle it may well explain why there were a number of Irish-language manuscripts in the family library at Maynooth Castle *circa* 1500. One of these manuscripts was a copy of the Munster manuscript, the *Psalter of Cashel*. Those in Desmond's scribal circle claimed to have seen this manuscript and copied from it although it is not mentioned directly in the *Book of the White Earl* proper.[27]

During the vacancy in the Kildare title it was not the earl of Desmond who tried to annex the Kildare lands but Kildare's old enemy, Thomas Butler, the Earl of Ormond.[28] Under Ormond's managerial eye, the Kildare estates were better documented and a number of documents survive describing the Maynooth area. Most importantly, an extent of 1451 and fragments of court rolls and accounts, together reveal a great deal about the world of the manor and its tenants.[29] The most substantial group of buildings on the manor, as reflected in these documents, was the village of Maynooth. The extent for Maynooth included lands and buildings that were not in the village itself but, allowing for this, it seems that the number of tenants in the village was about 50 – or about the same as it had been in the early fourteenth century. At a period when urban life in the Pale was contracting due to the declining population and pressure from the native Irish, this is an indication of vitality in the urban element of manorial life at Maynooth. Moreover, the large number of pleas for debt in the few surviving records of the manor court, suggest that a vigorous exchange economy had taken root. That the region as a whole may have been prospering while other areas were contracting, is borne out by other evidence. In 1483 a grant of an extra market day to be held in the town implies increasing trade.[30] Money was spent on architectural improvement: the ground floor of the castle was radically altered in the early fifteenth century, and the church at Laraghbryan was significantly improved with the insertion of a rood loft.[31] However, this situation was unstable – the village population was very fluid – between the extent of 1451 and the 'Kildare Rental' in 1518–19 there was little continuity of surnames – pointing to a highly mobile society in which land was readily available and people in short supply.[32]

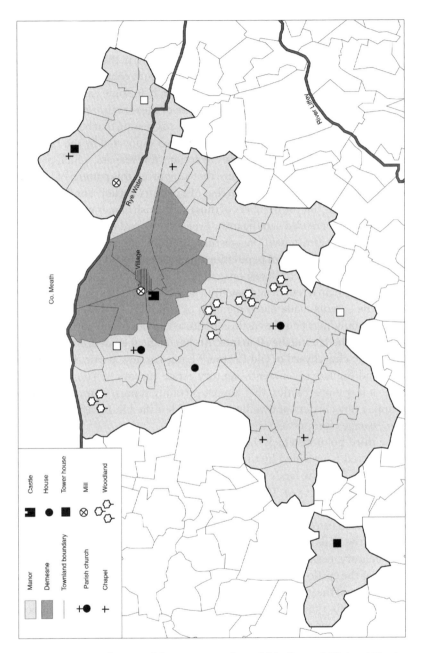

Legend:

Castle · House · Tower house · Mill · Woodland

Manor · Demesne · Townland boundary · Parish church · Chapel

MAP 3 *The Manor of Maynooth in c.1450. Based on British Library, Additional Charter 62, 253; Paul Dryburgh and Brendan Smith, 'Handbook and Select Calendar of sources for medieval Ireland in the National Archives of the United Kingdom' (Dublin, 2005), pp 23–41, 263–5 and archaeological evidence.*

Whereas the extents of the 1320s had only described the demesne, that of 1451 shows a greater concern with the lands outside it. For example, a mill was recorded at Old Carton that did not previously appear in the extents and which remained working until at least the early seventeenth century. The land of the manor was recorded as parcelled into units which, in some cases, were recognisably modern townland units. At least some of these maintained stable acreages in surveys into the seventeenth century – suggesting that boundaries were well-defined and were remembered. This is also supported by the fact that at the manor court there were a number of actions for trespass, which presumes clear boundaries. The social structure that supported this pattern of landownership had changed somewhat from that of a century earlier. The 'betaghs' as a class disappeared, but the numbers of those with Irish names within the manor as a whole had increased significantly. Free tenants had mostly been replaced with the simpler term 'tenant', suggesting a simplification of the tenurial structure (possibly in the wake of population changes as a result of the Black Death (as in England) or possibly a response to the Irish revival). Each townland had at least one principal tenant and usually a number of smaller tenants. However, none of the extents made much mention of buildings on these lands. Clearly the church buildings and the castle constituted an important part of the building stock on the late medieval manor. Archaeological evidence adds a towerhouse in the churchyard of Old Carton.[33] Later surveys, particularly the Civil Survey and the late seventeenth-century estate surveys of Thomas Emerson include a few more 'castles' that almost certainly represent tower-houses. In addition, a few clusters of dwellings can be identified in Laraghbryan, where four messuages (properties) were described.

The third point at which the structure of the manor of Maynooth can be reconstructed is provided by the survey of the FitzGerald family lands *circa* 1540, that is, after the lands were confiscated following the abortive rebellion of Silken Thomas in 1534. This evidence can be supplemented with a rental of Kildare lands dating from 1518–19.[34] Many of the features that have already been described can be readily identified: the demesne (specified at 320 acres), the castle, the mills and the village. There had been changes since the mid-fifteenth century, notably the construction of a chantry chapel, probably in the grounds of the castle, founded in 1515 and the building of the Council House, which reflected the growing role of the Kildares in national politics.[35] However, the value of this 1540 survey is that it allows us to peer inside the units that made up the manor and glimpse something of how they worked. In most cases the survey specified the land use of individual townlands, confirming the impression of earlier evidence that this was a landscape heavily dominated by arable farming. In the extents of the early fourteenth century some 87 per cent of the agricultural demesne was given over to tillage, a high figure in the context of the Dublin hinterland.[36] This is hardly surprising given the proximity of

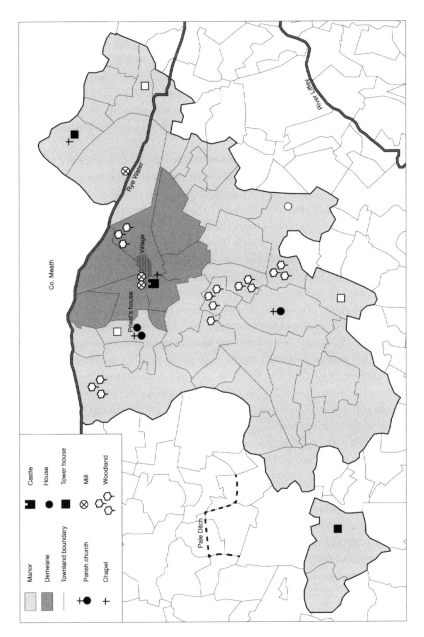

MAP 4 *The Manor of Maynooth in c.1540. Based on Gearóid Mac Niocall (ed.), 'Crown Surveys of Lands, 1540–1' (Dublin, 1992), pp 132–42, 279–84; R. C. Simington, 'The Civil Survey: VIII County of Kildare' (Dublin, 1952) and archaeological evidence. For further details on the Pale ditch see Seamus Cullen, 'The Pale in the Donadea area', in Oughterany, no. 1 (1993), pp 9–22.*

the manor to the city of Dublin, the inhabitants of which required feeding from the countryside around them. The royal manor of Esker, to the east of Maynooth, certainly seems to have sent substantial quantities of grain into Dublin in the early sixteenth century; and Dublin-glazed pottery found in Maynooth Castle demonstrates trade between the manor and Dublin.[37] In the case of Maynooth, the presence of two mills in the survey and possibly a third at Old Carton, hints though that increasing amounts may have been processed into flour for local consumption.

Despite this apparent dominance of arable husbandry there are clues that the survey may conceal other activities. In most cases the townland acreages given in the survey tally roughly with those given in the Civil Survey of the 1650s and Thomas Emerson's surveys in the late seventeenth century. However, in a number of townlands, especially those on the edges of the manor, the areas given in the survey are much lower than in later accounts. In the case of Barrogstown (or Ballybarry) the survey gives 123 acres and the Civil Survey has 126 acres, yet Emerson gives it as 206 acres. Again, Smithstown and Johnstown are given as 106 acres in the survey, 100 acres in the Kildare Rental but 238 acres by Emerson.[38] In almost all cases where there are significant differences between the sixteenth-century survey and Emerson's account this can be explained by the enclosure of common land, as at Moneycoole and Toolestown. It seems that many townlands on the edge of the manor may have had a significant commonage attached to them, sometimes in adjoining County Meath, on which cattle were raised.[39] This common pasturage was not recorded in the 1540 survey, but its use would suggest a larger cattle-raising element on the margins of the manor than may appear at first glance.

The settlement pattern that underpins this economic structure is only hinted at in the survey. Significant clusters of houses were rare – only Laraghbryan and Taghadoe could muster eight and nine cottages respectively, and given their status as church sites of some antiquity they inevitably attracted settlement. Most townlands (with the exception of Maws) could manage only three or four cottages with the average being about three. Such scattered settlement does not suggest the sort of co-operative effort required in working open field agriculture, and the indications of the survey were that land was parcelled out to one or more landholders in each townland.

The portrait of the manor of Maynooth in the 1540 survey represents the apogee of the medieval landscape. Thereafter, significant changes began to take place in the way in which the manor was organised. The attainder of the Fitz-Geralds in the wake of Silken Thomas's rebellion meant that the estates passed out of the hands of the family and, while the lands were restored in 1552, new interim managers brought new ideas. By the time of the survey of 1540, the demesne had been leased out and the labour services that had been drawn on to work it had been commuted into cash. Customary tenures were gradually replaced by leases that regulated the relationship of landlord and tenant. The departure of the FitzGerald family after the wars of the 1640s saw yet further changes. By the late seventeenth century the demesne was in the process of being broken up and new townlands, usually with English names such as Rail Park, were created as a result. It was the eastern end of that new landscape that was, in turn, reshaped to create the pleasure ground around Carton in the 1750s and which marked the return of the Kildare family to Maynooth (albeit on a new site) as one demesne replaced another. The evolution of the landscape of Maynooth before the middle of the eighteenth century is, therefore, a complex story that requires a leap of the imagination to visualise Carton before Carton. It is a reminder that the engagement of the Kildares with their landscape was a dynamic process, one that mirrored the history of the family itself.

NOTES

1   Giraldus Cambrensis, *Expugnatio Hibernica*, ed. A. B. Scott and F. X. Martin (Dublin, 1978), pp 142–3.

2   Paul MacCotter, *Medieval Ireland: Territorial, Political and Economic Divisions* (Dublin, 2008), pp 174–6.

3   Gearóid Mac Niocaill (ed.), *The Red Book of the Earls of Kildare* (Dublin, 1964), no. 1; W. L. Warren, 'John in Ireland, 1185' in John Bossy and Peter Jupp (eds), *Essays Presented to Michael Roberts* (Belfast, 1976), pp 11–23.

4   *Excavations 1999*, p. 132.

5   Geoffrey Keating, *Foras feasa ar Éirinn*, ed. David Comyn and P. S. Dinneen (4 vols, London, 1902–14), vol. i, p. 115.

6   *Cath Ruis na Ríg for Boinn* (Dublin, 1892), pp 54–5, 104–5.

7   Pádraig Ó Riain, 'Boundary Association in early Irish society', in *Studia Celtica*, vii (1972), pp 12–29.

8   For details of battles see John O'Donovan (ed.), *Annala Ríoghachta Éireann: Annals of the Kingdom of Ireland by the Four Masters* (7 vols, Dublin, 1851), s.a. 776; Seán Mac Airt and Gearóid Mac Niocaill (eds), *The Annals of Ulster (to AD 1131)* (Dublin, 1983), s.a. 781. For Moneycooley see, *Excavations 2004*, pp 203–4. The date of the medieval church in Old Carton may be much older than the existing late medieval structure.

9   Mac Niocaill (ed.), *The Red Book*, nos 69–73, 88.

10   Ibid., nos 119–21, 134,

11   Ibid., no. 120.

12   Detailed in Arnold Horner, 'Carton, Co. Kildare: a case study in the making of an Irish demesne', in *QBIGS*, xviii (1975), pp 45–104; idem, 'Land transactions and the making of Carton demesne', in *JCKAS*, xv: 4 (1974–5), pp 387–96.

13   Mac Niocaill (ed.), *The Red Book*, nos 119, 120.

14   Edited in Ailbhe Mac Shamhráin, *Church and Polity in Pre-Norman Ireland: The Case of Glendalough* (Maynooth, 1996), pp 198, 238–9. For a possible earlier affiliation of Laraghbryan see, Thomas Charles Edwards, 'Erlam: The patron saint of an Irish church', in Alan Thacker and Richard Sharpe (eds), *Local Saints and Local Churches in the Early Medieval West* (Oxford, 2002), pp 282–4.

15   Richard Butler (ed.), *Registrum prioratus Omnium Sanctorum* (Dublin, 1845), pp 16–17; Charles McNeill (ed.), *Calendar of Archbishop Alen's register* (Dublin, 1950), p. 68.

16   McNeill (ed.), *Calendar of Archbishop Alen's register*, p. 71.

17   Michael O'Neill, 'The medieval parish churches of Kildare' in William Nolan and Thomas McGrath (eds), *Kildare: History and Society* (Dublin, 2006), pp 169–71.

18   Charles William FitzGerald, *The Earls of Kildare and Their Ancestors* (Dublin, 1857), pp 34–5.

19   James Mills (ed.), *Calendar of the Justiciary Rolls, or Proceedings in the Court of the Justiciar of Ireland ... 1308–14* (Dublin, 1914), p. 218.

20   *Calendar of Documents Relating to Ireland, 1285–92* (London, 1879), pp 109.

21   *Excavations 2003*, p. 250.

22   *Rotulorum Patentium et Clausorum Cancellariae Hiberniae Calendarium* (Dublin, 1828), nos 41, 55.

23   R. C. Simington (ed.), *The Civil Survey, A. D. 1654–56*, viii: *County of Kildare*, Irish Manuscripts Commission (hereafter IMC), (Dublin, 1952), p. 7.

24   *Excavations 1967*, p. 18; Margaret Murphy and Michael Potterton, *The Dublin Region in the Middle Ages* (Dublin, 2010), p. 206.

25   *Calendar of Entries in the Papal Registers Relating to Great Britain and Ireland: papal letters, 1455–64* (London, 1921), pp 262–3.

26   'Book of the White Earl', Bodleian Library, Oxford, MS Laud. Misc. 610.

27   Gearóid MacNiocaill (ed.), *Crown Surveys of Lands, 1540–41, with the Kildare Rental Begun in 1518*, IMC (Dublin, 1992), p 356.

28   Edmund Curtis, *Calendar of Ormond Deeds* (6 vols, Dublin, 1932–43), iii, pp 83–5.

29   British Library, Additional Charter 62,253; Paul Dryburgh and Brendan Smith, *Handbook and Select Calendar of Sources for Medieval Ireland in the National Archives of the United Kingdom* (Dublin, 2005), pp 238–41, 263–5; The National Archives, London, SP 46/183, ff 43, 237 SC6/1238/17–20.

30   *Calendar of the Carew Manuscripts preserved in the archiepiscopal library at Lambeth 1515–74* (London, 1867–73), p. 321.

31   *Excavations 1999*, p. 132; O'Neill, 'Medieval parish churches', pp 179–80.

32   Mac Niocaill (ed.), *Crown Surveys of Lands*, pp 280–3.

33   *Excavations 2000*, p. 167. There may have been some associated settlement evidenced by pottery scatters, see *Excavations 1996*, p. 53.

34   Mac Niocaill (ed.), *Crown Surveys of Lands*, pp 132–42, 279–84.

35   Walter FitzGerald, 'Carton' in *JCKAS*, iv (1903–5), pp 23–4.

36   Murphy and Potterton, *The Dublin Region*, p. 288.

37   Raymond Gillespie, 'Small worlds: settlement and society in the royal manors of sixteenth-century Dublin', in Howard Clarke, Jacinta Prunty and Mark Hennessy (eds), *Surveying Ireland's Past* (Dublin, 2004), pp 204–5; Murphy and Potterton, *The Dublin Region*, p. 454.

38   Arnold Horner, 'Thomas Emerson's Kildare estate surveys 1647–97', in *JCKAS*, xviii (1994–9), pp 412, 418.

39   Simington, *The Civil Survey*, p. 7. Commonage rights clearly fluctuated over time as new areas were colonised by local groups as is clear in an early seventeenth-century case involving Carton; see FitzGerald, 'Carton', p. 33.

CHAPTER 3

The Kildare Ascendancy

Mary Ann Lyons

The period from *c*.1478 to 1534, when the 8th and 9th earls of Kildare exercised unrivalled political authority in the lordship of Ireland and ranked among the wealthiest landed magnates in the entire Tudor realm, was undoubtedly the most illustrious chapter in the FitzGerald dynasty's history. This essay traces their steady ascent to this position of exceptional wealth and influence, and explores the circumstances that precipitated their dramatic demise and that of their residence at Maynooth in 1534–5.[1]

Thomas FitzGerald (d. 1478), father of Gerald (1456–1513), also known as Gearóid Mór or The Great Earl, is credited with laying the foundations for his dynasty's remarkable ascendancy. In 1454, when the fortunes of the English in Ireland were at their lowest ebb, Thomas succeeded as 7th earl and set about salvaging his ancestral inheritance which had become so wasted during the earldom's abeyance (since 1432) its value barely exceeded £250 a year. In addition to serving as governor of Ireland for over 11 years between the 1450s and 1470s, Thomas made significant progress in re-establishing his dynasty's effective control over the western frontier of the English Pale and recovered several former FitzGerald holdings, notably the manor of Rathangan in west Kildare. By the late 1400s thanks to his efforts and those of his successor Gerald, the Kildares had forced neighbouring clans to retreat from south Kildare and Carlow.[2]

After succeeding his father in 1478, Gerald continued to augment the familial estates in Kildare, Dublin and beyond, whilst emerging as the most powerful figure in the lordship of Ireland. However, his ascent was punctuated with a succession of serious challenges, particularly during the early years of his career, which coincided with serious political instability and intrigue that marked the closing phase of the English War of the Roses (c. 1455–87). The Kildares' track record as staunch Yorkist supporters, which had greatly enhanced Gerald's career prospects during the reigns of Edward IV (1461–83) and Richard III (1483–85), would later compromise his political position.

When Gerald, aged 22, became 8th earl of Kildare, he was elected by the

Irish Council to serve as deputy-governor of Ireland. However, King Edward IV considered Gerald too young and inexperienced to hold such a senior post on a permanent basis; Gerald thought otherwise. When Edward replaced him with an outsider, Lord Grey, Gerald and his allies in the Dublin administration successfully obstructed Grey's efforts to govern. Both men asserted their right as deputy-governors, each presiding over rival parliaments. In the end, Gerald was re-appointed as deputy-governor in 1479. In the immediate aftermath of this débâcle, relations between Edward IV and the earl stabilised, and Gerald devoted his energies to providing impartial government – which he hoped would justify Edward's confidence in him. For the remainder of Edward's reign, Gerald gained considerable wealth and political influence both in English and Gaelic parts of the country. Having been confirmed as deputy-governor by Richard III in July 1483, he exercised unprecedented control over the Irish Council, even appointing his brother, Thomas, as chancellor in defiance of the king's wishes.

By 1485, however, a new danger to his position emerged with England under threat of invasion by the pretender to the throne, Henry Tudor. Fearing that if Henry became king, his Yorkist associations would militate against his re-appointment as deputy-governor, the earl had parliament pass an Act in June 1485 which effectively ensured his election in the event of Henry succeeding to the throne. With Henry's accession in August 1485, the mutual mistrust between Kildare and the new king was evident – the earl hesitating to recognise Henry as the legitimate monarch.

Less than two years into Henry's reign, in the summer of 1487, Kildare and his brother, Thomas, colluded in a plot to secure the Crown for an apparent Yorkist claimant who was, in fact, Lambert Simnel (the son of an Oxford joiner impersonating Edward, Earl of Warwick). Furthermore, Kildare supported the subsequent Yorkist invasion of England, supplying 4,000 Gaelic foot soldiers under Thomas's command. However, at the battle of Stoke in June 1487 Thomas was killed and Henry Tudor emerged victorious. Kildare's short lieutenancy came to an abrupt end. The following month he took an oath of allegiance to Henry VII and was pardoned by the king. In the years that immediately followed, Kildare remained aloof in his dealings with the king, even refusing to answer a summons to court in 1490. When in November 1491 a second Yorkist pretender arrived in Cork and won widespread support in Munster, Kildare remained suspiciously inactive as deputy-governor. Henry's response was to dismiss both Kildare and several of his supporters from office. As Henry consolidated his hold on the English Crown, Gerald FitzGerald's prospects for regaining his political influence seemed bleak.

It soon became apparent, however, that Kildare's influence on the island far outweighed that of his two successors – Archbishop Walter Fitzsimons and Sir James Butler, Earl of Ormond who jointly held the governorship of Ireland in

1492–3. The situation deteriorated when the king's efforts to cultivate Sir James Ormond as a counterweight to Kildare sparked the outbreak of another round in the longstanding Butler–FitzGerald feud, and gave rise to serious unrest in the Pale. By mid-1494 the king had effectively defused these tensions, and when in September 1494 Henry VII appointed a new deputy-governor, Sir Edward Poynings, Kildare was co-operative with the new appointment, assisting Poynings in negotiating settlements with Gaelic chiefs. However, Poynings soon accused the earl of inciting the Irish to oppose him. Consequently, Kildare was arrested in February 1495 and charged with plotting Poynings's assassination and other treasonous activities. Having been attainted by the Irish Parliament he was dispatched to England, but within days of his arrest Gerald's kinsmen set about demonstrating to Henry that without the earl's cooperation, Poynings could not govern Ireland. Indeed, in Kildare's absence, Poynings found it difficult even to maintain the status quo and in late December he was recalled and sailed for England.

Once again Henry VII faced the problem of how best to govern Ireland, and what to do with the earl of Kildare whom he still detained at court. Notwithstanding his reservations, Henry acknowledged that Kildare was the only magnate capable of providing the cheapest, most effective government of Ireland, and that he was invaluable in any attempt to reduce Gaelic Ireland to the Crown's authority. He therefore resolved to re-appoint Kildare as deputy-governor. As a sign of favour, Henry permitted Kildare to marry his first cousin, Elizabeth St John, in 1496 (the earl's first wife, Alison, having recently died). At the same time Gerald entered into an agreement with Henry which ensured that throughout the rest of his time in office, the Crown's interests would be assiduously protected. Gerald also managed to remain on reasonably peaceable terms with his old rival, Earl Thomas of Ormond. The English Pale was relatively peaceful and prosperous during this period, and effective royal government was extended more firmly and continuously over a wider area of the island than it had been for almost a century. As a guarantee of his good behaviour, the earl's young son and heir, Gerald, the future 9th earl, was sent to the English court where he was brought up. Following his return to Ireland in autumn 1496, Kildare campaigned extensively throughout Ireland, leading progresses to Carrickfergus (1503), Galway (1504) and Limerick (1510); indeed, Henry acknowledged his resounding victory at the battle of Knockdoe, County Galway, by investing the earl with the special military honour of Knight of the Garter in 1505.

Following his accession to the throne in 1509, Henry VIII appointed Gerald deputy-governor and later governor, and the two men appear to have had a mutually beneficial relationship. The earl continued to conduct campaigns aimed at asserting his authority over Gaelic lords right up until the time of his death – it was whilst engaged in a routine campaign against the Gaelic O'Carroll of Offaly in August 1513 that he was shot by one of the O'More clan of Leix as he watered his horse in the River Greece at Kilkea in south Kildare. Severely debilitated by his injuries he was moved in slow stages, via Athy, to Kildare town where, after lingering for a few days, he died on 3 September in his fifty-seventh year. His body was brought to Dublin and honourably interred in Christ Church cathedral, in his own chapel on the north-side of the high altar.

The 8th earl had 14 children (eight boys and six girls, all of whom survived him) from his two marriages – both of which had significantly augmented his estates in Ireland and England. At the time of his death in 1513, Kildare was Ireland's richest magnate – his annual estate income amounting to approximately £1,800 – with large holdings in Counties Kildare, Meath, Carlow and east Ulster and his seat being Maynooth Castle.

Throughout his career Gerald FitzGerald's readiness to use his unrivalled strategic position at the nexus between the English Pale and Gaelic lordships, together with his readiness to use his allies and tenants for military service in defending the Pale, provided the Crown with a cheap and effective form of provincial government. His success as governor can be attributed to his unique capacity to reconcile the divergent interests of successive English monarchs, the Englishry and the Gaelic Irish. Whilst serving as the king's leading representative in Ireland, he built up cross-border alliances with Gaelic chiefs, many of which were copper-fastened by marriage alliances. He exercised unrivalled influence over his Gaelic contemporaries (from whom he extracted protection money) and was adept in manipulating his dual roles as the king's governor and as a leading nobleman to his own private advantage, careful to portray all campaigns that he undertook at his own expense against the Gaelic Irish as being in the king's name and interest. As such he greatly increased his dynasty's wealth, landed estates and political influence.[3]

Some contemporaries hostile to Gerald dismissed him for his lack of knowledge and learning, and for his unsophisticated upbringing. The earl does appear to have been more accustomed to the outdoors, preferring hawking and horse-riding to reading. Yet, he was a man of civility: his home at Maynooth was lavishly furnished; he had a library; he spoke English; his relationship with the Gaelic Irish intimates that he was proficient in the Gaelic language; and he was at the very least capable of signing his initials.

Certain sixteenth-century commentators, such as the Dublin chronicler, Richard Stanihurst, were favourably disposed towards Gerald. Stanihurst described him as 'open and plain', stating that 'notwithstanding his simplicity in peace', Gerald was a man of great 'valour and policy in war'. He portrayed Gerald as 'a mighty man of stature full of honour and courage' whose name 'bred a greater terror to the Irish than other men's armies'. He was 'of the English well beloved; a good Justiciar, a suppressor of the rebels, a warrior incomparable; towards the nobles that he fancied not, somewhat headlong and unruly'.[4] The account of Gerald featured in the Gaelic *Annals of the Four Masters* identifies similar traits, describing the earl as being 'a knight in valour, and princely and religious in his words and judgements'.[5] The demise of 'the unique Foreigner who was the best and was of most power and fame and estimation ... and was of best right and rule and gave most of his own substance to the men of Ireland' was lamented in the Gaelic *Annals of Ulster*.[6]

Gerald, the 9th earl (1487–1534) (Plate 1: Portrait of Gerald FitzGerald, *c*.1530), having been raised at the English court between the ages of eight and 16, was well-spoken, witty and, unlike his father, scholarly. He received a decidedly English education, gaining exposure to the classics and to the new vernacular Renaissance literature. He also acquired a valuable insight into the operation of court politics and diplomacy that was to stand him in good stead in later years. Most important of all, his sojourn at court brought him into direct personal contact with leading courtiers and officials of Henry VII, and with young men who later became members of Henry VIII's government. Throughout his life, Kildare maintained contact with many of these courtiers – sending them gifts as tokens of their continued friendship.

By 1503 the time had come for Gerald, aged 16, to return home. Soon after his marriage to Elizabeth Zouche, the young couple departed for Ireland accompanied by his father (the 8th earl) who was returning from a brief visit to court. Anxious to involve his son in government immediately, in February 1504 the earl secured Gerald's appointment as treasurer in the Dublin administration. Following his father's death in September 1513, Gerald became 9th earl of Kildare and was elected deputy-governor by the Irish Council. Two months later he was elevated to the position of lord deputy by Henry VIII, who invested him with the same powers he had granted the 8th earl three years previously.[7]

Aged 26 when he succeeded his father, Gerald was a handsome, cultured young man of refined taste. Stanihurst regarded him as 'nothing inferior to his father in martial prowess', 'a wise and prudent man in war, valiant without rashness, and politic without treachery; ... a suppressor of rebels, ... [who] heaped no small revenue to the crown; enriched the king's treasure; guarded with security the Pale; continued the honour of his house, and purchased envy unto his person'. The chronicler also remarked Gerald's 'great hospitality', which was, Stanihurst claimed, unequalled by any of his contemporaries.[8] The new earl had a reputation as a prominent patron of Gaelic learning. A devout Christian, he always had priests in his retinue whilst on campaigns and was a generous benefactor to both secular and religious clergy. Furthermore, he was widely recognised as 'the greatest improver of his lands in this land',[9] and his assiduous stewardship of his ancestral estates and finances is evidenced by his decision in 1518 to compile the 'Kildare Rental' which records details of contracts, terms of leases, tributes, duties, fees, and other matters pertaining to his properties.[10]

From the time he succeeded as earl down to 1519, Gerald was left to govern in a manner similar to his father – Henry VIII maintaining an attentive but largely aloof involvement in the administration of his lordship in Ireland. However, the first serious murmurings of discontent concerning Kildare's governance came in 1515 when William Darcy, acting as spokesman for a group within the Dublin administration, presented Henry VIII with a list of complaints regarding the earl's alleged abuse of his position as lord deputy. Fortunately for Gerald, on this occasion these criticisms were met with an indifferent response from the king. It was also in 1515 that rumblings of what was to develop into a major feud between the Kildare and Ormond (Butler) dynasties first sounded, in a quarrel over the latter's dynastic inheritance. The intense animosity that this stirred between the two noblemen persisted throughout the 1520s and early 1530s, while Ormond's senior position in the Irish Council and his influence both in Ireland and at the English court seriously undermined Kildare's political authority.

The 9th earl's political fortunes took a turn in 1519 when Henry VIII suddenly developed a lively interest in the governance of Ireland and summoned Kildare to court to discuss recent complaints he had received from disgruntled Palesmen. Gerald's answers clearly did not satisfy Henry – he was summarily dismissed and replaced with an English nobleman, Thomas Howard, Earl of Surrey (later created Duke of Norfolk). Although detained in England by order of the king, Gerald's sojourn was fortuitous: while at court that he met and married his second wife, Lady Elizabeth Grey, daughter of Thomas, Marquis of Dorset, his first wife having died in 1517.

During his absence from Ireland, Kildare engaged in behind-the-scenes plotting with his Gaelic allies to ensure that Surrey's attempt to govern Ireland without his support would fail. So exasperated was Surrey by Henry's failure to provide him with the resources he needed to carry out his grandiose plans for subjugating Gaelic Ireland, he wrote to the king requesting that Kildare be sent back to Ireland. To Kildare's great relief, Surrey was recalled in September 1521. Nevertheless, Henry refused to consider reinstating Gerald to the vacant position of lord deputy of Ireland, and, in a provocative move, appointed Gerald's rival (and brother-in-law), Sir Piers Roe Butler to the position in 1522. However, Piers found it impossible to defend the English Pale from his base in Kilkenny, and soon he too requested that Kildare be permitted to return to Ireland to provide the necessary defence. Henry succumbed, and on New Year's Day 1523, having been detained in England for almost three and a half years, Gerald returned to Ireland, accompanied by his new wife, Elizabeth. He had been instructed to pacify his own county of Kildare and to cooperate with Ormond. However, from the outset Kildare showed himself unwilling to work with his brother-in-law who held the office to which Kildare felt entitled. Soon the two were again locked in conflict, Kildare behaving as though he were lord deputy. Throughout 1523–4 the feud grew more intense. Eventually, in May

1524, Henry dismissed Ormond from the deputyship and reinstated Kildare. In July of the same year, the two earls signed a peace agreement.

The following month Kildare took up duty as lord deputy, but soon discovered that his position was coming under increasing scrutiny from London. Furthermore, by September cracks in the accord between the two earls were becoming apparent: throughout 1525 and early 1526 both engaged in mutual defamation. By August 1526 Henry, exasperated by their quarrelling, summoned them to court. Although Piers Roe proved amenable and was allowed return to Ireland in 1528, Kildare was truculent under interrogation by Henry's secretary, Cardinal Thomas Wolsey, and was therefore detained for another three and a half years (until 1530). Throughout this period Kildare repeatedly pointed to the extremely disturbed state of the lordship of Ireland, presenting it as conclusive proof of his dynasty's unique capacity to govern Ireland in the king's name. But in July 1528 Henry discovered that Kildare had sent a letter to his daughter, Lady Slane, in Ireland, urging that his nephew, Con Bacach O'Neill and his son-in-law, O'Connor, should invade the Pale. Henry had Kildare imprisoned in London and re-appointed a reluctant Piers Roe Butler as lord deputy. Kildare's connivance failed to secure his reinstatement. Released on bail, he took up residence at the duke of Norfolk's home at Newington in Middlesex.

Meanwhile, in Ireland Butler's administration had once again fallen into serious trouble. Having tried unsuccessfully to govern the country with a 'Secret Council' in 1529, Henry VIII resolved to send his former master of the ordnance, Sir William Skeffington, as lord deputy. In response to pressure from Kildare's influential in-laws, the Greys, as well as from the earl of Wiltshire, Thomas Boleyn, and the duke of Norfolk, Henry decided to allow Gerald to return home under strict instruction that he cooperate with Skeffington. On 24 August 1530 Kildare, in the company of Skeffington, landed in Ireland. For almost a year the two worked well while engaged on separate campaigns to suppress opposition in the lordship. However, by early summer 1531 relations again turned sour as Kildare showed himself incapable of sharing power and, to complicate the situation, the FitzGerald-Butler feud re-erupted. Having railed against his subordination to Butler in the early 1520s, Kildare now refused to suffer the indignity of being second to Skeffington, a commoner.

Skeffington's position as lord deputy became increasingly redundant as Kildare mobilised support within the Irish Council, while simultaneously securing the backing of his two influential court allies: Norfolk and Wiltshire. By April 1532 Skeffington's deputyship was doomed, and in response to a series of complaints about his administrative malpractice, Henry dismissed him. Concluding that the lordship could be governed more economically and effectively by Kildare, he was re-appointed as lord deputy on 5 July 1532 for what was to be the last time.[11]

In 1533, therefore, the Kildare dynasty was once again at the helm of Ireland's political life and Maynooth Castle was the locus of political power. As Ray-mond Gillespie's essay in this volume shows, significant additions were made to the castle precincts during Gerald's lifetime – notably a chantry chapel and the Council House, reflecting the family's standing as Ireland's premier politi-cal dynasty at the apex of their power. The earl enjoyed an annual income of well in excess of £2,000 Irish – ranking his dynasty among the top ten of Tudor nobility. His household and lifestyle clearly reflected that status. The Geral-dine castles at Maynooth, Kilkea and Portlester were lavishly furnished with all the trappings of immense wealth, not least of which was a vast collection of silver and gold plate held in each castle – the heirlooms of generations of FitzGeralds. Since their marriage in 1520, Gerald and his second wife, Eliza-beth, had lived at Maynooth Castle along with their five children and Gerald's son, Thomas, and four daughters from his first marriage. Richard Stanihurst painted a picture of domestic contentment in the household, testifying to the earl's devotion to his spouse:

> this noble man was so well affected to his wife, the Lady Gray, as he would not, at any time, buy a suit of apparel for himself, but he would suit her with the same stuff. Which gentleness she recompensed with equal kindness.[12]

The furnishing and decoration of their home was in a distinctly Renais-sance style, no doubt owing to both his wives' English aristocratic background and to Gerald's upbringing at court. Gerald had in his possession a portrait of himself purportedly executed by Hans Holbein the Younger. The family had a substantial library containing Latin, English, French and Irish works, a number of these very recently published. In the 1530s the interior of the castle was lit by candles mounted on gold candlesticks, some bearing the earl's coat-of-arms, and contained 'such a store of beds, so many goodly hangings, so rich a ward-robe, such brave furniture ... household stuff and utensils' that it was recog-nised as 'one of the richest earl's houses under the Crown of England'.[13] Even their kitchen utensils attested to the FitzGeralds' affluence: a gilded strainer for oranges, ornamented goblets and salt cellars, spoons decorated with figures of men, women, mermaids and animals, a great horn embellished with silver and gilt, two great serving platters (one gold and one silver), a powder box for various spices, a gilded container for green ginger, a decorated ostrich egg, a bottle in the shape of a heart, several small pots from which to drink ale, and a number of gilded standing cups. The family dressed in accordance with the latest, contemporary English fashions and had a sizeable collection of jewelry. Among the personal effects belonging to the earl's wives and his daughters were a look-ing-glass adorned with silver and gilt, an adder's tongue made of gilded plate and a gilded figure of a lion. Several of the household's more exotic utensils and valuable items of furniture were imported from Spain and Turkey.[14]

Yet while the FitzGeralds enjoyed a life of luxury at Maynooth, storm clouds were gathering on the political horizon in England during the early 1530s. This was a particularly sensitive time for Henry VIII who had pressing domestic problems as he wrestled with Pope Clement V's refusal to grant him a divorce from his wife, Catherine of Aragon, so preventing his marriage to Anne Boleyn. It was Henry's new secretary, Thomas Cromwell, who presented him with a solution to his problem – suggesting that all ties with Rome be severed. That way Henry would have his divorce, marry Anne and greatly increase the Crown's wealth while Cromwell would have the opportunity to remodel the government of the Tudor realm, including Ireland.

Himself of humble social origins, Cromwell was suspicious of over-mighty noblemen such as the Percys and Dacres in northern England and the earl of Kildare in Ireland, whom he believed wielded too much power independent of the Crown. In 1534 he devised a blueprint for reform of the administration in Ireland entitled *Ordinances for the Government of Ireland* which aimed to limit the autonomy enjoyed by Kildare in governing the lordship. While it was not Cromwell's intention to destroy the Kildare dynasty, the 9th earl and his son, Silken Thomas, were not prepared to relinquish their hold on the coveted deputyship and their influence within the Irish Council. Historians now contend that it was therefore the FitzGeralds' reaction to the policy, rather than the policy itself, that brought about their downfall in 1534–5.[15]

In the autumn and winter months of 1533, opposition to Kildare's governance was steadily mounting both in the Irish Council and at court. Fearing that he might again be removed from the lord deputyship, the earl transferred the king's munitions from Dublin Castle to his own castles, especially Maynooth. This pre-emptive move was designed to enable him to cause disturbances in the Pale in the event of his again being dismissed. Henry responded by summoning Kildare and Butler to court. There, Cromwell hoped to persuade Kildare to comply with his proposed governmental reforms. As a gesture of goodwill and reassurance, the king allowed Gerald to name his own deputy during his absence from Ireland. Gerald nominated his son, Thomas, Lord Offaly, and departed for the court where he made his appearance in March 1534.[16]

Henry's courtiers were struck by Gerald's feeble state, remarking how he was 'sick both in body and brain ... [from] the shot of a harquebus, which he received a long time ago'. It was rumoured that 'there is no hope of his recovery' and that he was 'not like[ly] to live long'.[17] By May 1534 Gerald was convinced that he was set to lose his dominance in governing the lordship. He was dismissed from the deputyship, replaced by Skeffington, and prevented from returning to Ireland. The earl's claim to liberty jurisdiction over County Kildare was dispensed with and his authority to exercise jurisdiction over neighbouring Gaelic clans or disobedient English lords curtailed.

From May onwards events unfolded rapidly. Gerald dispatched some of his retinue, including family members, to Ireland to advise his son, Thomas, on the planned course of action designed to subvert the reform measures. Henry had also summoned Thomas to court, but the earl instructed his son not to trust the king's councillors who he believed would advise Thomas to travel to England where his life could be in danger. Gerald and Thomas reckoned that by resorting to the ploy of staging a demonstration of Kildare indispensability, they could force Henry and Cromwell to reverse, or at least postpone, their plans for reform in such a way as to accommodate Geraldine dominance.

Acting on his father's instructions, on St Barnabas's Day, 11 June 1534, Thomas arrived at a meeting of the king's council at St Mary's Abbey in Dublin accompanied by up to 1,000 horsemen and foot soldiers. In a gesture of protest, he threw down the sword of state on the council table, resigned his office as deputy-governor and renounced the king's policies. While in the eyes of the FitzGeralds this may have amounted to a show of indispensability, Henry took an altogether different view. Thomas's action came at a particularly delicate time: Henry was openly at loggerheads with both the pope and the Holy Roman Emperor, Charles V, Catherine of Aragon's nephew, over the divorce controversy and Cromwell was gingerly steering through parliament a battery of reforms to legalise the break with Rome. Henry, therefore, was in no humour for indulging the Kildares in (as he saw it) their show of defiance. Angered especially by Thomas's solicitations for Charles V's support for what he portrayed as a Catholic crusade, Henry had the earl imprisoned in the Tower of London on 29 June. Gerald's wife, Elizabeth, who had travelled to England the previous October to intercede to have her husband's recall rescinded, remained with him constantly throughout his imprisonment. The murder of the FitzGeralds' opponent, Archbishop John Alen, in Dublin by Thomas's supporters in late July sent a clear message that the Kildares intended to persist with their defiant stance.[18] During his imprisonment Gerald remained entirely supportive of his son's actions, invariably praising him and showing 'great contentment at his present work, only wishing that he [Thomas] was older and more experienced in warfare'.[19] When the earl, aged 47, died and was buried in St Peter's Church in the Tower on 2 September 1534, his 21-year old son, then in open rebellion in Ireland, succeeded him as 10th earl of Kildare.

Between August and early October 1534, Thomas FitzGerald besieged Dublin Castle; in mid-October Sir William Skeffington's 2,300-strong army arrived in Dublin. During the winter months FitzGerald adopted a defensive strategy, and from mid-December 1534 to early January 1535 both sides observed a truce. However, Thomas's forces steadily weakened, and by the time full campaigning resumed in the spring of 1535, he had lost the initiative. As early as September 1534 Thomas had taken the precaution of transferring most of the family's possessions from Maynooth Castle to another of their fortresses at Lea in Leix; the family too vacated the castle. By February 1535 he had fortified Maynooth with most of his munitions, reinforced the castle's garrison and was actively recruiting Gaelic forces in anticipation of the inevitable siege. In March Skeffington's forces were penetrating into Kildare from their garrisons around the Pale borders and skirmishing occurred around Maynooth. On 18 March, Skeffington's men laid siege to the Geraldine castle.[20]

Contemporary accounts of the taking of Maynooth Castle feature conflicting details. Richard Stanihurst, the historian Sir James Ware and various Gaelic annalists all claimed that the castle was betrayed by its constable, Christopher Paris. According to Ware, Paris gained access to the interior of the castle by making the guard on duty drunk. Stanihurst recounted how, the morning after the taking of the castle, Paris received Skeffington's thanks and payment for his great service to the Crown – before being beheaded since no agreement had been made that his life would be spared.[21] Not surprisingly, Skeffington made no reference to foul play in his report to Henry VIII on the capture of the castle. He explained that they bombarded the castle day and night, until between four and five o'clock in the morning on the 23 March they managed to penetrate the walls. (Plate 2: the ruinous keep of Maynooth Castle.) On gaining entry to the interior, the English forces killed approximately 60 of Kildare's men. Skeffington then raided the keep from which the dean of Kildare, the constable of the castle (Paris), Donough O'Dogan (Kildare's master of the ordnance), a priest named Sir Simon Walshe and one of Kildare's captains, Nicholas Wafer, along with 37 gunners and archers, surrendered and were taken prisoner. Skeffington ordered the execution of those captured. On the morning of 25 March they were examined. That afternoon they were arraigned before the provost marshal and captains and, on the strength of their confessions, 25 were immediately beheaded and one hanged in front of the castle gate. In line with the custom of the time, the heads of the more important prisoners were placed on the castle turrets as trophies of victory.[22]

The capture of the Kildares' fortress and the summary execution of several of the family's closest advisers dealt a shattering psychological and practical blow to Thomas's campaign and credibility. Skeffington immediately occupied the castle. Thomas fell back to the woods and bogs in the west of his territory, and in vain prolonged his campaign into the summer months, still hopeful of receiving military aid from the Holy Roman Emperor, Charles V. It was Thomas's solicitations for foreign aid that made Henry VIII determined to suppress the rebellion. News of the fall of Maynooth spread to the continent. By August County Kildare was desolate, and unsafe for the fugitive earl: Piers Butler, Earl of Ossory, was stirring up unrest amongst Kildare's allies, many of whom submitted to Skeffington. Thomas, accompanied by his brother-in-law, Brian O'Connor, was forced to take refuge in the woods and bogs of Allen in northwest Kildare. With Skeffington threatening to pursue them with a force of 1,000 kerne, they surrendered on 24 August 1535. The circumstances of Thomas's surrender to his uncle-in-law, Lord Leonard Grey, who had recently arrived in Ireland as marshal of the army, are controversial. It is said that in return for surrendering, Thomas was promised that his life would be spared. However, while satisfied by the capture of FitzGerald, Henry was displeased at the conditions of his submission. He therefore resolved to have Thomas and leading male members of the Kildare Geraldines executed after an appropriate interval of time. Thus, after Thomas arrived at court in October 1535, he was arrested and imprisoned in the Tower cell in which his father had died over a year before. Thereafter, five of his uncles, two of whom had assisted Skeffington and another who had not participated in the revolt, were brought to England and imprisoned in the Tower. In July 1536 an act of attainder against Thomas and his five uncles was passed in the English parliament. All six were executed at Tyburn on 3 February 1537. Thomas's uncles were hanged, beheaded and quartered; Thomas was hanged and beheaded, his body buried in the priory of the Crutched Friars situated on Tower Hill.[23]

Although Thomas's half-brother, Gerald,[24] was restored to some of the ancestral lands and, in 1554, to the earldom, the Kildares never regained their former prominence as Ireland's most powerful political dynasty – a reality starkly reflected in their derelict castle. Maynooth Castle lay in such a ruinous state following the confederate wars of the 1640s that, in the late 1730s when Robert FitzGerald, 19th Earl of Kildare (1675–1744), considered restoring it as his private residence, he was forced to abandon the idea and instead resolved to upgrade the house at Carton.[25]

NOTES

1   This essay draws extensively on the following scholarly studies of the Kildare ascendancy and restoration: Laurence McCorristine, *The Revolt of Silken Thomas: A Challenge to Henry VIII* (Dublin, 1987); S. G. Ellis, *Reform and Revival: English Government in Ireland, 1470–1534* (Woodbridge, 1986); idem, *Ireland in the Age of the Tudors, 1447–1603: English Expansion and the End of Gaelic Rule* (London and New York, 1998), chs 3–6; idem, *Tudor Frontiers and Noble Power: The Making of the British State* (Oxford, 1998 edn), chs 4 and 7; M. A. Lyons, *Gearóid Óg, Ninth Earl of Kildare* (Dundalk, 1998); idem, *Church and Society in County Kildare, c.1470–1547* (Dublin, 2000); V. Carey, *Surviving the Tudors: The 'Wizard Earl' of Kildare and English Rule in Ireland, 1537–1586* (Dublin, 2002); Colm Lennon, *Sixteenth-Century Ireland: The Incomplete Conquest* (Dublin, 2005 edn), chs 3–4; see also entries for the earls in the print and online editions of the *Oxford Dictionary of National Biography* (hereafter *ODNB*) and *Dictionary of Irish Biography* (hereafter *DIB*).

2   Ellis, *Tudor Frontiers*, pp 107–21.

3   Ellis, *Ireland in the Age of the Tudors*, pp 70–114; idem, *Tudor Frontiers*, ch. 4; idem, 'FitzGerald, Gerald, Eighth Earl of Kildare (1456?–1513)', *ODNB*, online edn (http://oxforddnb.com.view/article/9554) (accessed 3 Oct. 2011); M. A. Lyons, 'FitzGerald, Gerald (Gearóid Mór) (1456/7–1513)', *DIB*, online edn (http://dib.cambridge.org/viewReadPage.do?articleId=a3148) (accessed 3 Oct. 2011).

4   *Holinshed's Chronicles of England, Scotland and Ireland*, ed. H. Ellis (6 vols, London, 1807–08), vol. vi, p. 275.

5   *Annála Ríoghachta Éireann: Annals of the Kingdom of Ireland by the Four Masters, from the*

Earliest Period to the Year 1616, ed. John O'Donovan (7 vols, Dublin, 1851; repr. New York, 1966), vol. v, p. 1327.

6   *Annála Uladh: annals of Ulster ...: a chronicle of Irish affairs ..., 431 to 1541*, ed. W. M. Hennessy and Bartholomew MacCarthy (4 vols, Dublin, 1887–1901), vol. iii, p. 507.

7   Lyons, *Gearóid Óg*, p 9, 18, 20; S. G. Ellis, 'FitzGerald, Gerald, Ninth Earl of Kildare (1487–1534)', *ODNB* online edn (http://www.oxforddnb.com/articles/9/9555) (accessed 3 Oct. 2011); M. A. Lyons, 'FitzGerald, Gerald (Gearóid Óg, Garrett McAlison) (1487–1534)', *DIB*, online edn (http://dib.cambridge.org/viewReadPage.do?articleId=a3152) (accessed 3 Oct. 2011).

8   *Holinshed's Chronicles*, vol. vi, p. 309.

9   *State Papers Henry VIII* (11 vols, London, 1830–52), vol. ii, p. 300.

10   Gearóid Mac Niocaill (ed.) *Crown Surveys of Lands, 1540–41, with the Kildare Rental begun in 1518* (Dublin, 1992), pp 232–357; for analysis of the rental, see Ellis, *Tudor Frontiers*, pp 125–32.

11   Lyons, *Gearóid Óg*, pp 49–50; Ellis, 'FitzGerald, Gerald, Ninth Earl of Kildare', *ODNB* online; Lyons, 'FitzGerald, Gerald (Gearóid Óg, Garrett McAlison)', *DIB*, online.

12   *Holinshed's Chronicles*, quoted in Charles William FitzGerald, *The Earls of Kildare and Their Ancestors from 1057 to 1773* (Dublin, 1858), pp 125–6.

13   *Holinshed's Irish Chronicle*, ed. Liam Miller and Eileen Power (Dublin, 1979), p. 278.

14   Mac Niocaill, *Crown Surveys*, pp 314–17.

15   Lyons, *Gearóid Óg; Ellis, 'FitzGerald, Gerald, Ninth Earl of Kildare'*; S. G. Ellis, 'FitzGerald, Thomas [Silken Thomas], Tenth Earl of Kildare (1513–1537)', *ODNB* online edn (http://www.oxforddnb.com/view/article/9586) (accessed 3 Oct. 2011); Lyons, 'FitzGerald, Gerald (Gearóid Óg, Garrett McAlison)'; idem, 'FitzGerald, Thomas ('Silken Thomas') (1513–37)', *DIB* online edn (www.http://dib.cambridge.org/viewReadPage.do?articleId=a3191) (accessed 3 Oct. 2011).

16   Ibid.; McCorristine, *Revolt*, pp 51–63.

17   *Letters and Papers, Foreign and Domestic, Henry VIII* (21 vols, London, 1862–1932), vol. vii, no. 530.

18   McCorristine, *Revolt*, pp 65–78; Lyons, *Gearóid Óg*; Ellis, 'FitzGerald, Gerald, Ninth Earl of Kildare'; Ellis, 'FitzGerald, Thomas [Silken Thomas]'; Lyons, 'FitzGerald, Gerald (Gearóid Óg, Garrett McAlison)'; idem, 'FitzGerald, Thomas'.

19   *Calendar of Letters, Dispatches and State Papers Relating to the Negotiations Between England and Spain, Preserved in the Archives at Simancas and Elsewhere, 1485–1558* (13 vols, London, 1862–1954), vol. v, no. 87.

20   McCorristine, *Revolt*, pp 81–109; Ellis, 'FitzGerald, Thomas'; Lyons, 'FitzGerald, Thomas'.

21   McCorristine, *Revolt*, pp 109–10.

22   McCorristine, *Revolt*, pp 110–11; Ellis, 'FitzGerald, Thomas'; Lyons, 'FitzGerald, Thomas'.

23   McCorristine, *Revolt*, pp 112–31; Ellis, 'FitzGerald, Thomas'; Lyons, 'FitzGerald, Thomas'.

24   J. Barry, 'FitzGerald, Gerald 11th Earl of Kildare', *DIB*, online edn (http://dib.cambridge.org/viewReadPage.do?articleId=a3150) (accessed 3 Oct. 2011)

25   Terence Dooley and Conor Mallaghan, *Carton House: An Illustrated History* (Celbridge, 2006), p. 15.

CHAPTER 4

Mabel Browne, Countess of Kildare, and the Restoration of the House of Kildare, 1552–1610

Carol O'Connor

In 1552, at a masque held at the court of King Edward VI (1537–53), Gerald FitzGerald, later 11th Earl of Kildare (1525–85) met his future wife, Mabel Browne (c. 1536–1610).[1] As a member of the prominent Browne family, Mabel's pedigree and background were to prove perfect for the political ambitions of the young heir to the Kildare dynasty.[2] At the height of their power, the FitzGeralds of Kildare had been the foremost aristocratic family in Ireland, but Silken Thomas's 1534–35 rebellion demolished the Geraldine power network and left a huge void in the hitherto Kildare-dominated political arena. When Gerald returned to restore the earldom in the 1550s, the established structures of power and governance in Ireland had been significantly altered in the years since his half-brother's rebellion. Out of favour at the English royal court, the task of restoration relied heavily on both his return as head of the local Geraldine power base and on the favour of court alliances. Connections such as those with the Browne family were thus of crucial importance to the future of the Kildare inheritance – none more so than the influential role Mabel Browne would come to play in court negotiations on Kildare's behalf. As a woman Mabel did not have access to formal agencies of government or political office, however, her position as a member of the social elite held the key to her influence.[3] Now, as a member of the FitzGerald family, Mabel integrated her courtly education with the traditional bonds of loyalty, pride and allegiance that were instilled in each family member, regardless of gender, to actively promote the house of Kildare.

Mabel Browne was the daughter of the distinguished courtier Sir Anthony Browne (c.1500–48), and his first wife, Alice, herself a daughter of the courtier, Sir John Gage.[4] Anthony was a close confidant of Henry VIII and a member of the Privy Council; as such he secured the titles of Master of the Horse and

Knight of the Garter. Remaining close to the monarch throughout his career he was duly appointed as an executor of Henry VIII's will and as a guardian of his children, Edward and Elizabeth.[5] Little is known of Mabel's early years, but given the status her father attained it is reasonable to assume that she grew up and was educated at the Tudor court. Her mother died in 1540, but Anthony re-married in 1542 at the age of 60. His second wife was Elizabeth FitzGerald (1528–89), the 15-year old daughter of the 9th earl of Kildare, affectionately known as 'the fair Geraldine' in recognition of her admired beauty.[6] This marriage not only set in motion the close relationship which Elizabeth and Mabel would come to maintain, but also the important role that the Browne family would play in restoring the FitzGerald name.

Mabel's marriage to Gerald FitzGerald in May 1554 continued the Kildare tradition of establishing successful political connections through marriage. Beyond the importance of local alliances maintained through the Geraldine network, Irish matrimonial connections within the English court ensured a necessary pro-Kildare faction there – both the 8th and 9th earls had utilised this strategy by marrying English wives. The Roman Catholic court of Queen Mary (1516–58) provided the means for the FitzGerald-Browne alliance to positively impact the future of the diminished Kildare earldom; the abandonment of the Protestant Reformation ensured that the connections of the ardently Catholic Browne family, strongly contributed to the earl's renewed political standing. Not only had Mabel's father been a leading recusant, but the Browne family were also relatives of the influential Cardinal Pole, papal legate to England, and from 1555, Archbishop of Canterbury.[7] As a reward for their devout Catholicism, Mabel's brother, Anthony, was elevated to the peerage as Viscount Montagu in 1554. In her own right, Mabel Browne held a notable position at the Marian court as one of Queen Mary's gentlewomen of the privy chamber. Such a prominent position allowed Mabel admission into the inner circle of court politics, as the privy chamber provided female members of the aristocracy with significant political influence.[8]

It was within this realm of the female privy chamber that Mabel formed a close bond with Elizabeth FitzGerald (her step-mother and sister-in-law). Although raised at court, Elizabeth continued to be a strong Kildare supporter, with her first marriage to Mabel's father playing an important role in paving the way for her brother, Gerald, to return to court. Another solid Kildare marital alliance was forged when, after the death of Mabel's father in 1548, Elizabeth married Edward Clinton who held the post of Lord Admiral. The bonds of sisterhood established in the royal court were a further aspect of the alliance which Mabel Browne and Elizabeth FitzGerald used to promote the Kildare faction. The friendships they maintained as gentlewomen of the privy chamber would prove consistently influential to the future of the house of Kildare, and largely owing to their efforts Gerald was eventually received into favour and knighted on 25 April 1552.[9] In 1554 he was restored to the title of earl of Kildare and baron of Offaly.

The 11th earl of Kildare and his countess, Mabel, were given permission to return to Ireland in 1556. For a noblewoman brought up in such close proximity to the restraints of the royal court, marriage to an Irish aristocrat offered Mabel the means to escape court politics, where women's lives and interests were closely dictated by centuries of tradition. Ireland offered the countess greater freedom to carve an individual public persona under the guise of Kildare politics. Once settled in Ireland, Kildare immediately sought to reconstruct the crucial Geraldine alliance network. The traditional role of the earls of Kildare in local politics had largely been diminished in the intervening years since the 1534 rebellion. Attempts by the 11th earl to regain FitzGerald hegemony met constant opposition from the office of the lord deputy, and would continue to do so throughout his career.[10] In the early months of 1557 Mabel attended court and entered into negotiations on Kildare's behalf in a bid to restore both lands and the jurisdictional and military rights traditionally held by the Kildare title.[11] Drawing significantly upon her previous position in the privy chamber, and with the strategic help of Cardinal Pole, Mabel was not sent by Kildare merely as a decoy while he fulfilled more pressing matters – she was sent as the more influential courtier. However, Queen Mary was not willing to grant her requests without seeking the involvement and advice of the earl of Sussex, her new lord deputy in Ireland.[12] The queen requested that the deputy and council of Ireland consider the matter 'with the more speed, for that the Countess is attending an answer there to her great charges'.[13] Mabel's 'charges' included the return of traditional Kildare jurisdiction over territory in Offaly, although this proved incompatible with impending plans for a Laois–Offaly plantation. However influential Mabel may have been at court in 1557, the Kildare earldom did not have the political leverage to override the authority of the lord deputy and regain the full liberty of the county of Kildare.

The early 1560s progressed well for the FitzGeralds and Kildare successfully managed to reassert control over a number of Gaelic lords. In 1567 Gerald began a second major attempt to recover Kildare lands. The earl and countess's diligent efforts in complying with the new queen, Elizabeth I (1533–1603), proved successful, and in 1569 the FitzGerald's were fully restored when an act of parliament was passed to reverse the Kildare attainder: the earl of Kildare, his brother and sisters were all fully recalled 'to their blood'.[14] It was not merely a formality that the women of the family were included in the act, but rather an indication of the contribution the FitzGerald women had made to the political position of their family. However, Kildare's rise was short-lived; the Desmond and Butler rebellions of the early 1570s, together with a strong anti-Geraldine movement among some Palesmen, led to the arrest of Gerald in May 1574 after accusations of involvement in a plot to undermine English government, and, more specifically, the office of the lord deputy.[15] Queen Elizabeth, however, was lenient in her treatment of Gerald and Mabel – despite the fact that evidence consistently suggested there was an element of truth in the allegations. It was reported in January 1576 that the queen was so well-disposed towards the earl and countess that to 'signify the Queen's pleasure' towards Gerald 'the Lady Kildare might have free access to the Earl her husband' – which included permission for them 'to lye together, a thinge unusuall' in such cases.[16] The state papers also record that 'the queen will show further favour to the earl in a few days', an indication that she was willing to grant pardon to Kildare.[17] This came on 13 February 1576 when the queen granted 'Lady Kildare license to return to Ireland to take charge of the earl's lands during his absence'.[18]

The leniency shown towards Kildare once again points to his wife's influence at court and, indeed, that of his sister, Elizabeth, now countess of Lincoln, who was also a member of the queen's privy chamber. Mabel was given permission to see to Kildare's affairs, with Sidney, the new lord deputy, 'instructed to assist her in these endeavours and ... to ensure that Kildare's interests be protected in his absence'.[19] As warfare brutally ravaged the estate, Mabel assumed a pivotal position in keeping control of the lordship. On her return to Ireland in October 1576 she wrote to Kildare of the happenings in his absence. She recounted that not only were 'his most serviceable servants detestably murdered', but that his lands had decayed and that if she 'should depart the country, all would run to wreck' as even the Geraldine alliance was in jeopardy.[20] When Gerald finally returned to Ireland in 1578 it was to a devastated lordship, and to the reality that, although Kildare rights had been restored, the Kildare power base held by his father and grandfather was no longer tenable, due mainly to the changing nature of Irish politics.

While the Kildares' religious persuasions had proved politically advantageous in the court of Queen Mary, they were to prove less so in the latter years of Gerald's career at the court of Queen Elizabeth. When Gerald returned to Ireland it was assumed that he would adopt a traditional Kildare leadership role in support of the Catholic cause, this widespread impression was no doubt furthered by Mabel's stance as an ardent Catholic. However, Gerald, as a representative of the Crown in Ireland, grew increasingly ambiguous in his own admission of faith, while Mabel continued to manage a household that fully represented her support for the Catholic or Counter-Reformation.

Mabel and Gerald had five children: Gerald or Garret, Lord Offaly; Henry (who would become the 12th Earl of Kildare); William (who would become the 13th earl); Mary who married Christopher Nugent, 9th Baron of Delvin; and Elizabeth who married Donnchadh MacConcobhair O'Brien, 4th Earl of Thomond. An early influence upon the FitzGerald children was the chronicler, Richard Stanihurst, who was appointed as a tutor to the young FitzGerald heir, Garret, Lord Offaly. Although Stanihurst did not entirely commit himself to the

Counter-Reformation until after his time with the FitzGeralds, his Catholic beliefs would certainly have been a dominant aspect of his involvement in Mabel's household. It was even reported that there was the possibility of a plot to assist in the removal of Lord Offaly to Spain, in order to have him brought up in the Catholic household of Jane Dormer, the Duchess of Feria, and to marry him to the Infanta Isabella, daughter of the Spanish king, Philip II. Stanihurst's later confession claims that the countess was innocent of the plot, but it is known that the countess did have a relationship with the Spanish duchess – they were companions in the English court of Queen Mary.[21]

As the Counter-Reformation took hold in Ireland, Mabel increasingly came into her own, expressing opinions that were decisively in opposition to Gerald's allegiances to the Protestant crown. However, the religious zeal that occupied the Kildare household resonated with the more overtly public demonstrations that dominated Ireland in the late 1570s and the 1580s. Mabel remained staunchly committed as a religious activist, supporting the Counter-Reformation movement from her castle at Rathangan, County Kildare. Rathangan had become known as a 'safe-house' for those engaged in recusant behaviour, and Mabel harboured a number of renowned dissident priests including Fr Robert Rochford and Fr Compton, while Nicolas Eustace, a relative of the rebel Viscount Baltinglass, was her private chaplain. Mabel was also associated with Dr Nicholas Sander, the papal legate and a notable Counter-Reformation missionary, who had arrived in Ireland with James Fitzmaurice FitzGerald.[22] Mabel's frequent communication with the Counter-Reformation movement was widely acknowledged among her peers in Elizabeth's court. In 1581, for example, it was reported, that 'her majesty is not ignorant of her [the countess] harbouring known papists combined with Sander in her house', that Rochford had an 'open passage' at 'Rahangan where his books were left' and that Nicholas Eustace 'who for the most part [was] kept at Rahangan, but would depart thence to gentlemen's houses and there at mass swear men to join the rebels or at least not to be against them'.[23] In addition, Mabel's brother, Charles Browne, was a member of the papal force that landed at Smerwick, County Kerry, in September 1580; it is significant that his connection to Mabel was recorded upon his arrival: 'the countess of Kildare's base brother has come with the Italians'.[24]

Gerald's failure to stop the Baltinglass rebellion (a Catholic revolt in the Pale led by James Eustace, Viscount Baltinglass) in 1580, coupled with his association with Stanihurst, and indeed, Mabel's recusant activities, led to accusations of treason against the earl and his eventual imprisonment. Mabel was thus left to transfer her energy once more into securing her husband's assets and renewing the management of the Kildare estate, with the help of her confidante and ally, the countess of Lincoln. In January 1581 the joint lobbying of the FitzGerald women proved successful, with the countess of Lincoln described as being such 'an earnest suitor that the countess of Kildare may have

GERALDVS·FILIVS·GERALDI· COMES·
KILDARIE· ÆTATIS·43·Å DNĨ·1530·

Chapter 3 Garret Oge, 9th Earl of Kildare. Painting purportedly attributed to Holbein.
Courtesy of President, St Patrick's College, Maynooth.

Chapter 3 Ruins of the keep of Maynooth Castle.

Chapters 6, 7, 8 Arthur Devis (1712–87), *Lord and Lady Kildare Laying Out the Park at Carton* (1753).

Courtesy of Mallaghan family.

Chapter 7 Ceiling of the Gold Saloon, Carton House.
Courtesy of Mallaghan family. .

Chapter 8 The service staircase, Carton House.
Courtesy of Mallaghan family.

Chapters 7, 8 and 9 Allan Ramsay (1713–84), *Emily, 1st Duchess of Leinster.*
Courtesy of Mallaghan family.

Chapter 9 Wine cistern supplied by the Dublin silversmith, Thomas Sutton (1727).
A rare survival in terms of Irish silver of this period.

Courtesy of the Dallas Museum of Art, The Karl and Esther Hoblitzelle Collection,
gift of the Hoblitzelle Foundation.

Chapter 9 The Ante-Room at Carton House. The Leinster catalogue was devoted to the
picture collection and reveals that over 220 pictures hung on the walls at Carton.

Chapter 9   A number of the Cuyp paintings that hung at Carton represented equestrian subjects, including *Men on Horseback*. It has recently been acquired by the National Gallery of Ireland.

Chapter 10   The Carton sextet by Thomas Roberts and William Ashford (1775–9) on display at the National Gallery of Ireland, 2009.

Photo courtesy of Raymond Keaveney and the National Gallery of Ireland.

Chapter 10 Thomas Roberts (1747–77), *Bold Sir William (a Barb), an Indian Servant, and French Dog in the Possession of Gerald FitzGerald*, 1772.
Private collection.

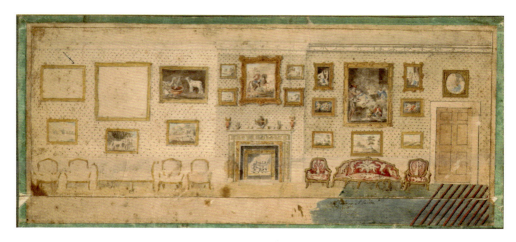

Chapter 10 Anonymous, *The Drawing-Room at Carton House*, *c*.1800.
Private collection.

licence to repair to England, and that she may have the custody of all her hus-band's evidences of his lands and money, found in the house at the time of the earl's arrest'.[25] On 1 February 1581, Mabel herself requested 'friendship to be shown to her husband in his trouble', attesting his 'innocence' and asking 'that he may be heard before the Privy Council in England'.[26] The countess contin-ued to petition relentlessly for Kildare, writing to court on 3 April to express 'her sorrow at not being admitted to her majesty's presence'.[27] Kildare was detained in the Tower until his release in June 1583. His earlier court connec-tions and crown service served him well in that the queen was seemingly reluc-tant to destroy Kildare, thus he was spared a traitor's death. Through continued perseverance Mabel too regained royal favour, and by March 1600 it was noted that the countess was 'attending her majesty'.[28] Being admitted to personally attend the queen was no easy feat during a time when Elizabeth operated a determinedly restricted privy chamber. Meanwhile, Gerald, the 11th earl, had died in November 1585, leaving Mabel to assume the role of matriarch of the FitzGerald lordship – a position she occupied for the next 25 years.

Mabel's personal life, beyond her public duties as countess of Kildare, was not without suffering. Her eldest son and heir to the earldom, Lord Offaly, died in July 1580, five years before the death of her husband. Her second son, Henry (d. 1597), who succeeded as the 12th earl, described his new earldom with a certain despondency: 'the greatness of my ancestors' titles remains to me, but their estate of living altogether decayed'.[29] Further tragedy was to befall Mabel with the premature deaths of Henry and his brother, William (d. 1599), who had succeeded as the 13th earl. William's death also resulted in the transfer of the line of succession to a collateral branch of the FitzGerald family, the earl-dom being inherited by Gerald (d. 1612), a nephew of the 11th earl. Mabel, the dowager countess of Kildare, now relied upon the relationship she maintained with her daughter, Mary, and son-in-law Christopher Nugent, Baron of Delvin. Delvin was an ardent recusant, having been imprisoned with the 11th earl fol-lowing the Baltinglass insurrection; it was he who kept Mabel in close contact with the Catholic elite.

While priests, Jesuits and seminarians had been banned from practice in Ireland in 1605, many, with the assistance of patrons such as Mabel, remained in the country. In 1606 the administration voiced suspicion regarding the 'con-triving innovation' of Irish priests who were believed to 'withdraw the hearts and obedience of the people, who otherwise of themselves are well affected in peace and good settlement'.[30] It was also thought that a number of priests in Ireland had forged a papal bull in an effort to contribute to the Catholic Refor-mation mission in Ireland. This was coupled with reports of many priests 'who come to this kingdom ... who run from place to place, spreading naughty and seditious reports'.[31] One such priest thought to be affiliated with this movement was Francis Barnaby, who at this time was residing with Mabel in her home at

Maynooth Castle. Originally from Yorkshire, he was ordained in 1598 at the English College in Rome.[32] He had a notable career, travelling in an official capacity between Paris, Rome and London. Not much is known of his activities from 1603 until it is recorded in 1606 that he came to Ireland as chaplain to the dowager countess of Kildare. Upon his coming to Maynooth, Lord Deputy Chichester reported that Barnaby apparently 'names himself Wentwourth, and remains at Maynouth with the old countess of Kyldare, and lives in show of a gentleman'. Barnaby had obtained 'the kings pardon, with liberty to live and remain in the kingdom of England', leaving Chichester to 'abstain from further troubling' him, especially following Barnaby's role in persuading the 'Lord and Lady of Delvin to resort to the church, and to do some other good offices'. Chichester credited Barnaby with 'being a man of discreet carriage and good understanding, he hath won a great opinion among them [the Delvins], and out of that may work much with this people'.[33] (Notably, Barnaby signed the oath of allegiance in Dublin in 1612, an act that was consistent with the allegiance he continually professed to the Crown despite his Catholicism.) Although Barnaby was in good repute with the administration for his allegiance to the Crown, Mabel's associations with the Roman Catholic community continued to go without reprimand, highlighting the ambiguous attitude taken by the administration towards religious dissent. The following September, 1607, Chichester even reported that 'the countess of Kildare lies now at his house together with the lady dowager of Delvin and her children, to whom many priests do resort'.[34] Although the countess's continued affiliation with the Catholic cause was monitored by court officials, her female aristocratic position appears to have brought with it more leverage to act outside the restraints of early seventeenth-century law and reform in Ireland.

The final years of Mabel's life were dominated by a legal suit between the FitzGeralds of Kildare and Mabel's granddaughter, Lettice Digby. Lettice was the only daughter of Mabel's eldest son, Gerald, who had died in 1580. Mabel's husband, the 11th earl of Kildare, had failed to put a deed of entail in his will to stipulate the direct succession of the earldom along the male line – thus enabling his granddaughter, Lettice, to make a claim as heiress. Although heiresses were exceptional, it was possible for a female member of the family lineage to inherit land and title. Following the early deaths of three successive earls by 1597 the Kildare estate was burdened with three, substantial jointure claims. However, it was the legality of Mabel Browne's jointure and, in particular, the three significant lordship manors of Woodstock, Athy and Portlester, that instigated the jointure and inheritance battle with her granddaughter. In 1599, Lettice laid her claim as heir-general to the estates of her grandfather, and began a legal dispute that would financially dominate and cripple the lordship for over two decades.

In 1602 Lettice officially filed her complaint in the court of castle chamber 'against Gerald, the new earl of Kildare, the countess dowager and her attorney Henry Burnell, charging them with fraudulently altering the will of the eleventh earl'.[35] The dispute was extensively reported within aristocratic circles, with many accounts notably favouring the position of the 'innocent' dowager countess Mabel. Central to the case was Mabel's attorney, Henry Burnell, who was accused of forgery. Burnell, like many of Mabel's acquaintances and confidents, was a recusant leader and had been an active Pale agitator in the late 1570s and 1580s. The Digbys petitioned that Burnell, acting on behalf of Mabel, had forged a deed of jointure originally dated 7 September 1566 and made changes to the deed. The bill claimed that on the death of her husband in 1585, Mabel had consulted Burnell and 'demaunded what was Best to be don for hir and hir Childrens Advancement'.[36] Burnell advised her that 'he should insert into the testament a deed of entail to the heirs male of the deceased earl, which he then forged',[37] ensuring that the inheritance of the estate would benefit Mabel and her children, thus disinheriting Lettice. The bill also attested that years later Burnell had once again asked to see the jointure and, with 'the consent of the countess dowager added a certificate of execution by livery and adornment' along with the names of the 11th earl's servants who were long since dead, as witnesses. Records of the incident consistently attest to the countess being 'iynocante of any thought of harme or guyle' and her not 'knowinge nor Suspectinge the unlawfullnes of such practises nor the mischyeffes that might ensue such fraudulent devises'.[38]

The suit attracted such widespread notice that in July 1606 the lords of council expressed a direct concern regarding the controversy, as they were informed 'that if the old lady Mabel, Countess Dowager of Kildare, should happen to die during the pendancy of this controversy, there might be some extraordinary course used for obtaining possession of the lands of the said lady by violence'.[39] Mabel evidently held the balance of power and control in the case; powerful officials acknowledged her peace-keeping position in Ireland and were reluctant to recognise her role in the controversy. Instead, they offered her a scapegoat in the form of Burnell's forgery and plea of innocence. Mabel directly made reference to the controversy in a letter to the lord deputy dated 7 December 1608. The letter began with the countess asserting her competence in the matter and that she was of 'a clear conscience, free from the least imputation that might bring her loyalty in suspicion'.[40] She also referred to the 'manifold miseries inflicted upon her by God's divine appointment', a statement which acutely reminds the historian of the situation which faced the countess in her final years – division among her blood relatives; and, in turn, the declining management and prosperity of her lordship. Mabel also referred to her ailing health: she was 'through weakness and age, not able, these two years past, to bear company out of her chambers'.[41] The countess advised the lord deputy of her relationship with the aforementioned Francis Barnaby, the Catholic priest, whom she had welcomed into her home and whom she described as 'a gentleman whose employment in her causes has given her great comfort'.[42]

While Mabel apparently questioned the integrity and trustworthiness of those around her, both Gerald, the 14th earl of Kildare, and the Digbys likewise questioned Barnaby's role at Maynooth Castle; the earl described him as having 'careful endeavours in all her affairs, together with some good offices used by him between her and himself, as to have so far her good will that she only trusts him with all her business'.[43] Mabel was evidently well aware of the Digbys' efforts to dominate the management of her affairs and to secure Barnaby's banishment from her household, mentioning to the lord deputy that 'some men, more beholden to her than himself, taking the same in ill part, have suggested some matter against him [Barnaby] of purpose to remove him from her'.[44] Despite being bedridden she was just as well-equipped as the Digbys to fight for her jointure and, indeed, assert her own judgment on the situation. The determination of the Digbys in their suit against the countess became so notorious, both in London and Dublin, that the councils in both kingdoms attempted to avoid making a final judgment on the case.[45] However, while Lettice's claim as heir-general was left to common law, the allegation of forgery was finally dealt with at the court of the castle chamber on 3 February 1609. The court directly examined the aforesaid forgeries and determined that the endorsements 'shalbe Damned and never geven in Evidence to prove any Execution of any Estate to be Passed Accordingly in or by the said deed of feoffment'.[46] According to Jon G. Crawford, a historian of the court of the castle chamber: 'this interlocutory decree in a property dispute was certainly an unusual exercise of its prerogative authority by the court, showing once again its interest in the final disposition of the earldom and its estates'.[47]

The ruling fined Burnell for forging the endorsements, while the countess was acquitted of any involvement 'owing to the clumsy manner in which the original bill was drawn',[48] so the 'Court ffindeth noe Cause to Censure the said Countesse for her said offence'.[49] However, the issue was not laid to rest with this ruling. Gerald, the 14th earl of Kildare, filed another bill with the court of castle chamber, suing both his aunt, Mabel, and his cousin, Lettice, for conspiracy against the bill which entitled him to the succession of the earldom. While this bill was acquitted by the court in February 1609, the final outcome of the Kildare-Digby suit was not decided upon until King James I (1566–1625) passed judgment on 11 July 1619. While rejecting Lettice's claim as her grandfather's heir-general, the king awarded her the possession of significant FitzGerald manors and the title, baroness of Offaly – heralding a new era in the management of the FitzGerald estate as the property of a member of the Protestant elite.

When Mabel died in 1610 having outlived the majority of her children, she left behind a renewed scramble for the jointure lands she fought so hard to protect. Her death marked the end of the dominance of the Kildare lordship in the governance of Ireland, as the earldom failed to overcome its financial burdens and the division of a once-strong and united family. Although few sources attest to Mabel's own personal thoughts or insights, the evidence that does remain depicts a strong woman, well-educated in the politics of the day, who actively embraced her own beliefs along with the various duties which her position as countess required of her. Described by the 14th earl, her nephew-in-law, as 'a gracious adversary such as that good lady who is, I must confess, for her years and calling deserveth all honourable regard',[50] Mabel was well-regarded and respected by her contemporaries. Her accomplishments extended far beyond the assumed domestic role of an aristocratic wife, and she warrants remembrance as an active participant in the restoration of the house of Kildare at a critical period in its history. However, her life, along with those of numerous female family members, has largely been overlooked in favour of the exploits of male counterparts. Nevertheless, there is much scope for the restoration of many generations of women to the long and rich history of the FitzGerald family.

NOTES

1   Judy Barry, 'FitzGerald, Gerald 11th Earl of Kildare', *Dictionary of Irish Biography* (hereafter *DIB*), online edn (http://dib.cambridge.org/viewReadPage.do?articleId=a3150) (accessed 3 Oct. 2011).

2   Charles William FitzGerald, *The Earls of Kildare and Their Ancestors From 1057 to 1773* (2 vols, Dublin, 1858), vol. i, p. 206.

3   Mary O'Dowd, *A History of Women in Ireland*, (Harlow, 2005), p. 18.

4   William B. Robison, 'Browne, Sir Anthony (*c.* 1500–1548)', *Oxford Dictionary of National Biography* (hereafter *ODNB*), online edn (http://www.oxforddnb.com/view/article/3665) (accessed 7 Oct. 2011).

5   James Graves, 'Notes on an autograph of the fair Geraldine', in *Journal of the Royal Society of Antiquaries of Ireland*, ii (1873), p. 565.

6   Henry Howard, Earl of Surrey, 'Description and praise of his love Geraldine', in Liam Miller and Eileen Power (eds), *Holinshed's Irish Chronicle: The Historie of Irelande from the First Habitation Thereof, unto the Yeare 1509, Collected by Raphaell Holinshed, & Continued till the Yeare 1547 by Richarde Stanyhurst* (Dublin, 1979), p. 79.

7   Vincent Carey, *Surviving the Tudors: The 'Wizard' Earl of Kildare and English Rule in Ireland, 1537–1586* (Dublin, 2002), p. 58.

8   Natalie Mears, 'Politics in the Elizabethan privy chamber: Lady Mary Sidney and Kat Ashley', in James Daybell (ed.), *Women and Politics in Early Modern England, 1450–1700* (Aldershot, 2004), p. 67.

9   FitzGerald, *The Earls of Kildare*, p. 206.

10   Carey, *Surviving the Tudors*, p. 60.

11   Ibid.

12   Council to the Lord Deputy, 20 Mar. 1557, *Acts Privy Council, Eng.*, vi, 67.

13   'The Deputy and Council of Ireland to Philip and Mary, 3 July 1557', *Calendar of the Carew Manuscripts Preserved in the Archiepiscopal Library at Lambeth, 1515–1574* (London, 1867-73), p. 264. Hereafter cited as Cal. Carew MSS, 1515–1574.

14   *Cal. Carew MSS, 1515–1574*, p. 400.

15   Carey, *Surviving the Tudors*, p. 168.

16   'The Council to the Bishop of London, January 1576', *Calendar of the State Papers relating to Ireland in the reigns of Henry VII, Edward VI, Mary and Elizabeth, 1574–1588* (London, 1860–1912), p. 89. Hereafter cited as *Cal. S.P. Ire.*

17   Ibid.

18   Ibid.

19   Carey, *Surviving the Tudors*, p. 175.

20   Mabel, Countess of Kildare to the Earl of Kildare, 25 Oct. 1576, *Cal. S.P. Ire., 1574–1588*, p. 100.

21   A. J. Loomie, *The Spanish Elizabethans* (London, 1963), p. 96.

22   Elizabeth Ann O'Connor, 'The Rebellion of James Eustace, Viscount Baltinglass, 1580–81' (MA thesis, St Patrick's College, Maynooth, 1989), p. 68. See also J. H. Pollen, 'Dr Nicholas Sander, sixteenth-century Catholic controversialist', in *English Historical Review*, 6 (1891), pp 36–47.

23   Chancellor Gerrarde to Walsyngham, 18 Feb. 1581, *Cal. S.P. Ire., 1574–1588*, p. 287.

24   St Ledger, Sept. 1580, ibid., p. 254.

25   Walsyngham to Lord Grey, 29 Jan. 1581, ibid., p. 283.

26   Mabel, Countess of Kildare, to Walsyngham, 1 Feb. 1581, ibid., p. 285.

27   Mabel, Countess of Kildare, to Walsyngham, 3 Apr. 1581, ibid., p. 285.

28   Warrant from the Queen to Sir George Carey, 12 Mar. 1600, *Cal. S.P. Ire., 1600*, p. 37.

29   Petition of the Earl of Kildare to Queen Elizabeth, Sept. 1596, *Cal. S.P. Ire., 1596–1597*, p. 134.

30   Chicester to Salisbury, 29 Mar. 1606, *Cal. S.P. Ire., 1603–1606*, p. 439.

31   Ibid.

32   William Joseph Sheils, 'Barnaby, Francis (b. 1573, d. in or after 1621)', *ODNB*, online edn (http://www.oxforddnb.com/view/article/67452) (accessed 2 June 2008).

33   Chicester to Salisbury, 29 Mar. 1606, *Cal. S.P. Ire., 1603–1606*, p. 439.

34   Chichester to Salisbury, 10 Sept. 1607, *Cal. S.P. Ire., 1606–1608*, p. 269.

35   Jon G. Crawford, *A Star Chamber Court in Ireland: The Court of Castle Chamber, 1571–1641* (Dublin, 2005), p. 337. Crawford's edition provides a full transcription of the proceedings of the suit.

36   Ibid., p. 493.

37   Ibid., p. 337.

38   Ibid.

39   Lords of Council to Lord Deputy and Council, 14 July 1607, *Cal. S.P. Ire., 1606–1608*, p. 219.

40   Mabel, Countess of Kildare, to the Lord Deputy, 7 Dec. 1607, ibid., p. 346.

41   Ibid.

42   Mabel, Countess of Kildare, to the Lord Deputy, 7 Dec. 1607, *Cal. S.P. Ire., 1606–1608*, p. 346.

43   Kildare to Salisbury, 8 Jan. 1608, ibid., p. 393.

44   Mabel, Countess of Kildare, to the Lord Deputy, 7 Dec. 1607, ibid., p. 346.

45   Crawford, *Star Chamber Court*, p. 310.

46   Ibid., p. 496.

47   Ibid., p. 337.

48   Ibid.

49   Ibid., p. 496.

50   Garrett, Earl of Kildare, to Sir Robert Cecil, 24 June 1601, *Cal. S.P. Ire., 1600–1601*, p. 398.

CHAPTER 5

The Making of the Geraldines
The Kildare FitzGeralds and their Early Historians

Colm Lennon

As part of their drive to power in Irish political life at the end of the Middle Ages, the Kildare FitzGeralds forged an image of themselves as a family with a glorious past. We know that, *c.* 1500, Garret More (Gearóid Mór), the 8th Earl of Kildare, sought definite details of the connection between the Gherardini family of Florence and the Irish FitzGeralds. Giraldus Cambrensis, the famous historian of the arrival of the Normans in Ireland and an ancestor of the FitzGeralds, had associated the family very closely with the valiant struggle for the conquest in his famous work, *Expugnatio Hibernica*, written before 1200. This was not available in print until the 1580s, but it circulated widely in manuscript form in the late medieval period, along with his *Topographia Hibernica*, the highly influential perspective on the geography and inhabitants of Ireland. It is very significant that there were two copies of Giraldus's works in the library of Maynooth Castle in the early sixteenth century. True to the FitzGeralds' cultural dualism, one was in Irish and the other in English, although it is not clear whether both the *Expugnatio* and the *Topographia* were represented. When the generic name for the family, Geraldine, first came into usage is not clear; a sonnet by Henry Howard (1517–47), Earl of Surrey, in praise of Eleanor, 'the fair Geraldine', dates from the 1530s. The widespread adoption of the appellation, 'Geraldines', by the later sixteenth century however, was an early modern form of quasi-journalistic acceptance of the power and prestige of the family – not unlike 'the Kennedys' in the United States of America in the twentieth century.[1]

The exercise in careful self-presentation was successfully directed by the earls down to the revolt of Silken Thomas in 1534 and with greater difficulty thereafter. Garret Oge (Gearóid Óg), the 9th Earl, employed bards and musicians amongst his entourage to bolster the family's position in the Gaelic world; as did Gerald, the 11th Earl, in the later sixteenth century. In the early decades of the century, Philip Flattisbury of Johnstown, County Kildare, was retained by the 8th and 9th earls as their archivist and historian. He compiled a collection of their documents and transcribed annals of the early Anglo-Norman period, including a panegyric on the earl of Kildare. In his catalogue of the 'learned men' of Ireland, Richard Stanihurst, writing in the 1570s described Flattisbury as 'a diligent antiquary'. Stanihurst himself, an Oxford-trained humanist, was employed by the 11th earl as schoolmaster to his children and he became an important chronicler of the FitzGerald family and their place in Irish history. By the time he wrote his histories in the 1570s and 1580s, the FitzGerald family of Kildare was slowly emerging from a period as social and political outcasts, and he found himself very much in the role of Kildare apologist. In that capacity Stanihurst exercised an enormous influence over the historical narrative of the early sixteenth century, which has lasted almost to the present. Only very recently has the popular story of the impetuous rebel, Silken Thomas, and his helpless and heart-broken father, Garret Oge, been discredited by rigorous investigation of the evidence by modern historians.[2]

This essay examines the way in which the family history of the FitzGeralds was used by various Elizabethan historians to reflect their diverse and conflicting attitudes to the governing of Ireland. Most of them drew heavily upon Giraldus Cambrensis's *Expugnatio* as a source for the early family story, as well as the annals compiled by Philip Flattisbury. An important landmark was the compilation in the 1570s and 1580s of the famous Holinshed's *Chronicles*, which contains the first printed history of Ireland. This multi-authored and multi-layered work had its first edition in 1577, and, such was its success, it was brought out in an expanded second edition in 1587. The coverage of the history and geography of Ireland, which was extensive, was contributed to by several authors, including Richard Stanihurst. These scholars worked against the backdrop of an intense, ideological debate about whether Ireland should be reformed politically by peaceful means under the leadership of the older English population; or treated as an English colony and subjected to plantation and suppression by newly-arriving English. As the best-known Anglo-Norman family, it is not surprising that the FitzGeralds should figure prominently in the historical narrative given their former dominance; and likewise that attitudes to the issue of their continuing political role coloured the discussion of the future of the Irish polity come as no surprise.[3]

One of the earliest historians to contribute to this discourse was the English scholar, Edmund Campion, who composed his manuscript *Histories of Ireland* in a period of ten weeks while staying in the Dublin home of the Stanihursts in 1570–1. Drawing upon state and private records, as well as copies of both *Topographia* and *Expugnatio*, Campion's work was divided into two 'books': the first contained six chapters of descriptive material, mostly drawn from *Topographia*, as well as the history of Ireland down to 1169; the second continued the historical narrative down to 1570. Campion's work was infused with the spirit of Christian humanism which saw the Gaelic Irish as reformable by educative and persuasive means, and as partners – ultimately – of the 'Old English' in a newly-constituted kingdom of Ireland. Among the exemplars of loyal service of the Crown, Campion included the Geraldines: as conquerors in the depiction of Giraldus Cambrensis, as governors as recorded in Flattisbury's annals, and as lord deputies as evidenced in the state papers to which he had access. Campion's vision for Ireland as conveyed in his *Histories* was for a unified polity in which the Old English, led by the FitzGeralds (and indeed the Butlers), as well as the newer English under the wise leadership of Henry Sidney, his patron, would share the task of reforming the Gaelic Irish, to bring them to embrace the legal, social and cultural norms of an anglicised state. Campion's work remained in manuscript until its publication in 1633, but it enjoyed wide circulation in the intervening decades.[4]

Among those to whom a copy of Campion's *Histories* became available was Christopher St Lawrence, the lord of Howth, who was compiling a large scrapbook of Irish history which subsequently became known as *The Book of Howth*. St Lawrence also used a version of Cambrensis's *Expugnatio* for his narrative of the Norman conquest of Ireland. In this respect, full play was given to the magnificence of the contribution of the Geraldines to the establishment of English rule in Ireland, and, in particular, that of Maurice FitzGerald, the founder of the dynasty in Ireland. His famous speech before battle is recorded thus in *The Book of Howth*:

> Not to delight nor to idleness are we come into this land, but for to show adventure and prove our strength upon peril of our heads. We dare not trust any, for we are so few. Though few men we be, yet well weaponed we are; we will out stoutly and assay our fortune upon our foemen: we shall never stand back.

In terms of political allegiances, the St Lawrence family was very closely aligned to the FitzGeralds of Kildare and Desmond. Moreover, Christopher was a leader of the Pale community who opposed arbitrary Tudor government, and a proponent of the ruling of the kingdom of Ireland by the native aristocracy – led by the earl of Kildare, and the Old English gentry, including the St Lawrences. In sponsoring the compilation of *The Book of Howth*, Christopher was making available a version of Giraldus Cambrensis's work in which the contemporary resonances were very evident. The greedy ambition of English newcomers in the present was implicitly comparable to the heedless arrogance of some of the early Norman barons – those who antagonised the Gaelic population – and it was left to the Kildares and their peers, then and now, to provide just leadership.[5]

Campion's *Histories* became the core narrative of the history of Ireland down to 1509 for the compilers of Holinshed's *Chronicles*; the Englishman's skeletal work being fleshed out with additional information from Philip Flattisbury and other chroniclers. In following Campion's historical thread, the Holinshed team gave full play to the Geraldines' contribution as highlighted by Giraldus Cambrensis. This is especially evident in the positing of the role of newcomers from England and Wales in the political and religious reform of the island from the twelfth century onwards. Generally speaking, the outline of Campion's perspective on the Norman settlement in Ireland comes through. While the principal aristocratic lineages such as the Geraldines and the Butlers appear often in the narrative as agents of good governance, the Gaelic are presented as the 'enemies', alien to the English colony. But the picture of the early Tudor lordship elicited from the final section of Holinshed's contribution in 1577 is decidedly bleak from the metropolitan perspective – it is without the optimistic and unitive coda of Campion's *Histories* which adumbrated a Christian, humanist programme of reform through education, supported by established and newly-arrived English. The emphasis instead is on Gaelic usurpation of 'Englishe countreys', and the degeneration of families such as the Desmond Geraldines into the 'enormities' of Irish expropriations and bastardised lineages.[6]

Holinshed's team recruited Richard Stanihurst to contribute a human geography of Ireland, as well as a history of Henry VIII's reign to the *Chronicles*. Stanihurst, who at the time was a member of the 11th earl of Kildare's household, had been working on editing the manuscript history of his mentor, Edmund Campion. Stanihurst's *A Playne and Perfect Description of Ireland*, reflects his own cultural identity as a member of the older English community. Pride of place among his gallery of the nobility and gentry of Ireland goes to the FitzGeralds. He translates Giraldus's famous paean of praise to the dynasty, including this passage:

> Who are they that scale the enemies forte? The Giraldines. Who are they that defend their countrey? The Giraldines. Who are they that make the enemie quake in hys skynne? The Giraldines. Who are they whom envy backbiteth? The Giraldines.

When grafted on to the Campion/Holinshed history of the Norman colonial enterprise, Stanihurst's contribution represents the flowering of the English reforming mission in Ireland through the accomplishments of their sixteenth-century successors. His last chapter in *A Playne and Perfect Description* – on the *mores* of the Gaelic Irish – ended with a prayer for the amendment of 'that rude people' through their coming to self-awareness of their miserable state, and through enlightened reforms propagated by those charged with their governance, especially the Old English nobility and gentry, most notably the FitzGeralds. Dismissing contemporary critics of the Geraldines, he prayed that for the good of that 'miserable countrey and noble progeny', 'suspicion be abandoned and malicious slaunders be squatted, so that that noble house be trusted, and consequently the batterd weale publique of Ireland reedified'.[7]

Apart from his own research, it is clear that one of the reasons for his being recruited to write the history of Henry VIII's reign in Ireland was his unparalleled access to written and oral records of the careers of the earls of Kildare in the earlier sixteenth century. Not surprisingly, the Kildare FitzGeralds dominated the narrative, both as active protagonists down to 1534 and as significant absentees thereafter. The careers of the 8th and 9th earls, Garret More and Garret Oge respectively, were recounted in detail, the former providing the introductory passage to the history of Henry's reign, beginning 'Geralde FitzGerald erle of Kildare, a mightie man of stature, full of honor and courage ...'. The real hero of the piece however, was Garret Oge, the 9th earl, who was presented as a wise and accomplished figure, sophisticated in his domestic milieu and astute in the public sphere. His duels at court with Cardinal Wolsey were major set-pieces, replete with verbatim speeches and gallery-pleasing performances. The key events of the insurrection of Thomas, then Lord Offaly, were conveyed in such a way as to shift the blame on to conspirators in the administration in Dublin and London, and to present Thomas as a hapless and gormless foil to these plotters. Garret Oge was exculpated from any guilt for the actions of his 'headlong hotspur' of a son, which 'smote him so deeply to the heart, as upon the report thereof hee deceased in the Tower [of London]'. Stanihurst went so far as to eliminate Thomas from the line of the earldom, despite his short-lived succession to his father, enabling him to claim that 'there was never any Erle of that house read or heard of that bare armour in the fielde agaynst his Prince'.[8]

So effective was Stanihurst as an apologist for the family in the face of accusations of 'treacherie' that his history attracted the scrutiny of the censors as the work went through the presses. The English Privy Council complained of 'many thinges ... falcelie recited and contrarie to the ancient records' in 'an historie of Ireland by one Stanhurste'. The controversial passages appeared on one leaf of the book and characterised the anti-Geraldine conspirators, the 'belweathers and caterpillars' of Thomas's overthrow, in scurrilous terms. The offensive allusions to the principal enemies of the FitzGeralds – Archbishop John Alen, his namesake, John Alen, master of the rolls, and Robert Cowley, an associate of the countess of Ossory – were to be excised before sales of the work could continue. While these deletions perhaps spared the feelings of the descendants of those impugned, especially the favoured Butlers of Ormond, they hardly constituted the rectifying of substantial falsehoods or errors, but the gratuitous comments may have been seen more as injurious to already-fraught Anglo-Irish relations in the later 1570s. It is significant that the restored 11th earl, Gerald FitzGerald, Stanihurst's patron, was ordered to ensure the historian's compliance with the wishes of the Privy Council. Gerald's boyhood and youthful adventures in exile in Italy and elsewhere, as the heir to the Kildare house, were graphically recounted in Stanihurst's history. In the person of his employer, Stanihurst may have discerned the ancestral Geraldine qualities of martial valour and cultivated taste that could be necessary were the earl to attain a full restoration of his family's political power in the government of Ireland.[9]

By the time a new edition of Holinshed's *Chronicles* was being planned for 1587, the decline of Old English political and cultural ascendancy, adumbrated in the summoning of the 11th earl of Kildare and his chronicler by the Privy Council, was well under way. Kildare was dead, and Stanihurst was himself an exile on the continent. Chosen to edit the Irish section of the *Chronicles* was the Englishman, John Hooker, a noted antiquarian from Exeter who had served as secretary to the adventurer, Peter Carew, in Ireland in the late 1560s. While he left the description and the historical section down to 1547 of the first edition intact, Hooker's original contributions were a full version of Cambrensis's *Expugnatio* in English translation, and a continuation of the history of Ireland down to 1586. As Hiram Morgan has shown, Hooker's translation is really an adaptation of the Welshman's work in the light of the political situation of Ireland in the 1580s. For example, in his commentary on Giraldus's laudatory passage about the contribution of his Geraldine connections to the conquest and settlement of Ireland, Hooker makes a distinction between the earlier demeanour of the family and their later disaffection:

> It is verie true that these Geraldines ... did dailie grow and increase to much honour: there being at this instant two houses advanced to the titles of earledoms, and sundrie to the estates of barons. And so long as they continued in the steps of their ancestors, they were not so honourable as terrible to the Irish nation: but when they leaving English government, liked the loose life of that viperous nation, then they brought in coine and liuerie, and a number of other Irish and divelish impositions, which hath beene the ruine of their honour, the losse of their credit, & in the end will be the overthrow of all their houses and families.

Having been an eyewitness to the events of the first Desmond revolt, Hooker, an evangelical Protestant, was completely dismissive of any claims of loyalty on the part of that branch of the Geraldines. In the decade between the first and second editions of the Chronicles, a neo-colonialist approach to Ireland had become entrenched in the Dublin administration. Hooker in his history echoed the alarm of the New English authorities at the conjoining of political disaffection with Catholic dissidence on the part of the older nobility and gentry in the rebellions in Munster and Leinster in the 1570s and 1580s. He looked to the New English servitors to finish the conquest of Ireland begun four centuries previously.[10]

In the period of less than 20 years within which the works discussed here appeared – from 1570 to 1587 – a radical shift in attitudes to the governing of Ireland had taken place; but the evolution of policy was not linear, as evidenced by the cacophony of voices in the 1587 edition of the *Chronicles*. The text pre-serves the strata of Campion's Christian, humanist reformism, Stanihurst's pro-Geraldine civic patriotism, and Hooker's English Protestant imperialism. In particular, the uses which the authors made of the Geraldines' history were consistent with their diverse outlook on Ireland's constitution and polity. Stan-ihurst's *Description* incorporates Giraldus's fulsome praise for his Geraldine connections, and endorses their continuing political ascendancy in his own time. The history of Ireland down to 1509 contains a positive appraisal of the FitzGeralds' role in the government of the medieval colony. It is bisected, how-ever, by Hooker's translation of the *Expugnatio*, adapted to reflect a neo-colo-nial mentality, while the theme of Geraldine untrustworthiness is consolidated in his history of the period 1547–86. This strikes a discordant note with the concluding section: Stanihurst's staunch defence of the FitzGeralds' ascend-ancy in early Tudor Ireland.

NOTES

1   Brian FitzGerald, *The Geraldines: An Experiment in Irish Government, 1169–1601* (London, 1951), pp, 156–7; for a discussion of the historiographical significance of Giraldus's works, see Hiram Morgan, 'Giraldus Cambrensis and the Tudor conquest of Ireland', in idem (ed.), *Political Ideology in Ireland, 1541–1641* (Dublin, 1999), pp, 22–44; for the catalogue of the library in Maynooth Castle, see Gearóid Mac Niocaill (ed.), *Crown Surveys of Lands, 1540–41, with the Kildare Rental Begun in 1518* (Dublin, 1992), pp 312–14, 355–6.

2   For Flattisbury, see K. W. Nicholls, 'Flattisbury, Philip (fl. 1503–1526), *Oxford Dictionary of National Biography* (hereafter *ODNB*), online edn (www.oxforddnb.com/view/article/9676) (accessed 3 May 2011); *Holinshed's Irish Chronicle*, ed. Liam Miller and Eileen Power (Dublin, 1979), p. 102; Colm Lennon, *Richard Stanihurst the Dubliner (1547–1618)* (Dublin, 1981), pp, 106–16; for a modern interpretation, see, for example, Laurence McCorristine, *The Revolt of Silken Thomas: A Challenge to Henry VIII* (Dublin, 1987).

3   Raphael Holinshed (ed.), *Chronicles of England Scotland and Ireland* (London, 1577; second edn, 1587).

4   See, *Two Bokes of the Histories of Ireland Compiled by Edmund Campion*, ed. A. F. Vossen (Assen, 1963); for a discussion of the context, see Colm Lennon, 'Edmund Campion's Histories of Ireland and Reform in Tudor Ireland' in Thomas M. McCoog (ed.), *The Reckoned Expense: Edmund Campion and the Early English Jesuits* (Rome, 2007), pp 75–96.

5   For *The Book of Howth*, see *Calendar of the Carew Manuscripts preserved in the Archiepiscopal Library at Lambeth, 1515–1624* (London, 1871) (quotation is on p. 55); for a recent analysis of the significance of *The Book of Howth*, see Valerie McGowan-Doyle, '*The Book of Howth*: The Old English and the Elizabethan Conquest of Ireland' (Unpublished Ph.D. thesis, NUI, Cork, 2005).

6   For a discussion of the shaping of the Irish sections of Holinshed, see Colm Lennon, '"A iagged hystorie of a ragged wealepublicke": Holinshed's Irish *Chronicle*', in Paulina Kewes, Ian W. Archer and Felicity Heal (eds), *The Oxford Handbook to Holinshed's Chronicles* (Oxford, 2012).

7   Ibid., pp 81, 115–16.

8   Ibid., pp 252–85.

9   Ibid., pp 317–41; *Acts of the Privy Council of England, x: 1577–8*, ed. J. R. Dasent (London, 1895), pp 114–15, 142–3; for a discussion of the relationship between Stanihurst and the eleventh earl of

Kildare, see Vincent Carey, 'A "dubious loyalty": Richard Stanihurst, the "wizard" Earl of Kildare, and English-Irish identity', in idem and Ute Lotz-Heumann (eds), *Taking Sides? Colonial and Confessional Mentalités in Early Modern Ireland: Essays in Honour of Karl S. Bottigheimer* (Dublin, 2003), pp 61–77.

10   For Hooker, see S. Mendyk, 'Hooker, John (*c.*1527–1601)', *ODNB*, online edn (http://www.oxforddnb.com/view/article/13695) (accessed 3 May 2011); Morgan, 'Giraldus Cambrensis and the Tudor conquest of Ireland', in idem (ed.), *Political Ideology in Ireland*, pp 37–41; Holinshed (ed.), *Chronicles*, 1587 edn, iii, pp 41–42.

CHAPTER 6

Creating a Landscape
Carton and its Setting

Arnold Horner

One of the great glories of Carton is its park. Enclosed by a wall almost eight kilometres (five miles) in length, the rolling parkland landscape surrounding the great house extends to almost 400 hectares (1,000 acres). The wider setting is most evident from the steeple tower to the east of the house. Looking across the wooded banks of the Rye Water, the river that bisects the park, the Dublin and Wicklow mountains provide an exuberant backdrop to the much more subdued and subtle variations within the park itself. As it is today, Carton park (or Carton Demesne to use its more formal title) is the outcome of over three centuries of interaction between man and nature. In the mid-1700s, the geometrical lines and avenues of the formal spaces created more than half a century earlier were largely swept aside in favour of the 'natural' appearance that still dominates. Further modifications were effected in the early nineteenth century and during recent decades. As the following review indicates, many of these changes are well-documented in maps and other records, thus ensuring that the splendour of the setting is complemented by the detail of the history.

The first major development of the house and grounds at Carton probably dates to the late seventeenth century. A generation earlier, when the Civil Survey was compiled in 1654–6,[1] Carton was already in the possession of the Talbot family, to whom it had been leased by the earl of Kildare in 1603.[2] The Civil Survey records the presence of a stone house on the lands of Carton which was estimated to have been worth £200 in the year 1640 (the year before the outbreak of the Great Rebellion and the subsequent turmoil). However, 'being now ruined and decayed', this house was now reckoned to be worth just £60. In addition there was to be found upon the lands of Carton, 'one chapel of ease, one ruined stone house with a garden and orchard thereunto belonging, one decayed water mill and one decayed dovehouse'. Lord Walter FitzGerald (1858–1923), writing about Carton in 1903,[3] speculated that at least some of these buildings were located at Old Carton, which has an old churchyard and which lies outside the present park. Wherever their precise location may have been, the descriptions do not suggest a substantial development. The former value of £200 on the Carton house contrasts with the £3,000 accorded the

79

'manor house' at Maynooth for 1640 and also with the £500 value given after it had been burnt and 'only the walls left standing'. Elsewhere in the barony of Salt, the stone house, garden and orchards at St Wolstans near Celbridge were valued at £2,000 in 1640. The house at Castlewarden near Kill was similarly valued, while Lyons and two other houses were valued at £1,000. Carton was clearly in a lesser league, being comparable in valuation to the castles at Barberstown, Confey and several other places in the barony.

Half a century later, those relativities had changed significantly. During the 1680s, Carton was in the possession of Richard Talbot, a prominent Jacobite who was briefly Lord Lieutenant under James II and whom the king created earl and later duke of Tyrconnell. For his support of James, Richard's extensive estates, including Carton, were forfeited to the crown. Following a decade under crown control, Carton was one of a large number of properties auctioned by the 'Trustees for the sale of forfeited estates' in 1703. With 403 (presumably Irish) acres at a rent of £150, Carton was described as having

> On it 1 very fine House, with all manner of convenient offices and fine gardens &c., being the Mansion-house of the late Duke of Tyrconnell, also a stone-wall'd square castle on that part of the town-land call'd Old Carton, eight houses and cabins, the land well fenc'd, most of it quick'd, it has good conveniency of fire and water.[4]

The purchaser, Major-General Richard Ingoldsby, who was Master-General of the Ordnance and later a Lord Justice of Ireland, paid £1,860 for the property, a sum which no doubt took account of the substantial improvements that had been effected since the time of the Civil Survey.

A well-known later painting and a map of the 1740s give impressions of how Carton may have looked in the early eighteenth century, with the improvements that had been made, probably while Richard Talbot was in residence. A further relatively little-noticed source corroborates these records and provides the earliest evidence of how the surrounds of Carton had been developed. The library of the earls of Leicester at Holkham, Norfolk, contains a vast collection of maps and drawings arranged in some 150 volumes. These volumes were assembled by John Innys (1695–1778), a London publisher and book-seller, and sold as a 'ready-made' collection to an aspiring earl of Leicester sometime around 1750.[5] Embedded amongst a series of Irish maps and drawings making up volumes 98 and 99 is 'A Resemblance of the Improvem[en]ts of Carretowne'. Undated and drawn to the large scale of four perches to an inch (1:1008), this manuscript map is inscribed on the verso as 'A Draught of Carton, the Duke of Tyrconnell's house'. Drawn on the grid of one inch squares characteristic of most of the maps compiled during 1700–02 by the surveyors for the Trustees of the Forfeited Estates, this map may have been compiled to complement the more general small-scale Trustees' map of Carton by Thomas Higginson. Only a photograph of this latter map now survives.[6]

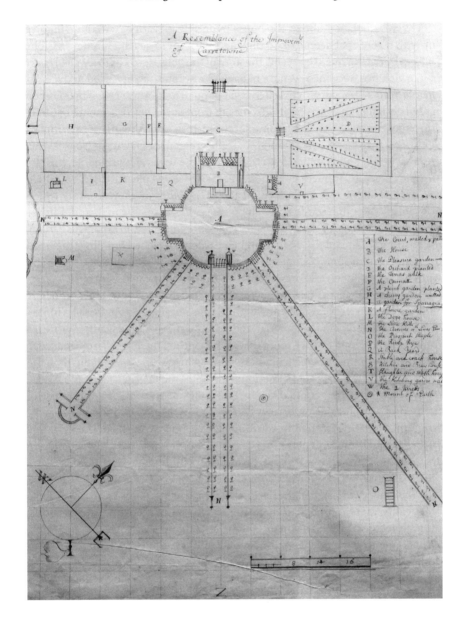

FIGURE 1 *'A resemblance of the Improvem[en]ts of Carretowne', perhaps drawn for the Trustees of the Forfeited Estates, c.1700, cartographer unknown. Part of collection of maps and drawings at Holkham, Norfolk.* By permission of Viscount Coke and the Trustees of the Holkham Estate

The 'resemblance' shows the house in outline elevation, without windows but with a roof that seems to be tiled and with up to seven chimneys visible. Flanked by two turrets at each end, the front of the house looks onto a walled court from which five tree-lined avenues radiate. The avenues are arranged in the fashionable 'bird's foot' pattern that had been popularised by the renowned French garden designer Le Nôtre. Some distance in front of the house a 'mount of earth' is located; this may have been some sort of historical earthwork, for example a motte, or it may have been a mound specially created for viewing purposes. Further away still, and at an angle to the front is the tower, identified here as the 'prospect steeple'. Immediately to the rear lay a walled pleasure garden, which was flanked to one side by an orchard and to the other by a terrace walk which overlooked the plum garden, in which there was a small canal, and, further away, the walled cherry garden. Smaller enclosures included an asparagus garden, the flower garden and the walled kitchen garden. Detached buildings included the 'dog house' at some distance to the main house, and nearer to it, a stable and wash house, a kitchen and brew-house, and a slaughter and wash house.

This plan suggests that late-seventeenth century Carton was aesthetically and functionally very much in line with contemporary fashion. With its blocks of walled gardens, its small canal and its straight avenues leading outward from the house area toward more distant prospects, the immediate landscape resonated with the geometrical idiom then fashionable. At the same time the range of out-buildings and functional gardens meant that Carton had the many accessories that could be expected alongside a large mansion-house of the period. Trustees' estates records for County Meath in 1700–02 demonstrate that what developed at Carton was just one expression, if a very fine one, of a much more general late seventeenth-century trend in the Dublin area, and perhaps across Ireland, toward the building of elegant houses and the ornamentation of their surrounds.[7]

Who may have designed the Carton landscape of the 1680s is unknown. In its practicality, in its approach to enclosure and in its linkage with water features, the architectural historian, Finola O'Kane, sees the strength of an Anglo-Dutch, as opposed to a more elaborate French, influence on the baroque garden design.[8] In the 1690s, during the time the property was being maintained by the state, the architect, Sir William Robinson, made some repairs to the house, while John Gregory, 'gardener at Carrtowne', was being paid 'for looking after the house and gardens'.[9] Much later again, in the 1750s, the walled 'Gregory's garden' is portrayed on John Rocque's map of Maynooth village. Perhaps Gregory represents a contemporary link between Maynooth and Carton.[10] In this context, it may be interesting also to note that in the late 1650s Wentworth, 17th Earl of Kildare, had given a lease for a nursery at Maynooth.[11] What became of this is again not known, but it does suggest that interest in planting and gardens was part of the local scene.

The Ingoldsby family were the proprietors of Carton for almost four decades until 1739. During that period, only limited changes appear to have been made to the garden landscape around the house. Henry Ingoldsby, who inherited the estate in 1712, bought trees, plants and seeds for the gardens. The gardeners he employed included John Dodson, a Major Sawyer, and George Lamb, who was brought from England in 1724. Although some extensions may have been made to the area of walled garden north-west of the house, 'the Carton garden remained that of a typical provincial nobleman at the turn of the ... century, who favoured an Anglo-Dutch style of garden in preference to a more French-Italianate continental model.'[12]

This is the landscape so vividly displayed in the 1730s painting of Carton that is attributed to William van der Hagen. Here one can readily appreciate the scale of the formal avenues and the extent of the various gardens to the rear of the house. This is a painting that creates a powerful impression although it may also incorporate some departures from reality. As represented on a near-contemporary map of 1744, the extent of the rear gardens seems less. More significantly, the background of rolling hills is represented as if it lies to the north-west. In fact, the hills appear to closely resemble the Dublin mountains as they might be seen looking away from the house to the south-east.

In 1739, Robert, the 19th Earl of Kildare, purchased Carton from the Ingoldsby family. His purchase was part of a programme to equip the Kildares with city and country residences fully in keeping with the status and image they wished to project as the premier peerage in Ireland. Kildare House (now Leinster House) in Dublin was being designed by Richard Castle and was already under construction. Now Carton offered a convenient location for a country mansion close to Dublin. Castle was commissioned to oversee the enlargement of the house, and various craftsmen were engaged to ensure a state of the art decoration. Alongside, an ambitious programme was developed for the remodelling and enlargement of the park and, a few years later, for (as is discussed in chapter 13) the redevelopment of the village most associated with the estate, Maynooth. Robert died in 1744 and was succeeded by his son, James (1722–73). While James and his wife Emily (1731–1814) – from 1767 the Duke and Duchess of Leinster – resided there, some of the most significant developments were effected at Carton.

The planning of the enlarged park started in the early 1740s. From early on, a master plan must have been in place that visualised a major enlargement about the axis of the Rye Water. The property purchased from the Ingoldsbys had been the townland of Carton, including the area around Old Carton churchyard. Although taking in the area leading to the steeple, much of this land was flat or of subdued relief, with limited potential for the creation of a 'natural' rolling landscape of the type then becoming fashionable.[13] The best land for such a landscape, along parts of the Rye Water, lay outside the direct

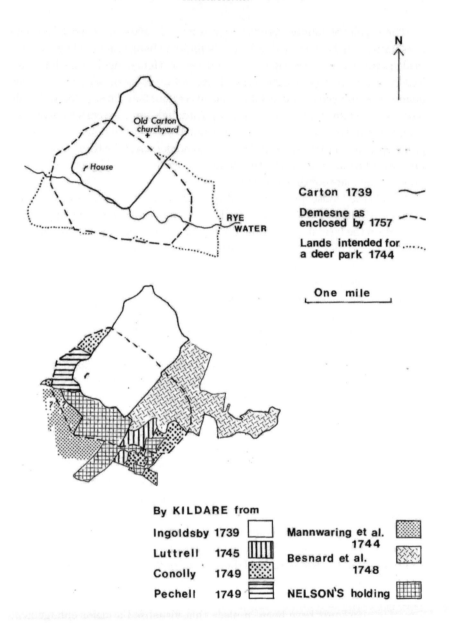

N
↑

Carton 1739 ⌒

Demesne as
enclosed by 1757 ╌╌╌

Lands intended for ·······
a deer park 1744

One mile

By KILDARE from

Ingoldsby 1739	☐	Mannwaring et al. 1744	▨
Luttrell 1745	▥	Besnard et al. 1748	▨
Conolly 1749	▨		
Pechell 1749	▤	NELSON'S holding	▦

FIGURE 2 *Growth of Carton (top), the new park compared to the original Carton townland, (above) lands added 1739–49. First published in the 'Quarterly Bulletin of the Irish Georgian Society', vol. 18 (1975), p. 55.*

control of the Kildares, and had to be acquired by purchase or exchange. As a result of five transactions during the 1740s the land in Kildare ownership doubled, extending into several neighbouring townlands and including a small exchange of lands with the Conolly estate based at Castletown.[14] The lands acquired are all shown on a map of 1744 depicting 'the demesne of Carrtown together with a map of the adjacent lands intended for a deer-park'. Compiled by Charles Baylie and John Mooney this unusual map focuses particularly on the topography of the proposed park.[15] A series of 'clouded spots' identify the rises within the park, with more precise data being given at various 'spot heights'. Reference panels give the names of townlands, and of fields within the proposed development, and also list the bearings from the prospect steeple of various more distant but prominent features and gentlemen's seats. With its emphasis on physique and inter-visibility, this large map must have been a key document in planning the park.

The development of Carton came at significant cost. The initial purchase from the Ingoldsbys involved an outlay of £8,000, and a further £7,500 was needed to acquire the lands of Kellystown and Criefstown, including a substantial section making up the eastern part of the new park. A further very significant ongoing expenditure was demanded with the far-reaching make-over of the landscape. Nonetheless, work proceeded rapidly, with the removal of many of the established features. Most of the gardens north-west of the house were taken away to leave a view across open grassland to the small wooded glen of the Glashrooneen. On the south-east side, in front of the house, the court, its walls and railings, and four of the five avenues, as well as the mount of earth and some small canals, were to be swept away. Only the north-east avenue was maintained as the principal approach to the house from the Dunboyne road. As early as 1750 Emily, then countess of Kildare, was writing that she 'was excessively impatient to see how the lawn looks, now that some of the hedges and ditches are taken away'.[16] The south-east view was now across open grass-land, planted with small irregular stands of trees. In the distance, the Dublin mountains might be seen, while nearer at hand the 40-metre high obelisk, built by the Conollys in 1740–41, appeared near the skyline.

John Rocque completed the first of several exceptionally fine maps of the new park in 1756–7. The frontispiece to his volume of maps of the 'manor of Maynooth' features a view of Carton with the avenue leading to the steeple apparently still intact, but the subsequent map of the park in this volume shows it removed.[17] A new perimeter wall had been established, new lodges had been built at each of the four entrance gates, and several roads which previously passed through the park had been re-routed. There had also been extensive planting, with a belt of trees and shrubs sheltering a perimeter boundary walk and a labyrinthine 'wilderness' being developed along the downstream section of the Rye Water. Extensive enclosures now occurred only to the north-east of the main house, where a new home farm area included a gardener's house, a 'hott wall', a large (3.6 ha/9 acres) kitchen garden, a 2ha. nursery and several paddocks. Away from the house, the only group of buildings to remain, apart from the prospect steeple, were the cottage and outbuildings south of the river in Waterstown. These had been leased to Richard Nelson, one of the earl's legal representatives, and he continued to reside there until his death in the 1760s.

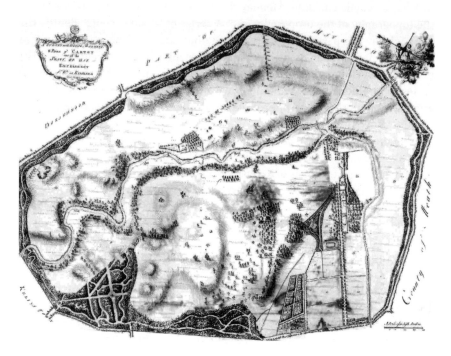

FIGURE 3 *The newly enclosed park as it appears on John Rocque's map of 1757 (Cambridge University Ms Plans x.4).*

A huge transformation had been achieved, much of it apparently guided by the direct involvement of James and Emily. They took a close interest in landscape developments in England, but efforts to directly involve a leading garden designer, most notably the renowned Lancelot 'Capability' Brown (1716–83), appear to have been unsuccessful. Brown allegedly rebuffed the Kildare invitation with the comment he had 'not yet finished England'. However, as Finola O'Kane shows, the celebrated work of Charles Hamilton (1704–86) at Painshill Park in Surrey appears to bear comparison with Carton and may have been a significant influence. As early as 1750, James was acknowledging the directions offered by Hamilton 'to lay the ground to grass', and when Emily visited Painshill in 1757 she found that 'nothing was ever so lovely as Mr. Hamilton's park'.[18]

FIGURE 4 *View of the house in 1760. Detail from John Rocque's map, NLI Ms 22,003 (A).*

Work on the park continued throughout the 1760s, much of it being driven by the continuing enthusiasm of Emily. She liaised with the noted botanist, Peter Collinson (1694–1768), hired gardeners, and promoted a policy of planting great variety, of mixing foreign trees with natives.[19] A particular focus was now the development, only partly successful, of water features. By the early 1760s, a previously narrow feeder channel to a reservoir north-east of the house had been widened, to create a 'New River' extending from the park wall. On this 'sheet of water' a boat house was built, with a Chinese bridge being added nearby, presumably a response to the increasing popularity of Chinese-style gardens. With additional tree planting, the home farm was effectively camouflaged from the park while at the same time a shady retreat was created near the house. The outcome certainly satisfied Emily. Writing to her husband in London, she commented on the beauty of the New River, adding 'one turn of it is a masterpiece in the art of laying out ... I defy Kent, Brown or Mr Hamilton to excel it'.[20]

The Rye Water posed a greater challenge. From the commencement of planning for the new park, the river seems to have been recognised as a significant feature, yet it cut only a narrow channel in a fairly broad but slightly incised valley, with the result that it was hidden below the level of much of the park and

87

could not be seen from the house. Water was ideally an exciting component of 'natural' vistas, an enhancement to the rolling lawns and the background trees and mountains. But surveys by Captain (later General) Vallancey (1726–1812) demonstrated that extensive changes would be needed if the river was to be visible from the house – in places the ground might have to be smoothed and lowered up to eight metres (25 feet), or else the river had to be raised that amount.[21] By constructing a series of weirs, it proved possible to widen the river to about 30 metres (100 feet) and to create several small islands. An elegant five-arch bridge, probably designed by Thomas Ivory (1732–86), was built across the river in the mid-1760s. At Waterstown in the same period, the cottage was re-developed

FIGURE 5 *A surveyor taking a line of sight from the portico at Carton, looking toward the Rye Water. Detail from NLI Ms 22,004.*

as an ornamental woodland feature, no doubt influenced by the then fashionable poetic garden trend. But the view of the river from the house demanded too much.

Bernard Scalé's map of 1769 shows Carton toward the end of the period of major transformation,[22] shortly before the death in 1773 of James and the departure of Emily. The ambience of the park is also captured in a series of paintings (some of which are discussed in chapters 9 and 10) by Arthur Devis (1753), Thomas Roberts (*c*.1770) and William Ashford (1779).[23] About this time too, the celebrated traveller and writer Arthur Young offered an extensive account of the landscape developed under James and Emily. Ranking the park amongst the finest in Ireland, he described:

> ... a vast Lawn, which waves over gentle hills, surrounded by plantations of great extent, and which break and divide in places, so as to give much variety. A large but gentle vale winds through the whole, in the bottom of which a small stream has been enlarged into a fine river, which throws a cheerfulness through most of the scenes: over it a handsome stone bridge. There is a great variety on the banks of this vale; part of it consists of mild and gentle slopes, part steep banks of thick wood; in another place they are formed into a large shrubbery, very elegantly laid out, and dressed in the highest order, with a cottage, the scenery about which is uncommonly pleasing; and farther on, this vale takes a strong character, having a rocky bank on one side, and steep slopes scattered irregularly, with wood on the other. On one of the most rising grounds in the park is a tower. From the top of which the whole scenery is beheld; the park spreads on every side in fine sheets of lawn, kept in the highest order by 1,100 sheep, scattered over with rich plantations, and bounded by a large margin of wood, through which is a riding.[24]

In the final decades of the eighteenth century, William Robert, the 2nd Duke of Leinster, appears to have been more occupied by politics than by parks. Nonetheless the role of the Rye Water was again reviewed in 1788. A sketch plan was made of the downstream part of the river valley, leading into Kellystown, apparently with the intention (never fully implemented) of creating a new road into the park from the Luttrellstown (County Dublin) direction.[25] Section plans were also compiled that again highlighted the problems that had to be addressed if the river was to be visible from the house.

During the period 1810–40 Augustus Frederick, the 3rd duke, and from 1818 his wife Charlotte, renewed interest in the house and park, making some far-reaching changes. Richard Morrison (1767–1849), one of the foremost Irish architects, made extensive internal alterations to the house about 1817. Associated with these changes, the front of the house was moved to the northwest side and new approaches were laid out. On the south-east side, carefully spaced bushes and shrubs were planted on the lawn near the house. An extension of the ha-ha or sunken fence was made to separate the lawn from the rest of the park. Sunken fences, hedges, and small sections of wall also appeared elsewhere in the park, dividing it into five or six major units and presumably facilitating park management. In the 1820s a new plantation was added near the prospect tower. By 1837 (when the first Ordnance Survey map of Carton was made) the lawn had been further formalised by being laid out in four squares about a fountain. Alterations were also made to the kitchen garden which was reduced in size as the nursery was extended and as a new range of hothouses were built.

The major achievement of this period was the creation of a lake on the Rye Water. Around 800 metres in length and up to 100 metres wide, it extended from near the house as far as the cottage at Waterstown, where a dam had been built. At the dam a small picturesque waterfall straddled by a wooden bridge was created. The cottage itself was remodelled, with the shell room being made a feature. Following over a decade of active planning, the lake was completed in 1835. As a result, a greatly enlarged water area became a feature of the park. However the long-sought objective of making it possible to view the lake from the house remained elusive.

The creation of the park at Carton is a spectacular achievement, the outcome of a series of interventions over a 150-year period between the 1680s and the 1830s. The size of the park is so great that it can really only be comprehended from the air or indeed from a satellite. As a distinctive, superbly-landscaped topographical unit, it is a remarkable physical and cultural resource, comparable to (although smaller, 400 ha against 700 ha) the great Phoenix Park. As such it deserves to be valued and jealously protected. In recent decades, the landscape has proven resilient to the discrete development of golf courses and to the addition of some housing. To date, particularly around the house, along the river and from the steeple, the great vistas remain. If the park and its wall can be regarded as indicative of a past era of privilege and social exclusion, its landscape is now an enduring witness and heritage to the ambition and vision of the past, potentially an asset of incalculable value for the future. It is the setting that makes Carton.

NOTES

1   R. C. Simington (ed.), *The Civil Survey A.D. 1654–1656, viii: County of Kildare* (Dublin, 1952), p. 7.

2   Walter FitzGerald, 'Copy of a lease of Carton to William Talbot, Recorder of Dublin, 1603', in *Journal of the County Kildare Archaeological Society* (hereafter *JCKAS*), vi:6 (1909–11), pp 516–19.

3   Walter FitzGerald, 'Carton' in *JCKAS*, iv (1903), pp 1–33.

4   'A book of postings and sale of the forfeited and other estates vested in the trustees nominated and appointed by Act of Parliament 11 and 12 William III', National Library of Ireland (NLI), MS 3024, p. 32.

5   The Innys collection has the title 'A general system of cosmography or elements of astronomy and geography, illustrated by maps, plans and views. Collected from the most eminent authors, ancient and modern.' For its general significance see Pearce Grove and Helen M. Wallis, 'Discovery of the Rawlinson copperplate maps of the Americas and their related prints', in *The Map Collector*, 56 (1991), pp 12–21. Thanks are due to Dr Suzanne Reynolds, curator of manuscripts and printed books, Holkham, and to Mr W. O. Hassall, former honorary librarian at Holkham, for facilitating information on, and a viewing of, the Carton map.

6   Arnold Horner, 'Carton, Co. Kildare: a case study of the making of an Irish demesne', in *Quarterly Bulletin of the Irish Georgian Society* (hereafter *QBIGS*), 18 (1975), pp 45–105, especially pp 90–2.

7   Arnold Horner and Rolf Loeber, 'Landscape in transition: descriptions of forfeited properties in counties Meath, Louth and Cavan in 1700', in *Analecta Hibernica*, 42 (2011), pp 59–119. Also, Rolf Loeber, 'Irish hountry houses and castles of the late Caroline period: an unremembered past recaptured', in *QBIGS*, 16 (1973), pp 1–70.

8   Finola O'Kane, *Landscape Design in Eighteenth-Century Ireland: Mixing Foreign Trees with the Natives* (Cork, 2004), pp 90–8.

9   FitzGerald, 'Carton', p. 11.

10   However, 'Gregory's garden' may alternatively derive from the rector Revd Benjamin Gregory, who was the incumbent from 1719 to 1742.

11   Lease of house in Maynooth and 'little spot of ground called ye old haggard', 20 Sep. 1657, from Wentworth FitzGerald, 17th Earl of Kildare, and others to Patrick Dunn, Maynooth, gardener Public Records of Northern Ireland (PRONI), Leinster Papers, D3078/1/5/29. The orchard was to be planted with apple, cherry, pear, plum, peach and apricot trees – the kind of plants to be found in the walled areas near large houses in the late seventeenth century. Patrick Dunn was bound to 'from time to time remove ye one half of ye nursery trees & plant them into whatsoever place ye said Wentworth ... shall think fit'.

12   O'Kane, *Landscape Design*, p. 95.

13   D. Clifford, *A History of Garden Design* (London, 1962), esp. ch. 6. Also T. Reeves–Smyth, 'Demesnes', in F. H. A. Aalen, K. Whelan and M. Stout (eds), *Atlas of the Irish Rural Landscape* 2nd edn (Cork, 2011), pp 278–86.

14   A. A. Horner, 'Land transactions and the making of Carton demesne', in *JCKAS*, xv:4 (1974–5), pp 387–96.

15   Carton Maps, NLI, MS 22,500. See also A. A. Horner, 'Some examples of the representation of height data on Irish maps before 1760 – including an early use of the spot height method', in *Irish Geography*, 7 (1974), pp 68–80.

16   FitzGerald, 'Carton', p. 16.

17   Refers to the volume of maps making up 'A survey of the volume of the manor of Maynooth (1757)', in Cambridge University Library, MS Plans x.4. Another version of this volume, with more limited colour, is available at the NLI, MS 25,002 and does not feature this frontispiece.

18   O'Kane, *Landscape Design*, pp 113–4.

19   Reviewed at greater length in ibid., pp 107–17.

20   Emily FitzGerald to James FitzGerald, 10 Dec. 1762, in Brian FitzGerald (ed.), *Correspondence of Emily, Duchess of Leinster (1731–1814)* 3 vols (Dublin, 1949–57), vol. i, p. 150.

20   'Section thro the vale where the bridge is to be built at Carton [June 1763]', NLI, MS 22,504.

22   Carton Maps, NLI, MS 22,504 (A).

23   Shown in colour in O'Kane, *Landscape Design*, p. 103, 104, 110, 115.

24   Arthur Young, *A Tour in Ireland 1776–1779*, 4th edn, ed. A. W. Hutton (London, 1892), vol. i, pp 21–2.

25   Shown in Horner, 'Carton, Co. Kildare', pp 74–5.

CHAPTER 7

'French Horns Playing at Every Meal'
Musical Activity at Carton
1747–1895

Karol Mullaney-Dignam

Domiciliary entertaining or the hosting of social gatherings at home was the primary form of rural sociability for the Irish landed elite in the eighteenth and nineteenth centuries. Music featured as an integral aspect of elite social and cultural life during this period – conspicuously so at the large Palladian mansion begun at Carton in the late 1730s. The house was occupied from 1747 by James FitzGerald (1722–73), the 20th Earl of Kildare, and his wife Emily Lennox (1731–1814).[1] As James spearheaded the re-emergence of the FitzGeralds as Ireland's foremost political and social power, Emily encouraged the development of Carton as a centre of fashionable sociability. She was keen that their house should look 'pretty, and smart, and well furnished' and agreed with her friend Caroline Ponsonby (1719–60), a daughter of the 3rd duke of Devonshire, that many Irish landowners 'didn't care' if their houses were 'fit to receive company – provided they can stuff them, that's enough'.[2] Although it would take many years for Carton to be fitted up to Emily's taste, the FitzGeralds would host most of the prominent figures in contemporary society over the next century with music featuring as an agent of hospitality. By this time, the acquisition of musical goods and services and the provision of musical entertainments were attestations of socio-economic status.

James was, as Horace Walpole (1717–97) put it, 'first peer of Ireland'.[3] Alongside his seniority in the Irish House of Lords and a reasonably successful military career, he maintained substantial electoral interests and controlled a sizeable block of MPs in the Irish House of Commons. His wife was a daughter of the 2nd duke of Richmond (grandson of King Charles II of England), a sister-in-law of the politician Henry Fox (1705–74) and a god-daughter of George II (1683–1760). By virtue of these associations, James also acquired an English peerage, which carried the title Viscount Leinster of Taplow, Buckinghamshire, and a seat in the English House of Lords. While social connections evidently provided political influence, such influence also stemmed from the cachet gained by the provision of good hospitality and entertainment. As Toby Barnard has observed, these aspects of social life, usually overseen by women in the town or country house, complemented and assisted the political or business interests of their husbands. This generally implied that the more influential the male head of household, the greater the social responsibility of his female counterpart.[4]

As a well-connected, high-society family with recently renewed ties to the royal household, the FitzGeralds received invitations to the most exclusive social events in Dublin and London. It was essential that the various children living at Carton from the 1750s (in addition to their ever-increasing family, James and Emily reared Emily's orphaned sisters, Louisa, Sarah and Cecilia Lennox, who had been sent from England in 1751) received formal instruction in social courtesy and deportment, including dance steps, and lessons commenced with a dancing-master at a very early age. Dancing was a particularly necessary accomplishment for the upper classes, featuring at assembly-room balls and as part of the formal engagements of the vice-regal court at Dublin Castle and at court in London. Music in country houses typically occurred in connection with social dancing; one of the earliest recorded references to social dancing at Carton was a large invitational ball held on 29 April 1762. James had been elevated to the marquisate of Kildare the previous year and his wife was eager to impress, spending days before the ball rearranging the furniture of the various reception rooms. To her mind the ball 'went off well', although she complained to her husband of financial stringency on the part of the butler, leading her husband to reply: 'Stoyte was more careful than was quite right upon such an occasion'.[5] Though it is not known who supplied the music for the ball on this occasion, surviving musical works by a number of composers bear titles which suggest musical patronage by the family; those by the Neapolitan Francesco Bianchi (1752–1810), for instance, include *The Marquis of Kildare's March* and *The Marchioness of Kildare's Minuet*.[6]

Music featured in the social education and cultural edification of the FitzGerald children. It was, by the mid-eighteenth century, socially acceptable for young gentlemen to practice as musicians, singers and actors in an amateur capacity outside of the home, particularly for charitable purposes. Women, however, usually learned music simply for domestic diversion and tended only to play for the informal entertainment of relatives and friends. Together with dancing, painting, sewing, drawing and learning languages, music-making was among a number of requisite 'accomplishments' for women of rank. Musical practice in the home was deemed a suitable activity for alleviating idleness, but also considered appropriate as a means of female display. Singing and playing music often facilitated courtship; more importantly it indicated that an investment had been made in a young lady's social refinement and in her preparation for her future roles as wife, mother and hostess. Music was thus a significant agent in the formation and expression of female identity but even if their skills were applied on 'private' occasions at country houses like Carton, professional musicians were always employed for formal, 'public', invitational events.[7]

Music may also have featured in amateur theatricals staged by the FitzGeralds at Carton from the 1760s.[8] Among these were versions of John Gay's *The Beggar's Opera* (1728) and Charles Coffey's *The Devil to Pay* (1732). Although it is possible that the Carton productions were spoken-word adaptations, the choice of these particular ballad-operas (comedies in which songs, set to well-known traditional or contemporary melodies, alternated with spoken dialogue), hints that at least some of the parts might have been sung. While music, song and dance had long been aspects of theatre production in Ireland, a strong tradition of ballad-opera had developed in Irish theatres by the eighteenth century; actors were expected to have the ability to sing, while theatre orchestras offered the principal employment for professional musicians.[9] The evidence shows that the FitzGeralds were keen theatre-goers and were encouraged in this by Emily FitzGerald, whose own father had been involved in the promotion of Italian opera in London.[10] When in Dublin, Emily regularly took her children and her sisters to musical entertainments at the Crow Street Theatre which targeted quality clientele by offering ambitious, elaborately-staged productions and by insisting that strict etiquette be observed.[11]

Following the elevation of the marquis of Kildare to the dukedom of Leinster in 1766, the younger FitzGerald children were sent to reside at the family's seaside villa at Blackrock, south of Dublin city. The new duke was popular in Ireland, often publicly fêted for his patriotism and his opposition to attempts by successive viceroys to 'manage' the Irish parliament.[12] Whereas the family's urban residence, Leinster House, functioned as an entertainment venue capable of accommodating hundreds of people, it seems that Carton was reserved for lavish displays of sociability intended to showcase the house and its setting. The duchess planned 'moonlight' balls in the autumn while the duke held the habitual 'little hop at Christmas'.[13] Some of these social events were also intended for the socialisation of the older children, whose marriages would secure the further expansion of FitzGerald patronage networks and the future of the dynasty. The girls of marriageable age were guided in their preparations by their favourite aunt, and sometime guardian, Louisa Lennox (1743–1821). In 1758, Louisa had married Thomas Conolly (1738–1803), whose Castletown estate bordered Carton and whose house the FitzGerald children considered as another home. The Conollys, having no children of their own, indulged relatives and friends in a variety of entertainments and musicians were regularly hired to provide music for dancing. Balls held there in 1772 enabled Emily FitzGerald (1752–1818) and her sister Charlotte (1758–1836) to rehearse for their formal 'debut' presentations at Dublin Castle.[14]

As well as the close connection with Castletown, the FitzGeralds maintained firm ties in England where they spent time socialising with friends and relatives each year. The men of the family were educated in the most prestigious English schools and, like their ancestors, went on to participate in political or military life. Educated at Eton, William Robert FitzGerald (1749–1804), 2nd Duke of Leinster, developed his taste in fashionable diversions during his Grand Tour of the European continent, a cultural rite of passage for young men of title and wealth. Aside from viewing sites and objects of classical antiquity, Renaissance works of arts, fortifications and buildings of significance in the late 1760s, William also attended operas, concerts, balls and theatricals in the primary social centres in France, Italy, Austria and Germany.[15] Upon his return to Ireland, he immersed himself in the elite social life of Dublin city (which he represented in the Irish House of Commons). He succeeded his father as duke of Leinster in 1773 and two years later married Emilia St George (*c.*1753–98), a wealthy Irish heiress who was known to dance 'the most perfect, graceful minuet that a woman of fashion can dance'.[16]

Under Emilia's influence music featured as an accompaniment to daily dining at Carton with various visitors remarking upon it, notably Caroline Dawson (1750–1813), afterwards the countess of Portarlington, who commented on the 'French horns playing at every meal'. Although the repertory of the French horn was not noted, presumably the provision of such music at mealtimes was unusual enough in the late 1770s to elicit the comment.[17] Dinnertime tended to be a ceremonious occasion in any country house, necessitating a designated dining-room, formal dress and processional procedures based on social rank. At Carton however, all mealtimes appear to have occasioned this type of ceremony, leading Lady Dawson again to comment: 'Everything seems to go on in great state here, the duchess appears in sack and hoops and diamonds in an afternoon ... and such quantities of plate etc. that one would imagine oneself in a palace. And there are servants without end.' The duchess was typically bedecked in diamonds, while servants dressed in blue and buff uniforms served 'courses upon courses' of luxury foods, including chocolate, honey, coloured breads and cakes. In between mealtimes, guests were free to explore 'a whole suite of rooms' which appears to have included a designated music-room.[18]

Outside of the home, the FitzGeralds continued to patronise musical concerts and theatrical productions as well as a variety of charity balls. While many members of the landed elite were primarily motivated by social and philanthropic concerns in their attendance at musical entertainments in Dublin, William and Emilia displayed a genuine interest. Their children, who lived principally at Carton, had a daily routine which included dancing and music lessons.[19] Among the musicians who appear to have received the patronage of the family at this time was the keyboard virtuoso Philip Cogan (*c.* 1748–1833). Like many musicians, Cogan supplemented his primary income (as the organist at Dublin's

St Patrick's Cathedral between 1780 and 1810) by composing stage works, songs, piano concertos and keyboard sonatas, playing in theatre orchestras and teaching. His pupils included talented young men like Michael Kelly (1762–1826), an actor, singer, composer and theatrical manager who had a remarkable international career as a tenor and was one of the leading figures in British theatre around the turn of the nineteenth century. Cogan also taught Thomas Moore (1779–1852). Best known for his *Irish Melodies* which were published in several volumes in the early nineteenth century, Moore was a prolific poet, songwriter and entertainer – as well as being the biographer of Lord Edward FitzGerald (1763–98).[20] In 1780 Cogan was employed by the Conollys of Castletown and, given that both families shared a French dancing-master at this time, it is likely that he was also employed by the FitzGeralds.[21] This is borne out by the fact that the duchess was the dedicatee of Cogan's *Six Sonatas for the Harpsichord* published in London around 1782.[22]

Country house sociability seems to have been invigorated during the 1780s by the increasingly militarised state of the countryside. The depletion of Irish garrisons to bolster the British war effort in North America, and the French alliance with the colonies, had sparked a threat of foreign invasion in 1778. This situation brought into being the Volunteers, an armed civilian defence force organised into small, local corps commanded and paid for by prominent members of the landed gentry. For his part, the 2nd duke of Leinster commanded the 1st Regiment of Dublin Infantry Volunteers and was the Volunteer commander-in-chief until 1780. Military parades and choreographed reviews swiftly became part of the cultural milieu, as did military bands providing marching and ceremonial music. Volunteer officers also featured among those socialising at estates like Carton in this period, as did officers of the British army and navy, many of them relatives and associates of the FitzGeralds. Even though the Volunteers declined after 1783, and were eventually replaced by government militias in 1793, a martial presence continued to be felt in Irish social life. Regimental bands were used to provide musical entertainment at the country residences of their commanders where the repertoire included arrangements of the popular theatre and dance music of the day. Marching music, in turn, became part of the popular music canon; pieces like 'The Dublin Volunteers quick march' were among a selection of airs published in Glasgow in the 1780s.[23] The martial climate was reflected too in the titles of works associated with the FitzGeralds at this time, including *His Grace the Duke of Leinster's March and Quick Step* and *The Marquis of Kildare's Slow and Quick March* by the prodigious Thomas Simpson Cooke (1782–1848).[24]

Like his father, the 2nd duke of Leinster was a popular politician, upon whose support the vice-regal administration depended, and in 1783 he was conferred with the first knighthood of the newly instituted Order of St Patrick.[25] Entertainments offered by the FitzGeralds around this time ranged from small dinner parties to large fancy dress balls, many of which were held at Leinster House. Carton remained the primary venue for significant family celebrations, including christenings, comings-of-age and weddings. Individual musicians – such as pipers or fiddlers – typically played for the more informal dances, but the services of a band were usually required for large-scale, invitational balls when the numerous guests in attendance were entertained on the basis of social status. Thus, fiddlers might perform for guests of higher social rank in the drawing-rooms of the house, while a military band played to those of lower social rank in marquee tents pitched outdoors for the occasion, and an individual piper might be found playing in the servants' quarters. Although the leisure time and activities of servants were regulated at country houses, particularly in the ducal household at Carton (see chapter 8), dancing and alcohol consumption were sanctioned and financed by landlords on special occasions.

The christening of the duke's eldest son and heir, Augustus Frederick (1791–1874), was the occasion of a magnificent ball at Carton in December 1791. In the drawing-room, select guests watched 26 couples performing country dances to music provided by three fiddlers and a dulcimer-player (a stringed-instrument played by striking with small hammers).[26] Country dances had traditionally been performed outdoors in large square, circle ('round') or line ('long') configurations, but by the eighteenth century the formalisation of dancing among the landed elite in urban venues meant that these were now mostly practised indoors by four, six or eight couples. Where indoor space allowed, as at Carton in 1791, versions of 'long' dances could be performed by a large number of couples arranged in two rows, men facing women.[27] These configurations, generally known as 'longways as many as will', still resembled the *rincífada* (long dances) danced outdoors by the Irish tenantry to jig music.[28] Nonetheless, 'refined' country dances were also popular in elite social circles; the duke's younger sister Lucy FitzGerald (1771–1851) was among seven couples, including members of the royal family, who performed them at St James's Palace, London, in June 1793.[29]

There were fewer grand displays of sociability at Carton during the 1790s for a variety of reasons, not least among them the dwindling finances of the 2nd duke. This was due in part to the number of siblings he had, whose requisite portions and jointures heavily encumbered the Leinster estate. The duke also began to clash with the vice-regal administration on issues of Catholic relief and parliamentary reform and was eventually removed from a number of key political and military offices.[30] Nonetheless, music and dancing still formed the basis of family gatherings as noted by the duke's sister, Lucy, in her diary in November 1796:

> We were a delightful party. Lady Edward was there the whole time and Edward backwards and forwards. We had beautiful dancing, and such a ballet called Didone. Lady Edward composed it mostly, I selected the music.[31]

'Lady Edward' was Pamela (*c.* 1773–1831), the wife of Lucy's older brother, Edward, one of the most high-profile members of the Society of United Irishmen, the revolutionary organisation which instigated the 1798 rebellion (see chapter 12). Of obscure origins, Pamela had grown up in France in the household of the Duke of Orléans, Louis Philippe Joseph d'Orléans (1747–93), an active supporter of the French revolution. She was raised by his mistress, Stéphanie Félicité Ducrest de St-Aubin (1746–1830), the countess of Genlis, who was renowned for her musical proficiency, particularly on the harp.[32]

Given the increasing indigence of the FitzGeralds, and their connection to a leader of the rebellion, Carton was compromised as a social venue for some years after 1798. In June 1799, one visitor described sharing with the recently widowed duke and his four unmarried daughters 'the shabbiest dinner I ever saw at a great man's table', though served on plate in order to keep up appearances.[33] After the duke's death in 1804, Carton remained largely uninhabited until Augustus, his heir, came of age. Music had featured prominently in the education of the 3rd duke who was, by all accounts, a highly competent musician, proficient on the violin, cello and double bass. A godson of King George III (1738–1820), Augustus was educated first by Revd Gilbert Austin at Woodville in Lucan, County Dublin, and later in England.[34] His coming-of-age in 1812 prompted renewed displays of sociability that showcased both the house and demesne – even though the duke himself was detained abroad there were festivities on the Carton estate and in the village of Maynooth. The *Freeman's Journal* reported: 'there was no scarcity of music, on every side the heart-cheering violin or the merry pipe was heard. The very excellent band of the Kilkenny militia was brought from Dublin on the occasion – many national airs were played in the course of the day.'[35] Military bands also featured at a huge fête held at Carton in July 1813 and were 'disposed at proper distances throughout the demesne' to play at intervals which began at 2p.m. More than 700 invitations had been issued to the 'nobility and gentry of Dublin and its environs for a magnificent breakfast', and over 30 spacious marquee tents were set up around the grounds, 'each containing tables covered with everything that the season could supply, that wealth could secure, and that taste and art could select and arrange'. Dancing began just after 7p.m., 'partly within, and partly without doors, and to various kinds of music' while 'tea, coffee, ices and every kind of refreshment continued to be supplied'.[36] Such hospitality was provided by – and expected of – landlords as public demonstrations of their power and prestige.

After his marriage, in 1818, to Charlotte Stanhope (1793–1859), a daughter of the 3rd earl of Harrington of Elvaston Castle in Derbyshire, England, and an accomplished musician, Augustus settled down to life 'in the quiet of his country seat among his own people'.[37] Having sold his Dublin town house, Carton was remodelled to designs executed by Richard Morrison (1767–1849), the chief result of which was the repositioning of the primary reception rooms to become south-facing.[38] Despite the fact that a previously designated music-room was apparently replaced by a new entrance hall, the main saloon (formerly the dining-room) became a hive of musical activity. Fittingly, the ceiling of this room had been decorated by the Lafranchini brothers in sumptuous stuccowork which featured Apollo, the god of music, playing a lyre. Given the musicality of the 3rd duke and duchess, music no longer featured simply as an accompaniment to dancing or dining at Carton, but rather prominently as an entertainment in its own right. In January 1822 the earl of Donoughmore reported attending a musical soirée in the saloon at which the duchess played 'a very fine organ' and the duke the double bass, while songs were sung by the wife of the duke's friend and former schoolmaster, Revd Gilbert Austin.[39]

Unsurprisingly, music was also represented in the library at Carton with numerous bound volumes of sacred and popular instrumental music by a variety of contemporary composers.[40] Music specifically associated with Carton and the FitzGeralds included works by Ferdinand Ries (1784–1838),[41] Frederick Southwell (1833–83),[42] and William Charles Levey (1837–94).[43] The 3rd duke of Leinster was personally acquainted with many musicians and patronised amateur choral and musical societies as well as charity concerts. Augustus was not only a patron of music but also an active and respected practitioner, prominent in the musical life of Dublin and London where he had acquired a residence on Carlton House Terrace. While in London ostensibly to attend to parliamentary business, in his free time he took lessons on the double bass with the virtuoso Domenico Dragonetti (1763–1846) with whom he developed a close relationship.[44] He performed alongside professional musicians in a variety of public contexts: in 1833, for instance, he was reported as the double bass player in the orchestra of the Brunswick Street Private Theatre in Dublin for a performance of Rossini's *opera buffa* 'The Barber of Seville'.[45] Lady Morgan wrote of a concert she attended at Dublin Castle in the 1830s where 'the duke of Leinster played his big fiddle and looked happy and amiable, and after each act pottered about, gathering the music, settling the lights'.[46]

Augustus was also responsible for cultivating the Irish music landscape, and propagated a degree of musical interchange between the cities of Dublin and London. In his capacity as Grand Master of the Freemasons of Ireland, for instance, he appointed the English organist, conductor and composer Jonathan Blewitt (1782–1853) as Grand Organist. Indeed, the duke exemplified the leadership of musical activity in the nineteenth century and, being a commissioner of national education for Ireland between 1836 and 1841, was particularly concerned with music education. From the 1860s he was president of the Irish Academy of Music in Dublin (founded 1848) for which he was largely responsible for securing annual government funding.[47] In 1872, moreover, it appears that he used his personal influence to acquire permission from Queen Victoria (1819–1901) to attach the prefix 'Royal' to the name of the Irish Academy of Music.[48]

The queen, a distant relative of the duke, had visited Carton as part of her first visit to Ireland in 1849. Cognisant of the devastation wrought by the Great Famine (1845–51), the earl of Clarendon, lord lieutenant of Ireland from 1847 to 1852, had advised that the visit 'would be of a strictly private character'. In a private letter to the duke of Leinster, he confided: 'if she came in state it would impose expense upon the nobility and gentry ... when all classes are suffering under a protracted visitation of Providence ... there will be no public ceremony.' He added that although the queen was disposed to 'put aside her general rule of not paying any visit to individuals' for a private lunch with the duke and duch- ess, they could 'be let off from the trouble and inconvenience' by pleading that 'it might cause jealousy if she made an exception in favour of Carton'.[49] Despite Clarendon's stated intention that the queen's 1849 sojourn would be 'private' in nature, contemporary newspaper reports reveal that it had much of the cho- reography and pageantry of a state visit. This was evident at Carton where the queen and her entourage arrived on Friday 10 August and walked around the gardens for about 20 minutes, serenaded by two military bands 'stationed on either side of the grounds', alternately playing 'a number of pleasing airs', such as '"God save the queen", "The Coburg march" and other national airs'.[50] The royal party repaired to the house for lunch while guests and onlookers were entertained in marquee tents pitched for the occasion.

After lunch the queen's party was conducted to the front lawn where they witnessed some dancing, including what the newspapers called 'a genuine Irish jig'. The jigs and reels, which went on for about half an hour, were danced by several tenants along with their wives and their daughters to music provided by at least one piper. The *Nenagh Guardian* reported that there was a piper called 'Sheridan, the well-known bagpiper of Kilcock' while the *Times* noted 'two veri- table Irish pipers'.[51] However, the Queen's Journal claimed that there were 'three old and tattered pipers playing'.[52] The *Illustrated London News* was at pains to present an image of a respectable Irish peasantry, emphasising that the dancing enjoyed by the queen was a genuine exhibition and that the dancers were 'disciples of Father Mathew', the leader of the temperance movement in Ireland.[53] Newspaper reports also indicate that musical activity at Irish country houses in the years after the Famine, revolved around social dancing at high- society gatherings, family celebrations involving estate employees and tenants, and occasionally house and demesne tours – as opposed to music recitals or concerts for committed audiences. The publication of reports of these 'private' events points to the fact that they were, as Paula Gillett has observed, 'less a sign of admiration for superb musical attainments than a statement of the power that could be demonstrated by highly conspicuous consumption'.[54] The FitzGeralds however did display genuine musical propensities. A sense of the centrality of musical activity in the 3rd duke's domestic life can be discerned from an article published in the *Freeman's Journal* as early as 1838 which stated:

His Grace lives a quiet and happy life in the bosom of his family. His tastes are chiefly musical; he is an accomplished player on the violoncello ... From this passion for music, probably, proceeds his somewhat whimsical exactness in regard to time. Almost every room in his princely seat of Carton has its clock, and each clock is regulated by the time-piece in the hall; and if the duke chances to observe two minutes' variation between any of these and their director in 'accordant harmony', an express is sent to Dublin for the watchmaker.[55]

Augustus and his wife inculcated a love of music in their children and in their grandchildren. Their younger son, Otho (1827–82), was a talented composer whose works, including *The Spirit of the Ball: A Galop* and *The Irish Steeple Chase Galop, or, Spirit of the Turf*, were published in Dublin in the 1860s.[56] His brother, Gerald (1821–86), was responsible for designing the organ case in the saloon which was executed in 1857. As well as being an officer in the Scots Guards, Gerald was an artist, accomplished musician and gifted composer – one of his compositions was hailed by the *Court Journal* as being 'on a par with the celebrated marches of the best composers; more we cannot say for this young nobleman's great musical talent'.[57]

Music and dancing continued to feature as aspects of edification and entertainment at Carton in the brief reigns of the 4th and 5th dukes of Leinster, significant family events continuing to provide occasions for musical entertainment and sociability. The marriage in 1847 of Charles William FitzGerald (1819–87), then Marquis of Kildare, to Caroline Leveson-Gower (1827–87), a daughter of the 2nd duke of Sutherland, was the occasion of a grand entertainment to which hundreds of 'the tenantry of His Grace's estate' had been invited. The Maynooth Temperance Band provided music for guests as they dined in a 'large barn adjoining the mansion', after which they participated in after-dinner sports on the 'pleasure lawn', including running in sacks, rolling in barrels and climbing poles. In the evening a ball was held in the loft of the barn; those who did not gain admittance danced on the lawn to the music of a harper and other musicians.[58] Until the death of the 3rd duke, in 1874, Charles and Caroline lived at Kilkea Castle where their children had a daily educational routine which included music; even while visiting at Carton the children continued their routine, rising every morning at 7.30 a.m. to prepare their lessons and read scripture before breakfast. Typically, Maurice (1852–1901) went to his music at 8.30 a.m. followed by his elder brother Gerald (1851–93) at 8.45 a.m.[59] In July 1884 their father, the 4th duke, was nominated as vice-president of the Royal College of Music, by the Prince of Wales (afterwards Edward VII), president of the college.[60] Entries in an extant household account book show that the servants at Carton continued to be treated to music and dancing at significant times of the year; for example a sum of £2 2s 6d was paid for 'music' for a 'servants' ball' held at Christmas, 1886.[61]

Gerald succeeded as the 5th duke of Leinster in 1887, having married Hermione Duncombe (1864–95), a daughter of the 1st earl of Feversham, three years previously. She was an accomplished keyboard player, taking lessons from the eminent Robert Prescott Stewart (1825–94) as late as 1891.[62] Although elite women had long been dissuaded from engaging seriously with music (in order to avoid appearing too 'masculine') or performing in public (to protect their reputations), by the 19th century it had become more acceptable for those with evident ability to study music academically. The main saloon at Carton continued to function as a designated music room wherein Hermione played both the organ and a grand piano for the entertainment of her closest friends, including members of the Lawless family who lived nearby on the Cloncurry estate at Lyons. Elizabeth (Daisy) Plunkett (1866–1944), countess of Fingall, of Killeen Castle, County Meath, a close friend of the duchess, recalled that there were 'wonderful musical evenings in that white and gold music-room which is one of the settings in which I remember her best.'[63] This type of sociability attracted far less contemporary attention than more public forms encountered at assembly rooms, theatres or the vice-regal court at Dublin Castle. Yet the evidence shows that in terms of repertoire and style domiciliary music-making was impacted significantly by the reception of professional performances in the non-domiciliary arena.

While access to music was more democratic by the twentieth century its production continued to necessitate specialist expertise and materials, ensuring its perpetuation as a marker of socio-economic status. Not all landowners displayed the musical proclivities or prominence of the FitzGeralds, but the majority engaged with music in some form or other. Musical activity embodied notions of propriety, promoted positive interactions with peers, supporters, servants and tenants, and even informed the design and decoration of spaces within the home. The fragmentary and sporadic nature of the available evidence – including materials relating to music – means that the historiography surrounding the Irish country house has tended to understate the extent and significance of domiciliary hospitality, entertainments and education in the eighteenth and nineteenth centuries. The study of music in the country house offers perspectives on the place of landowners in their local communities as well as the social and familial relationships fostered by music-making. It also provides a useful framework for investigating the lives and possessions of aristocratic families like the FitzGeralds of Carton.

NOTES

1   For biographical details on James and Emily FitzGerald, see, Eoin Magennis, 'FitzGerald, James, First Duke of Leinster (1722–1773)', *Oxford Dictionary of National Biography* (hereafter *ODNB*), online edn (www.oxforddnb.com/view/article/9965) (accessed 27 Aug. 2010); Rosemary Richey, 'FitzGerald, Emilia Mary, Duchess of Leinster (1731–1814)', *ODNB*, online edn (www.

oxforddnb.com/view/article/48893) (accessed 27 Aug 2010); Stella Tillyard, *Aristocrats: Caroline, Emily, Louisa and Sarah Lennox, 1740–1832* (London, 1994); Brian FitzGerald, *Emily, Duchess of Leinster, 1731–1814: A Study of her Life and Times* (London and New York, 1949); idem. (ed.), *Correspondence of Emily, Duchess of Leinster (1731–1814)* (3 vols, Dublin, 1949–57).

2   Emily FitzGerald to James FitzGerald, 7 July 1757, in FitzGerald (ed.), *Correspondence of Emily*, vol. i, p. 59.

3   Cited in Charles William FitzGerald, *The Earls of Kildare and Their Ancestors: From 1057 to 1773* (4th edn, Dublin, 1864), p. 284.

4   Toby Barnard, *Making the Grand Figure: Lives and Possessions in Ireland, 1641–1770* (New Haven and London, 2004), pp 71–80. Karol Mullaney-Dignam, 'Useless and extravagant? The consumption of music in the Irish country house', in Jon Stobart and Andrew Hann (eds), *Consuming the Country House* (forthcoming).

5   James FitzGerald to Emily FitzGerald, 6 May 1762, in FitzGerald (ed.), *Correspondence of Emily*, vol. i, p. 127; see also FitzGerald, *Emily, Duchess of Leinster*, p. 99.

6   Copies of these exist at the NLI (Joly Music Collection, JM 4041).

7   See Amanda Vickery, *The Gentleman's Daughter: Women's Lives in Georgian England* (New Haven, 1998), p. 242; Mullaney-Dignam, 'Useless and extravagant?'.

8   These theatricals featured servants and friends as well as family members, see: *The Private Theatre of Kilkenny with Introductory Observations on Other Private Theatres Before it was Opened* (privately published, 1825), pp 1–2; Louisa Conolly to Sarah Lennox, afterwards Bunbury, 30 Dec. 1760; 13 Aug., 24 Sept. 1771, Irish Architectural Archive (IAA), Conolly Letters, 94/136/1.

9   Brian Boydell, 'Music, 1700–1850' in T. W. Moody and W. E. Vaughan (eds), *A New History of Ireland, iv: 18th-Century Ireland 1691–1800* (Oxford, 1986), pp 570, 579–80. Harry White, *The Keeper's Recital: Music and Cultural History in Ireland, 1770–1970* (Cork, 1998), pp 27–8.

10   Elizabeth Gibson, 'Owen Swiney and the Italian Opera in London', in *Musical Times*, 125:1692 (Feb. 1984), pp 82–6.

11   For a description of such an outing see Emily FitzGerald to James FitzGerald, 16 Dec. 1762, in FitzGerald (ed.), *Correspondence of Emily*, vol. i, pp 155–6.

12   Magennis, 'FitzGerald, James', *ODNB*; FitzGerald (ed.), *Correspondence of Emily*, vol i, pp 34–46.

13   Louisa Conolly to Sarah Bunbury, 30 Aug. and 18 Dec. 1772, IAA, Conolly Letters, 94/136/1.

14   Karol Mullaney–Dignam, *Music and Dancing at Castletown, Co. Kildare, 1759–1821* (Dublin, 2011), p. 32.

15   See Elizabeth FitzGerald, *Lord Kildare's Grand Tour, 1766–1769* (Cork, 2000), passim.

16   Louisa Conolly to Emily Ogilvie, Dowager Duchess of Leinster, 29 Nov. 1775, FitzGerald (ed.), *Correspondence of Emily, vol. iii*, pp 163–4.

17   See *Gleanings From an Old Portfolio Containing Some Correspondence Between Lady Louisa Stuart and Her Sister Caroline, Countess of Portarlington*, ed. Mrs Godfrey Clark (2 vols, Edinburgh, 1895), vol i, p. 83.

18   Ibid. See also FitzGerald, *Emily, Duchess of Leinster*, pp 165–6; Desmond Guinness and William Ryan, *Irish Houses and Castles* (London, 1971 edn), p. 187.

19   Emily Coote to Lucy FitzGerald, 23 Oct. 1787, Public Records of Northern Ireland (PRONI), Strutt Papers, T3092/3/13.

20   Moore's *Irish Melodies* included poems such as 'The Minstrel Boy' and 'The Last Rose of Summer' which were set to traditional Irish tunes arranged by Sir John Stevenson

21   Castletown account book, 1778–88, Trinity College Dublin, Conolly Papers, MS 3955; Tradesmen's receipt book, 1778–1785, Trinity College Dublin, Conolly Papers, MS 3939.

22   *Six Sonatas for the Harpsichord ... Dedicated ... to ... the Duchess of Leinster*, National Library of Ireland (NLI), LO 2639/Bd.

23   James Aird (ed.), *A Selection of Scotch, English, Irish and Foreign Airs Adapted for the Fife, Violin or German Flute, vol. ii. Humbly Dedicated to the Volunteer and Defensive Bands of Great Britain and Ireland* (Glasgow, *c*.1785), p. 51.

24   *His grace the Duke of Leinster's March and Quick Step*, British Library, Music Collections, g.271.qq.(7.); *The Marquis of Kildare's Slow and Quick March Humbly Inscribed to His Lordship by Master T. Cooke*, NLI, Joly Music Collection, JM 4051. Another march bearing a reference to the duke of Leinster in the title features in the traditional music canon as does at least one reel, but it is not clear to which duke the titles refer. See Francis O'Neill (ed.), *O'Neill's Irish Music: 400 Choice Selections Arranged for Piano or Violin : Airs, Jigs, Reels, Hornpipes, Long Dances, etc., Most of Them Rare, Many of Them Unpublished* (reprint, Cork, 1987), p. 62; Breandán Breathnach, *Ceol Rince na hÉireann, 1* [The dance music of Ireland, 1] (Dublin,1963), p. 75.

25   Patrick M. Geoghegan, 'FitzGerald, William Robert, 2nd Duke of Leinster', *Dictionary of Irish Biography* (hereafter *DIB*), online edn (http://dib.cambridge.org/viewReadPage.do?articleId =a3195) (accessed 27 Aug. 2010).

26   'View of Lord Kildare's Ball' written by Mary FitzGerald to Charlotte Burgh, 26 Dec. 1791, NLI, Leinster Papers, MS 41, 552/32.

27   'A. D.' [unknown dancing master], *Country-Dancing Made Plain and Easy* (London, 1764), pp 19–21.

28   Helen Brennan, *The Story of Irish Dance* (Dingle, 1999), pp 16–20, 93–4; Mary Friel, *Dancing as a Social Pastime in the South-East of Ireland, 1800–1897* (Dublin, 2004), pp 44–5.

29   *Gentleman's Magazine and Historical Chronicle*, 63: 1 (June, 1793), pp 571–72. Lucy's letters reveal that she also liked to sing and play her harp.

30   Geoghegan, 'FitzGerald, William Robert', *DIB*, online edn (http://dib.cambridge.org/ viewReadPage.do?articleId=a3195) (accessed 27 Aug. 2010).

31   Entry for 20 Nov. 1796 in Lucy FitzGerald's journal for Oct.1796 to May 1797, reproduced in Gerald Campbell, *Edward and Pamela FitzGerald: Being Some Account of Their Lives Compiled From the Letters of Those Who Knew Them* (London, 1904), p. 111.

32   For details of Pamela's early life and influences see Stella Tillyard, *Citizen Lord: Edward FitzGerald, 1763–1798* (London, 1997), pp 142–52.

33   Entry for 3 June 1799 in the diary of Alexander Hamilton, 1793–1807, PRONI, Hamwood Papers, T3759/7/C/5/1.

34   Austin remained a life-long friend of the FitzGeralds. In 1836 the third duke purchased from him his prized Amati cello for £131 5s. See Gilbert Austin to Augustus FitzGerald, 15 Feb. 1836, PRONI, Leinster Papers, D3078/3/26/5.

35   *Freeman's Journal*, 25 Aug. 1812.

36   *Morning Chronicle*, 16 July 1813; *Freeman's Journal*, 16 July 1813.

37   *Freeman's Journal*, 26 June 1863.

38   FitzGerald, *Emily, Duchess of Leinster*, p. 281.

39   'From "Notices of the FitzGerald 1879": an account of the Earl of Donoughmore's visit to Maynooth and Carton, 5 & 6 Jan., 1822, and his expenses', PRONI, Leinster Papers, D3078/1/2/8.

40   Details of the music volumes previously held in the Carton library can be gleaned from various auction catalogues published in the twentieth century. See, for example, Bennett & Son, *Catalogue of a Collection of Important Books Selected from the Library at Carton, Co. Kildare ... Sold by Auction ... on Wednesday, 11th Nov. 1925 and Two Following Days* (Dublin, 1925). Some of the dispersed volumes – bearing embossed shelf or catalogue markings on the spines and 'Leinster'

autographs therein – appear to have been acquired by the NLI where they currently lie among the uncatalogued music materials. (The author wishes to express her gratitude to Dr Catherine Ferris, RISM Ireland/DIT Conservatory of Music and Drama, for drawing her attention to these volumes and to Ms Honora Faul, Dept of Prints and Drawings, NLI, for facilitating a viewing of same).

41   *Fantasia for the Piano Forte or Harp in Which is Introduced Two Much Admired Irish Airs,* *'Cailin Beog Cruite na mBo', 'Rose Tree in Full Bearing', Composed & Most Respectfully Dedicated (By* *Permission) to her Grace the Duchess of Leinster by Ferd. Ries* available at the National Archive of Irish Composers, a digital collection of historic piano music from the collections of the National Library of Ireland curated by the pianist Dr Una Hunt (www.naic.ie/record.xql?vtls= vtls000290740) (accessed 30 Mar. 2011).

42   *Le retour à Carton*, cited in Ita Hogan, *Anglo–Irish Music, 1780–1830* (Cork, 1966), p. 206.

43   A copy of *The Carton Galop by W. Levey Composer of the Celebrated Alliance Polka and* *Dedicated (by permission) to His Grace, the Duke of Leinster* can be found at the British Library (Music Collections, h.1314.(3.)).

44   Fiona M. Palmer, *Domenico Dragonetti in England (1794–1846): The Career of a Double Bass* *Virtuoso* (Oxford, 1997), pp 76, 87–8, 202, 233.

45   Unidentified newspaper clipping dated 1833, PRONI, Leinster Papers; D3078/6/1.

46   Lady Morgan, diary entry, 10 Dec. 1832, cited in *Times*, 12 Oct, 1874.

47   Richard Pine and Charles Acton (eds), *To Talent Alone: The Royal Irish Academy of Music,* *1848–1998* (Dublin, 1998), pp 79–84.

48   *Irish Times*, 20 Dec. 1872. See also Karol Mullaney–Dignam, 'State, nation and music in independent Ireland, 1922–51' (Unpublished Ph.D. thesis, NUI Maynooth, 2008), pp 59–76.

49   Lord Clarendon to the Duke of Leinster, 27 June 1849, PRONI, Leinster Papers, D3078/3/36/11.

50   *Times*, 13 Aug. 1849; *Nenagh Guardian*, 15 Aug. 1849; *Illustrated London News*, 18 Aug. 1849.

51   *Nenagh Guardian*, 15 Aug. 1849; *Times*, 13 Aug. 1849.

52   Cited in *Illustrated London News*, 18 Aug. 1849.

53   Ibid.

54   Paula Gillett, 'Ambivalent friendships: music-lovers, amateurs, and professional musicians in the late nineteenth century', in Christina Bashford and Leanne Langley (eds), *Music and British* *Culture, 1785–1914: Essays in Honour of Cyril Ehrlich* (Oxford, 2000), pp 321–40, 332.

55   *Freeman's Journal*, 9 Oct. 1838.

56   Copies of these can be found at the British Library (Music Collections, h.1458.s.(5.), h.721.m.(13.)).

57   *Court Journal*, 14 Feb. 1857. He was one of the composers featured in Arthur B. Leech (ed.), *Musical Album of the London Irish Rifle Volunteers* (Dublin, 1862).

58   *Freemans Journal*, 2 Nov. 1847.

59   Diary of [Lord] Offaly [afterwards 5th Duke of Leinster] 15 Dec. 1862, NLI, Lord Walter FitzGerald Papers, MS 18,852(1).

60   Charles Morley, Hon. Sec., Royal College of Music, Kensington Gore, London S.W., to the Duke of Leinster, 23 July 1884, PRONI, Leinster Papers, D3078/5/4/70.

61   Household account book, 1884–93, PRONI, Leinster Papers, D3078/2/13.

62   Robert P. Stewart to Lily Hutton, 28 Mar. 1891, cited in Olinthus J. Vignoles, *Memoir of Sir* *Robert P. Stewart* (London, 1898), p. 162.

63   Elizabeth, Countess of Fingal, *Seventy Years Young* (Dublin, 2009 edn), p. 179.

CHAPTER 8

'Till my Further Orders'
Rules Governing Servants at Carton
in the mid-Eighteenth Century

Terence Dooley

Arguably the decades of the 1750s and 1760s represented an age of conspicuous consumption at Carton as James FitzGerald, 1st Duke of Leinster, and his wife, Emily, completed the embellishment of their house and parkland, as well as the construction of a magnificent town house in Dublin and the adornment of another at 6 Carlton House Terrace in London. Mary Delany, a contemporary of fairly stringent moral outlook, rightly suggested that much of the extravagance was due to Emily whom she described as 'one of the proudest and most expensive women in the world.'[1] Emily would probably not have disagreed; in 1757 she signed off a letter to her husband: 'your tender, affectionate, fond, tho' extravagant wife'.[2] Moreover, in 1759, when James contemplated giving up his salaried position as master of the ordnance, Emily persuaded him to reconsider with the advice that: 'but think that one year's income of it pays all the expenses we are at here.'[3] As Ireland's premier aristocratic family, the FitzGeralds set – as much as followed – trends, thereby investing large sums of money in art, architecture, interiors and exteriors, to the extent that when James died in 1773 he left debts of £148,000.[4]

In order to further project their superior social standing, the FitzGeralds also employed an army of staff to run their houses and maintain the gardens and parkland. Toby Barnard has estimated that in the eighteenth century there were around 50 servants at Carton.[5] Even though most of these servants remain anonymous,[6] fortunately an extant 'household book' which covers the period from the early 1760s until James's death in 1773 has survived. The book reveals a great deal about the servants' daily chores, as well as describing the rules and regulations which governed the relationship between them and their employers at Carton.[7] In its own right the book represents a valuable part of the material culture of Carton in the eighteenth century – as a conception it was an important statement of the way in which James and Emily attempted to put order on their servants, at a time when they were also putting order on the architectural design of their home(s), their parkland, their estate town and their tenantry.[8]

The first entry in the household book was made in November 1764, three years after James had been created marquis of Kildare and two years before he became duke of Leinster. While it was James who signed off (as 'K', or later 'L') on all of the instructions and rules in the book, it is safe to surmise that given Emily's strength of character, the recognised calibre of her independent and well-educated mind and her role as chatelaine at Carton, this was just another aspect of life at Carton where she 'carefully steered Kildare towards decisions he later adopted as his own.'[9]

The paternalistic tone throughout the book suggests that James leaned towards being authoritative rather than authoritarian, even if he commanded the moral high ground in terms of how he expected his servants to behave: while he ensured that servants were 'fed at the proper hours' he simultaneously demanded that they 'behave decently and in a proper manner at their meals and in the servants' hall'. The servants are generally referred to as 'the family' suggesting some degree of interdependence in the relationship between employer and employees.[10] Unfortunately, the book offers no information about the servants' social backgrounds or their places of birth, although we can presume that the vast majority were Protestant and that the upper servants in particular came from respectable social backgrounds and, in all probability, from outside the immediate area of Carton. Emily employed her housekeeper, Mrs Clarke, in England; she epitomized the qualities Emily sought in her upper female servants: 'She seems a sensible, notable, genteel sort of woman; not fine but just the manner to create a little respect from the under servants and enters perfectly into our schemes.' Mrs Clarke was to receive £25 for the first year, and £30 thereafter, with a tea and sugar allowance and the use of a housekeeper's maid.[11]

Some of the lower servants may have been sons and daughters of local, Catholic tenant farmers or estate employees but, in general, the lack of employment opportunities for the local populace as upper servants was due to a number of factors: the material culture of eighteenth-century rural Ireland did not prepare a young man or woman for service in an aristocratic mansion; they were most likely inarticulate in the English language; their Catholicism may have been unacceptable; and as discretion was expected as the ultimate trait of a good servant, the danger of spreading gossip in the locality may have discriminated against them. At the same time, it was not easy to convince English servants or estate employees to move to Ireland; Emily wrote to her husband from England in 1757: '... tis such a difficulty to get them to go to Ireland; none but those who are undone and can't live here will [go].'[12]

The architectural design of Carton intentionally created spaces to allow the family to avoid coming into contact with servants. The original central block designed by Richard Castle contained the great reception rooms. The kitchen wing was purposely situated a distance removed from the dining area (which later became the saloon): on a practical level this prevented the cooking aromas reaching the dining room before meals were served; on another level it kept the lower servants well out of view (for a similar reason a series of tunnels ran beneath the house and out to various outbuildings). Only areas restricted to the upper servants occupied the spaces close to the main reception rooms – for example, the steward's room, the butler's pantry and his private bedroom and washroom. The butler's quarters were also adjacent to the plate room, where the family silver was kept. There were several ante-rooms nearer the principal apartments where footmen and those personally attending the master and mistress could wait, but those spaces were closed to lower servants.[13]

The architect Isaac Ware, who was at one time considered to remodel Carton, wrote in his *The Complete Body of Architecture* (1758) that keeping upper servants close to the family was acceptable: 'They can be suffered here because they are cleanly and quiet; therefore there is convenience in having them near, and nothing disagreeable.' But he continued:

On the other hand the kitchen is hot, the sculleries are offensive and the servants hall is noisy; these therefore we shall place in one of the wings. This is the conduct of reason; the housekeeper, the clerk of the kitchen, and other domestics of the like rank, will thus be separated from the rabble of the kitchen; they will be at quiet to discharge their several duties, and they will be ready to attend the master or lady.[14]

While upper servants (such as the steward, butler and housekeeper) may have had private quarters downstairs, the majority of domestic staff were accommodated in small bedrooms in the attic area of Carton – although if there were at least 50 servants and 19 children, space must have been at a premium – while the yard staff had accommodation over the stable yards. Here was a hive of industry catering for millers, tanners, brewers, granary workers, farriers, wheelwrights, chandlers, smiths, gentlemen of the horse, grooms, stable hands, lodgekeepers, gardeners and an army of estate labourers.

It may have been ongoing difficulties with managing such a large household that prompted James and Emily to set out the rules and regulations. There were times when Emily felt 'plagued by servants'.[15] This was generally when the duke himself was absent (and he was, it seems, more often away than at Carton), causing Emily to complain often, as on 22 May 1755 when she wrote to him: '... it was a month since you left us' and suggested it was 'high time for you to talk of returning to us.'[16] Two years before the first entry, Emily had written to him that Mrs Clarke (the English housekeeper employed the previous year) 'grumbles sadly about the maids; they won't get up in a morning, and she catches her death with cold going to call them.' Emily did not think that providing her with a bell to call them would be the answer, instead she suggested that

> the only way to get them up early was to make them go to bed early; that they won't do – why, because they have nothing to do, and so sit up gossiping and prating – give them work to do, make them mend and make the linen, you'll find they will be ready enough then to go to bed as early as you please.[17]

James and Emily saw the book as a necessary means to regularise their staff in a fashion which they may have deemed fair and equitable, but which was certainly devised within the confines of contemporary aristocratic attitudes towards service. When all the servants from Carton went to the races at Lyons and the estate farmer's mare cost him 'a great deal of money', Emily complained he was a 'foolish man', yet she would regularly tell her husband of having lost £20 in a single night playing card-games such as loo – the equivalent of the farmer's annual salary.[18]

The first regulations set down by James were 'Rules to be observed by the butler in regard to plate'.[19] This is noteworthy in itself, as the FitzGeralds had broadcast their re-entry into Irish elite society through the commissioning of spectacular silver services (see chapter 9).[20] The lengthy instructions to ensure the absolute care and cleanliness of the plate – 'well washed first in bran and water ... and 2nd to have a clean lather of soap and warm water ready with a brush for that purpose to wash it in' – emphasises its importance as a symbol of prestige and the family's intention to create an impression on their guests. Similarly, strict standards in the care of the linen – another measure of wealth in goods – had to be maintained to ensure proper and genteel presentation in the decoration of tables and bedrooms; thus the butler was instructed to send the table linen as soon as possible after dinner and supper to the housekeeper and to 'take great care they are not used to wipe things in the pantry' and to ensure that any table linen with holes or stains was to be returned to the housekeeper at once and new ones received.[21]

The butler at this time, John Stoyte, was generally well regarded by James and Emily, and was so well paid that he could eventually afford to reside in a grand house at the opposite end of the village of Maynooth (which in 1795 became the foundation house of St Patrick's College). Stoyte had to procure whatever was necessary, but he also had to be very careful to keep all the groceries locked up; he had to be 'very particular in having the sugar and salt in good order and when put to dry to take care the dust of the fire don't get in.' He was responsible for decanting all wines, procuring the water to be used at the table, drawing ales and beers, and cutting bread 'as short a time before dinner as possible.' Bad habits amongst kitchen staff had to be eradicated. The butler's pantry was effectively the physical space which acted as a buffer between the family and the under-servants, thus he should 'not by any means admit the pantry to be a meeting or gossiping place for the under servants' or allow any under-servant in the pantry 'without an order from either Lord or Lady Kildare'. He was strictly forbidden to allow strange servants or the footmen to dress in the pantry. At the same time he had to be courteous and respectful to fellow servants, to encourage them rather than criticise them, instruct them in the etiquette of the household and to leave all reprimanding to James and Emily. For whatever rea-son, the plate maid was singled out as a servant not to be 'used ill or rudely'.

Next, the book set out 'Rules to be observed by the steward at Carton'. As the overseer responsible for the running of the house and demesne, the stew-ard, Peter Bere, had to be resident. He had very comfortable quarters in the house and was well paid, probably around £100 per annum. It seems he often dined with the family; after one dinner in December 1762, Emily wrote to James of his 'grand company'.[22] More significantly, when the duke was devel-oping the village of Maynooth, he offered Bere long leases on town properties as an investment, so giving rise to Bere Street. (From the duke's point of view this ensured that Bere would have an influence over the town tenants; it was an extension of the complex patronage networks which operated on the estate with the duke in ultimate control.) At Carton, Bere rang the yard bell every morning and at other appointed times for servants and employees to start work, to break for lunch, to signify the end of the working day and so on. He was responsible for opening and locking the various gates, keeping 'idlers or others who have not any business' out of the yards and offices, and discourag-ing maid servants from having strangers around the house and yards.

These regulations suggest that vagabonds and other 'undesirables' often made their way to the house. In 1767, Leinster ordered that:

> Mary Kelly (commonly called Cocker Kelly) be not admitted within my park gates without my order in writing, upon any account either in my absence or oth-erwise. If ever I find she has been admitted I will stop a crown from the gate keeper at whose gate she has got in and if I cannot find it out from each gate keep-er half a crown.

Orders to that effect were posted in the gate lodges and shortly after the same instructions were given regarding Anne Strong and Mary McDermott. Who these women were is unknown but perhaps their 'profession' can be sur-mised. The steward was, in essence, the moral enforcer, and so James instruct-ed him: 'Not to allow of cursing and swearing about the house etc. or any riotous behaviour but everything done in the most quiet and regular manner.' He was charged with ensuring there should be no pilfering and was warned: 'To give the person who bakes, the different sorts of flour by weight, and to weigh the bread after being baked, to see the flour is not made away with or wasted.' The same applied to the grain which was sent for the 'making of good malt liquor.' The need to guard against pilfering was further suggested in an instruction of 25 August 1768, when the farm labourers were banned from loading coals into the sheds; from then on they were only allowed to measure what was delivered and 'if any is wanting they must pay for them.' On 28 August 1773 Leinster dismissed a number of car-men and labourers from Kellystown because he suspected them of making their way over the demesne wall and stealing wheat.

The steward was to carry out his duties 'without favour or affection to any body', and as far as James was concerned: 'the way to put all those things in execution is to show an example of regularity and sobriety etc.' He had a basic philosophy which he shared with his upper servants: 'be rather over strict at first as it is much easier to relax than to recover an authority over people, which must be done or the business will not go on as it ought.' Every aspect of duty at the house was expected to be carried out punctually and regularly; when the family was not in residence the steward was told that it was enough to clean the yard areas once a week but at other times it was deemed imperative that 'every place and thing to be kept neat, sweet and clean and in good repair'. James demanded: 'Nothing ... be put off till tomorrow which can be done today', and propounded that 'the way to do and have those things well done is never to think it well done enough if it can be done better.' Therefore, he finished his directions to the steward:

> The way to perform and get everything properly done is to be regular and not to do any thing but that all the world may know it, for once that anything is done that Lord or Lady Kildare is not acquainted with, and should be displeased if known, he puts himself in the power of others, and then all authority is over and not to be got again.

There were other instructions to the steward which point to both the importance of Carton to the local economy and, crucially, to how the FitzGerald family developed a paternalistic relationship with their tenantry, arguably in keeping with James's patriotic politics, in the wider sense of its definition. For example, the steward was instructed that 'when anything is to be bought, first enquire for it at Maynooth, and among Lord Kildare's tenants which, if not to be got there or among them as reasonable and as good as elsewhere, to get it where it is best and cheapest giving the preference to Lord Kildare's tenants.' Again, this 'shop local' policy had perhaps an element of ducal control – nothing maintained good local landlord-tenant relations as effectively as a sound, employment-based, local economy.

In terms of the general servant population there are only occasional references to remuneration levels, but working conditions are more broadly described. Food left over after the family had dined was to be brought to their table. The provision of a pint of ale was common practice in large households until the end of the nineteenth century; Jeremy Musson claims it was 'a kind of liquid bread, as ordinary water was then unhealthy to drink.'[23] A pint of ale was therefore allowed to all servants before ten o'clock at night but no later, except in the case of servants 'kept out beyond that hour by Lord or Lady Kildare, when in the country or by their orders.' A quart of ale was allowed to the cook at 11 o'clock in the morning, another quart at five o'clock, and a pint at nine o'clock at night was allowed to a wet nurse (considering that James and Emily had 19 children there must have been a few of these). Those servants lower in the hierarchy were allowed less ale: the laundry maid, for example, was only allowed a quart twice a week.

When the family were not in residence, dinner for the upper servants was to be served in the steward's hall, 'exactly at 4 o'clock to consist of one or two dishes, such as roast or boiled with garden things, mutton and broth, mutton chops, harrico or flashed roast or boiled pork with pease pudding and garden things or, steaks, roast or boiled veal with garden things when veal is killed at Carton.' Once a week they were to receive mutton or beef pie, and on every Sunday roast beef and plum (or alternative) pudding. Supper and breakfast was to comprise of meats left over from the previous evening's dinner, with potatoes, vegetables, cheese or eggs. The lower servants' dinner was to be served in the servants' hall at one o'clock – presumably, amongst other considerations, to allow them to serve the upper servants at four o'clock – to consist of boiled beef, cabbage or other vegetables and every Sunday they were to have a piece of roast beef followed by pudding. Every Thursday they could have boiled mutton with turnips or boiled pork and potatoes (with meat rationed to one and a half pound per week). For supper they were allowed bread and a quarter pound of cheese. Hospitality was extended to visiting servants and tradesmen who were to be fed beef, mutton chop, cold meat or cheese. Servants belonging to visiting gentlemen who were dining at Carton were also allowed a pint of ale. There was also provision for fish – 'which they should have once a week with potatoes and cheese' – possibly as a concession to whatever Catholic servants were employed.

There were evidently live-in and live-out servants. Those who were allowed board wages were not allowed 'to come to eat or drink in the house except, now and then, they and their wives may be asked to dinner on Sunday to live in harmony with them so far as to carry on their mutual business to Lord Kildare's advantage.' This also points to married servants at Carton (an unusual concession in comparison to English households), a fact remarked upon by Arthur Young during his 1770s tour of Ireland.[24] There were other perks for lower servants; for example, maids who washed their own linen and clothes and the ladies' maids who washed 'their small things' were allowed the use of the wash house and fires for drying them free of charge. Washing for other people could be taken in provided that they had 'not the Itch or some other distemper that may be catching.'

Up to the late 1750s the household book is made up mainly of rules and regulations for the indoor and yard staff, but for the early 1760s most of the entries are dedicated to lodge-keepers, the estate farm manager and the shepherds (who, for example, were to be fined sixpence out of their wages for every sheep and lamb found in the plantations). Indeed, it seems that James was becoming more stringent as the household book sets out a series of penalties from this time on: carters who took more than five and a half hours coming from Kildare (later Leinster) House – 'except a wagon or cart break down or any accident of that sort' – were to be stopped 2s 6d from their wages. He ordered: 'great care be taken to not let kitchen garbage or greens to be thrown in the ash hole, and if after this week, any be found in it I will order half a crown each time to be stopped from the kitchen boy'. In 1764 James ordered that from Candlemas Day (2 February), all the estate labourers were to begin work at dawn, have breakfast at 9 a.m., dinner at 1 p.m. and then 'to work as long as they can see'. He added: 'N.B. any workmen or labourers that don't conform to those my orders, let them be discharged.' In 1766, the pig boy, John Peppard, was sacked for no specified reason and the steward instructed that he was not to be re-employed in any other capacity 'upon any account ... till my further orders'. On 3 April 1767, at the solicitation of his wife, James forgave Thomas Rice who had earlier been dismissed and then permitted him to work with the planter on the condition that 'if ever he is seen about my house or any of my offices at Carton (exception pay nights in the office yard) [he] will be immediately discharged and never employed again, and whoever employs him in any shape in or about said house & offices shall be stopped 10s'. A year later in March 1768, James 'was so good as to forgive Thomas Rice entirely' – his probationary period over – and allowed Caleb Payne to permit him work in the brew-house. However, within a short time the unfortunate Rice had transgressed again – it may have been the case that he had a drink problem and the brew-house was not the place for him – and this time 'his Grace hath turned him away never more to be employed at Carton.'

There were unspecified reasons for the introduction of some regulations relating to outdoor staff. The following instructions of 25 April 1765 perhaps suggest some were prepared to move on during the summer to seek higher wages:

> ... any carter or labourer etc. that work as a constant man all the winter season and that leaves my work before the 24th of June following, shall be stopped four weeks pay in the office and their saying or making an excuse of being sick will be no apology unless there be an affidavit of the certainty of it by some other person.

In 1766 he ordered that all day labourers bring their spades and shovels to the office for inspection, threatening to stop 10s for every implement that was in bad condition, adding that this would become regular on the first pay night in every month: 'N.B. That there maybe no excuse, they will be provided with tools in the office and are to be stopped for the price.' Simple solutions were sought to problems: in 1766 he decreed that the estate ladders were all to be painted different colours – those used by the planters, green; those used by the gardeners, yellow; farmers, lead; lamplighters, blue and so on – pointing to an obvious reason for friction amongst employees. In more general terms, the changes in rules and regulations strongly suggest that James and Emily kept a very close eye on every aspect of the running of their household and demesne.

One of the most significant changes concerning servants' working conditions came on 21 March 1765 when James banned them from receiving vails (tips) in any of his houses. Up to that time the upper servants regarded (and expected) vails as a supplement to their annual wages, usually receiving them from visiting guests. James's decision needs to be considered in the wider context of the debate on vails which had been ongoing for some years. There were many contemporaries who railed against the practice. In 1760, for example, Jonas Hanway in his *Eight Letters to His Grace the Duke of ––– on the Custom of Vails-Giving in England* decried the fact that a guest such as a country parson might have to pay a vail equivalent to what would 'feed his large family for a week!'[25] When Hanway's letters were showed to George III (1738–1820), he also banned the acceptance of vails by his staff (a decision not universally popular with his servants), and its impact filtered down through the aristocratic ranks. Vails may, though, have been an issue at Carton long before this: in April 1759 Emily wrote to James that 'to save Lady Drogheda the tip she must have given our servants had they gone purposely to fetch her, I took a jaunt to town myself'.[26] Having banned vails, James agreed to give the following annual bonuses to his servants: £5 a year each to the housekeeper, *maître d'hôtel* (at Leinster House), cook and confectioner; £3 to the steward at Carton, butler, valet and groom of the chambers; £2 to the gentlemen of the horse. No allowances were made to livery servants or the under-servants.

In September 1766, two months before he was elevated to the dukedom, James ordered that 'for the future no strong beer be given to my servants upon their going to town or elsewhere; if they come home of a very wet night, I have no objection but have it to be done at discretion.' On 11 July 1769 he banned dancing in any part of the house without his or the duchess's permission, now believing that such 'occasions neglect, idleness and drinking and makes the family irregular.' He further insisted that servants not entertain company, and the steward's room was to be locked at 11 p.m. each night. The reason may have had something to do with a drink and/or company-keeping incident in the house, or the duke's increasingly high moral expectations in terms of how his servants presented themselves in front of his family and guests, certainly not wanting them to be an embarrassment. It is not clear if drinking was repugnant to the 1st duke, but certainly all of his successors up to the 5th duke seem to have been relatively abstemious; the 3rd duke was a known supporter and patron to Fr Theobald Mathew, the teetotalist reformer.

In the eighteenth century footmen had increasingly become the outward symbols of aristocratic status: 'an item of display in entrance halls and dining rooms – serving at the table where the aristocracy spent such vast sums on entertaining – as well as ornamenting expensively appointed family carriages in town.'[27] Up until James became duke in November 1766, there is no specific reference to them in the household book; then two months later, in January 1767, he instructed that he would allow footmen 'for a pair of black worsted shag breeches, for a fine felt hat with a silver chain loop and button and a horse hair cockade like to their present hats, twenty shillings a year. Those who do not choose to accept of it, to let me know that I may discharge them.' A few months later he ordered the steward that, from 1 April to 1 October, all footmen would be expected to 'wear clean leather breeches and at other times whenever they ride after said 1st of April. I shall stop one shilling for each time I shall see them without them without my leave in the country.' Later in 1767, the duke instructed that 'the footmen go ... and wait at the kitchen door to bring in dinner.' They had evidently become symbols of prestige at Carton. In January 1772 he instructed that the footmen at Leinster House were to receive £8 a year in wages and £4 bonus in lieu of vails at the end of the year. They were allowed an allowance of 30s. a year for leather breeches, shoes, stockings and boots. They were also promised a year's bonus wages for every five years worked in his employment.

Around the same time as his elevation to the dukedom, James also ordered that 'eight of the largest and best of my cart horses' be put into one of the stables in the farmyard and kept in that stable 'under the care of the two best of the carters.' They were to be fed more oats than the other horses, their heads and tails were to be kept well-cleaned and trimmed, and new harnesses were to be acquired for them. These were to be used to pull the newly-commissioned, large carriages that travelled to Dublin (and probably beyond to London). By then it was expected that 'three carts will be wanted to go out at the same time to Dublin' in which case the train was to be led by the best team. The overseer, Brown, was left in no doubt of the repercussions if he failed: 'I expect these things all done and not altered or changed without my being first acquainted with it, as I shall lay all blame upon you and will take no excuse for neglect.'

The loyalty bonus provided to footmen was symptomatic of a much wider problem in terms of retaining good servants. It was to be expected that many of the lower servants would have ambitions to move up the servant hierarchy, and one of the ways of doing so was to move to another house. As town houses grew in the heyday of Dublin expansion, more and more servants probably moved to the capital.[28] Thus, on 1 January 1767, James instructed that:

Elizabeth Kennedy, Anne Griffin and Thomas Farrell, kitchen people or any other kitchen people, who may succeed them, also each house maid, the footman, the steward's room man, pantry boy and lamplighter, and all other lower servants, shall be paid at the expiration of five years' service one entire year's wages over and above their yearly salaries.

On 1 January 1772 he proposed a schedule of bonuses for liveried servants (seven to ten guineas for five years' service depending on their place in the servant hierarchy) and five guineas to housemaids.

The Carton household book is an extremely important source, not only for what it reveals about the running of a country house and the functions of servants there, but also about the social expectations of James and Emily FitzGerald, particularly as they rose through the ranks of the aristocracy. As Jeremy Musson has found in relation to other aristocratic employers, they were certainly not 'as one-dimensional as their posed portraits might suggest, or as vacuous, haughty, thoughtless as characterisations in period drama would have us believe'.[29] The FitzGeralds were not completely consumed by high politics and leisure pursuits; they also invested considerable time and energy in running efficient households and ensuring the well-being, as well as the moral and spiritual development (albeit based on their own expectations) of their staff.

NOTES

1   Cited in Rosemary Richey, 'FitzGerald, Emilia Mary, Duchess of Leinster (1731–1814)', *Oxford Dictionary of National Biography* (hereafter *ODNB*) online edn (http://www.oxforddnb.com/view/article/48893) (accessed 1 Nov. 2012).

2   Emily to James, 6 June 1757, in Brian FitzGerald FitzGerald (ed.), *Correspondence of Emily, Duchess of Leinster (1731–1814)* (3 vols, Dublin, 1949–57), vol. i, p. 42.

3   Emily to James, 28 May 1759, in FitzGerald (ed.), *Correspondence of Emily*, vol. i, pp 97–8.

4   Eoin Magennis, 'FitzGerald, James, First Duke of Leinster (1722–1773)', *ODNB*, online edn (http://www.oxforddnb.com/view/article/9965) (accessed 1 Nov. 2012).

5   Toby Barnard, *Making the Grand Figure: Lives and Possessions in Ireland, 1641–1770* (New Haven and London, 2004), p. 84. From a return in 1884 we know that there were still 44 servants (including two pensioners, Andrew Murray and Mrs Brophy, receiving £30 and £12 respectively per annum) paid by the fifth Duke of Leinster, mainly at Carton, but also including seven at Kilkea and the London house. The staff included a house steward (James Bradley, £100 per annum), cook, (Mrs Harris, £60), valet (Bernard Flynn, £60), Dublin house housekeeper (Mrs Davis, £50), three gamekeepers (Donald McVicar, Francis Empey and William Molloy, £70, £55 and £25), cook (Mrs Baker, £60), two coachmen (Thomas Duffy and James Patterson, £46 and £30), hall porter (George Frost, £40), under butler (Charles Jordan, £35), two footmen (George Moreton and William ?Grove, £32), groom (Thomas Miles, £28), hall boy (Thomas Kieran, £22), pot boy (Patrick Byrne, £20), nineteen maids (house, kitchen, dairy, and laundry whose salaries ranged from £22 to £12), steward's room boy (Richard ?Darner, £18), coal boy (John Kavanagh, £12), clock-winder (Charles Hoey, £12), chimney cleaner (Michael Morris, £12), and parcel man (Patrick Russell, £8); servants' wages at Carton, Jan. 1884 (PRONI, Leinster Papers, D3078/2/13).

6   Some detail on names and place of origin of servants can be gleaned from Brian FitzGerald, *Correspondence of Emily, Duchess of Leinster* (3 vols. Dublin, 1949–57), especially vol. i.

7   The author would like to thank Maurice FitzGerald, 9th Duke of Leinster, for providing access to his copy of the household book, and to express his gratitude to Chris Hunwick, archivist at Alnwick Castle for providing information on the original at Alnwick; see Terence Dooley, 'Copy of the Marquis of Kildare's household book, 1758', in *Archivium Hibernicum*, lxii (2009), pp 183–220. The household book has also been the subject of Patricia McCarthy's 'Vails and travails: how Lord Kildare kept his household in order', in *Irish Architectural and Decorative Studies*, vi (2003), pp 120–39; see also Jeremy Musson, *Up and Down Stairs: The History of the Country House Servant* (London, 2009), especially pp 90–140.

8   Musson, *Up and Down Stairs*, p. 91; for how it may have ended up with the Duke of Northumberland, see Dooley, 'Copy of the Marquis of Kildare's household book, 1758', pp 186–7.

9   Magennis, 'FitzGerald, James, First Duke of Leinster (1722–1773)', *ODNB*, online edn.

10   It should be pointed out that there was nothing unusual about the use of the term 'family' to describe a household staff; in fact, it had been prevalent from at least the previous century; see J. T. Cliffe, *The World of the Country House in Seventeenth-Century England* (New Haven, 1999).

11   Emily to James, 13 Aug. 1761 in FitzGerald (ed.), *Correspondence of Emily*, vol. i, p. 100.

12   Emily to James, [?] June 1757 in ibid., vol. i, p. 43.

13   Richard Castle's floor plans for Carton, copies supplied by Mallaghan family; Barnard, *Making the Grand Figure*, p. 84; for an insight to the architectural design of servant quarters at the Palladian Florence Court, see Christina Hardyment, *Behind the Scenes: Domestic Arrangements in Historic Houses* (London, 1997 edn), pp 18–23.

14   Isaac Ware, *A Complete Body of Architecture* (originally issued in parts, 1756–57, 1971 edn), vol. iii, p. 413.

15   Emily to James, 17 Dec. 1762 in FitzGerald, *Correspondence of Emily*, vol. i, p. 157.

16   Emily to James, 22 May 1755 in ibid., vol. i, p. 21.

17   Emily to James, 10–11 Dec. 1762 in ibid., vol., i, p. 151.

18   Emily to James, 17 Apr. 1759 in ibid., vol. i, p. 61.

19   *Household Book*. All subsequent quotations, unless otherwise stated, are from the *Household Book*.

20   Barnard, *Making the Grand Figure*, p. 139.

21   Ibid., p. 259.

22   Emily to James, 14 Dec. 1762 in FitzGerald, *Correspondence of Emily*, vol. i, p. 154.

23   Musson, *Up and Down Stairs*, p. 128.

24   Cited in ibid., p. 129.

25   Cited in ibid., p. 133.

26   Emily to James, 24 Apr. 1759 in FitzGerald, *Correspondence of Emily*, vol. i, p. 61.

27   Musson, *Up and Down Stairs*, p. 96.

28   Ibid., p. 92.

29   Ibid.

CHAPTER 9

Desiring to 'Look Sprucish'
Objects in Context at Carton[1]

Alison FitzGerald

The starting point for this chapter is a nineteenth-century printed catalogue which lists pictures, plate, antiquities and other items found at Carton and three other properties belonging to the duke of Leinster. It was published in 1871, three years before the death of the 3rd duke, with a revised edition appearing 14 years later.[2] While printed catalogues of country house collections appeared in Britain in the first half of the eighteenth century, they only became popular for English country houses and the grander London town houses in the 1760s.[3] Ireland lagged behind in these trends, so, in an Irish context, the Leinster catalogue is not only early in date but also rare for this period. What then can it reveal about the collections of one of Ireland's most elite families, and the ways in which they acquired, valued and displayed luxury commodities like paintings and silverware?[4]

While catalogues of English private collections became increasingly sophisticated and extensive in the nineteenth century, the Leinster catalogue is generally more selective in its scope and laconic in its descriptions. Its title, *Notes on the pictures, plate, antiquities, &c. at Carton, Kilkea Castle, 13, Dominick Street, Dublin and 6, Carlton House Terrace, London*, clearly indicates that it was never intended to be a comprehensive guide to the collections. The 1871 catalogue is just 47 pages in length; the revised 1885 edition runs to 55 pages, probably necessitated by two principal factors: the initial edition may have had a limited print run;[5] and re-hangs and acquisitions may have rendered the earlier edition outdated. Concerning the second point, Charles William FitzGerald (1819–87) had succeeded to the dukedom in 1874, and the 4th duke and his wife seem to have extensively altered the room distribution of the paintings; as the earlier edition listed the paintings by room this would have rendered it largely redundant. Collectors also constantly intervened in the hanging arrangements of their pictures as works were added or removed, or fashions changed. A surviving watercolour dated to around 1800 for instance, purports to show the 'drawing room' at Carton.[6] It was probably intended as a proposed hanging plan for the layout of pictures on walls and indicates that symmetry and balance clearly played a major part in these arrangements. Such display considerations remained in vogue until late in the nineteenth century – as evidenced by the Carton catalogue editions of 1871 and 1885, both of which include dimensions. In the watercolour sketch, only two paintings can be identified: one an equestrian portrait by the Irish landscape artist Thomas Roberts (1748–77), which is not mentioned in either edition of the catalogue but remained in the ownership of the family;[7] the other a painting which was attributed in the catalogue to the Flemish artist, Frans Snyders (although later it was tentatively attributed to Giovanni Castiglione after being sold in Dublin in 1925).[8] There was evidently a desire to update information, particularly with respect to the attribution of paintings. In another example, a painting attributed to Rembrandt in the 1871 edition was given to the Flemish artist Wallerant Vaillant by 1885.

At the time these catalogues were published cultural tourism had become an increasingly widespread – and democratic – phenomenon in the British Isles.[9] They coincided with the publication of guides like *Walker's Hand-Book of Ireland: An Illustrated Guide for Tourists and Travellers*, which recommended Carton as one of a series of 'metropolitan excursions from Dublin'.[10] Walker's hand-book, which included rail routes, hotel recommendations and interesting places to visit, described Carton as 'a palatial mansion' with 'a great variety of paintings by the best masters'.[11] According to William Williams, Irish estates 'contributed to the establishment and development of Irish tourism in several ways. First of all, as in England, the big house and its surrounding gardens and parklands were among the first tourist attractions in Ireland'. However, as Williams points out, in Ireland tours were more likely to be restricted to gardens and demesnes and interior tours were rarely accommodated.[12]

The Leinster catalogue begins with a brief listing of a small portion of the plate at Carton. The contents of a cabinet that once belonged to Lady St George, mother-in-law of the 2nd duke, are more carefully itemised and include cameos and intaglios collected in Italy, medals, seals, 'freedom boxes'[13] and small sundry objects. One gets the impression that the possessions chosen for description were of historical importance or had family associations. This process of selection continues in the subsequent pages where a panoply of items from different parts of the house is brought to the reader's attention. These range from books and documents in the duke's study, to snowshoes and a sleigh brought back from Canada by Lord Edward FitzGerald in 1789. More systematic is the listing of miniature portraits of members of the FitzGerald and related families. However, the greater part of the catalogue is devoted to listing the picture collection at Carton on a room-by-room basis. The artist's name, his date of birth and death, the subject, and dimensions are given in nearly all cases. Occasionally there is some brief mention of provenance, date, or further amplification of the subject. The remainder of the catalogue is concerned with describing the collections at Kilkea Castle, the Dublin residence in Dominick Street, and the town house on Carlton House Terrace, London, which was leased to the 3rd Duke of Leinster in 1829 and occupied by the family until 1889.

Among the silver items singled out for more detailed description in the catalogue, the mace of the corporation of Athy illustrates the selective emphasis on objects which had historical significance or particular meaning for the family. Unusually, its provenance reveals that it was acquired three times by the FitzGeralds. It was purchased by the 20th earl of Kildare in the mid-eighteenth century and presented to the corporation. When the corporation was dissolved in the mid-nineteenth century it was purchased by the 3rd Duke of Leinster, who presented it to John Butler, late 'sovereign' of the corporation.[14] The 4th duke then acquired it from Butler's son in 1876. It is also mentioned repeatedly in the family's accounts and private papers, suggesting that it was valued on a number of levels, material and personal. In terms of market value it was appraised at £500 in 1888.[15] Similarly, a silver christening jug, presented by George II to his goddaughter, Emily Lennox (1731–1814), afterwards 1st Duchess of Leinster, was clearly a valued heirloom.[16]

Not surprisingly given their elevated position in Irish society, the FitzGeralds owned an impressive collection of plate. This included some very significant pieces acquired by the 19th earl of Kildare and his son, the 1st duke of Leinster.[17] The plate owned by the former included a wine cistern supplied by the Dublin silversmith, Thomas Sutton, a rare survival in terms of Irish silver of this period (see plate section).[18] Originally intended for cooling wine and later used for rinsing glasses, the Leinster catalogue reveals how the function and meaning of such objects could change over time. The vogue for silver cisterns reached a highpoint in the early eighteenth century but had fallen out of fashion by the 1730s, just a few years after the Kildare piece was made. By the late nineteenth century (when the catalogues were printed), the cistern had been redeployed as a table centerpiece. Similarly, a silver breadbasket, once a component of a larger table service had been transposed to a lady's dressing table, presumably as an elegant 'hold all'. The uses to which objects were put nuanced their meanings for owners. (A nineteenth-century watercolour in the Dunham Massey collection, shows the future 7th earl of Stamford using the Dunham Massey cistern as a 'bath', a play on the colloquial term for such objects.[19]) Another key piece, dating from the time of the 19th earl, was a silver fountain used by the family 'for washing glasses' (now in the Fowler Museum at the University of California).[20] It is unusual in having a flat back, a style derived from a continental form found more commonly in ceramic or pewter examples as part of water fountain and basin sets intended for personal ablutions.[21] The dimensions of the piece correspond with a number of references in the family's private accounts and, regardless of the context in which it was used, few Irish families could afford such luxuries.[22]

One curious omission from the catalogues is the famous Leinster dinner service, bought in London by the 1st duke of Leinster in the mid-eighteenth century at a cost of more than £4,000.[23] It would have certainly been used at Leinster House and was commented upon in the eighteenth century. The memoirs of the English dramatist, Samuel Foote, for example, describe the experience of a gala dinner there as like dining 'in a silversmith's shop'.[24] The service was still in the family's possession in the nineteenth century, and one explanation as to why it was not included may be that it was held in the bank as opposed to the house; items from the service were certainly listed in nineteenth-century bank receipts.[25]

As already noted, the greatest proportion of the Leinster catalogue was devoted to the picture collection and reveals that over 220 pictures hung on the walls at Carton.[26] Most of these were oil paintings on panel or canvas, but framed pastels and prints decorated the less important rooms of the house. Like all major collections it was accumulated over time, but it is no easy task to determine how and where most of the paintings were acquired. The catalogue states that the kernel of the collection was brought together by St George Ussher St George (1715–75), father-in-law of the 2nd duke of Leinster, who died in Naples in 1775. It is impossible to verify this claim or to distinguish the paintings – with the exception of portraits – that may have been bequeathed by Baron St George from those that came into the possession of the FitzGerald family via other routes. Prior to 1815 the best pictures were on display in the family's Dublin town house, Leinster House, where a specially designated gallery (now the chamber of Seanad Éireann) had been designed for the purpose by James Wyatt.[27] Thomas Malton described this room in around 1795, and listed eight works that he regarded as the most impressive:

> Over the supper room is the picture gallery, of the same dimensions, containing many fine paintings by the first masters, with other ornaments, chosen and displayed with great elegance ... the most distinguished pictures, are, *A Student Drawing from a Bust* by Rembrandt; *The Rape of Europa* by Claude Lorrain; *The Triumph of Amphitrite* by Lucca Giordano; two capital pictures of Rubens and his two wives, by Van Dyck; *Dogs Killing a Stag*; a fine picture of Saint Catherine; a landscape, by Barratt; with many others.[28]

Many of these attributions can no longer be substantiated;[29] most notably the painting attributed to Rembrandt (and presently in the Louvre in Paris) is now attributed to either the Leiden artist's contemporary, Jan Lievens, or to the French-born Flemish artist Wallerant Vaillant.[30] Indeed, the revised Leinster catalogue of 1885 re-attributed the painting to Vaillant, and a photograph taken around 1880 (see plate section) shows it hanging in an ante-room at Carton. Both editions however, claim that Napoleon Bonaparte had coveted the painting, a story that is in all likelihood apocryphal – though ironic given its current location in the French capital.

While paintings of different schools, periods and subjects are found in each room throughout the house, certain patterns do emerge in the Carton collection. The dining room, for example, was hung exclusively with family portraits – a tradition that had emerged in private homes in the late seventeenth century and continued right into the nineteenth.[31] Portraits were enormously important for the FitzGeralds, pictorially establishing their status and lineage.[32] As late as 1902 and 1905, attempts were made by the young 6th duke of Leinster to plug gaps in the family portrait collection or to find superior examples.[33] Surprisingly, the library at Carton was hung not with portraits of scholars and philosophers, as was the norm, but with large landscapes, and paintings of animals and fowl, placed high over the bookcases. One of the paintings which hung in this room, a market scene attributed in the catalogue to Frans Snyders and Jacob Jordaens, is now accepted as by Pieter van Boucle.[34] The major paintings hung in the principal reception rooms; bedrooms, studies and dressing rooms were typically decorated with pastels, watercolours, and prints. The duke's study, for example, was hung with 28 pastel portraits by Hugh Douglas Hamilton, mostly of family members. (Hamilton was one of a number of Irish artists to benefit from the 1st duke of Leinster's patronage.)

In terms of taste the catalogues reveal a clear preference for classical or ideal landscape paintings over naturalistic landscape art; and for views of Italy in particular.[35] The French artist Claude Lorrain, who spent most of his career in Rome, is regarded as the epitome of classical landscape representation. He did not paint nature as it was, preferring instead a perfected vision of the world: in his landscapes the sun is always shining, the hills gently rolling, with winding roads and rivers, classical temples, and manicured fields. One of the premier works from the Leinster collection was Claude's *Coastal Scene with Europa and the Bull*, which originally hung to one side of the fireplace in the saloon. The mythological figures would have complemented the stuccoed gods and goddesses carousing in the great Lafranchini ceiling there. Claude's painting was commissioned by a French nobleman, the duc de Lesdiguières, in 1634 and is now in the Kimbell Art Museum (see plate section).[36] Unlike the other major works from Carton which were auctioned or sold by private treaty in the 1920s, it remained in situ in the saloon until the 1970s – perhaps because it was encased in a stuccoed frame, it may have been regarded as part of the fixtures and fittings. Another painting located to the right-hand side of the fireplace – an ideal landscape painted by a member of the Dalens family, possibly Dirck Dalens (1688–1753) – was framed in the same way and has remained in place to this day. Claude's work was avidly collected in eighteenth-century Britain, (it has been estimated that *c.*1720 to *c.*1850, close to two-thirds of his paintings could be found there),[37] and this vogue extended to Ireland where, in addition to Leinster, the earls of Charlemont and Moira, both significant collectors, were reputed to own works by him.

Other classical landscape painters were also represented in the Carton collection. Hanging in the saloon was a pair of landscapes by another much-coveted
French artist, Gaspar Dughet. The work of Dutch Italianate landscapists, such as
Herman van Swanevelt and Willem de Heusch, who worked in a broadly similar
style to Claude and Dughet, are also listed. The eighteenth-century Irish landscapists, Thomas Roberts and William Ashford, whom the Leinsters commissioned to paint views of the Carton estate, used the same 'golden light'
compositional structure and idealising approach as these French and Dutch
artists of the previous century.[38] One of the most popular artists in the Carton
collection was the seventeenth-century Dutch artist Aelbert Cuyp. Unlike his
compatriots Van Swanevelt and De Heusch, Cuyp had never travelled to Italy yet
both his imaginary landscapes and his views of recognisable places in Holland
are peopled with Italian-looking shepherds and shepherdesses, and suffused with
the shimmering sunshine of the Mediterranean. Cuyp was also often bracketed
with Dughet and Claude in eighteenth-century writings on landscape art; he is
frequently referred to as the 'Dutch Claude' and was just as avidly collected.
According to the Leinster catalogue the FitzGeralds owned seven paintings by
Cuyp, including *Herdsmen and cattle*, which hung in an ante-room around
1880.[39] This painting must have been acquired before 1814, as it was one of two
Cuyps that the 3rd duke loaned to the Royal Irish Institute exhibition, in Dublin
that year. The family's fondness for Cuyp's work must have been well known:
after the 5th duke's death in 1893, his chaplain, Charles Ganley, published a
tribute where he singled out the work of Cuyp – and Joshua Reynolds – as the
most distinguished in his 'splendid collection'.[40] A number of the Cuyp paintings
that hung at Carton represented equestrian subjects, including *Men on Horseback* (see plate section, and recently acquired by the National Gallery of Ireland);
indeed, he has been called 'the quintessential country house artist'.[41] Images of
elegant riders participating in the ancient, noble sport of hunting, accompanied
by deferential servants, as well as bucolic paintings of animal husbandry
appealed to aristocrats living on their country estates. Still-lifes depicting
spoils of the hunt fitted into a similar demand for rustic subject matter, reflecting
the broader trends and fashions among the landed elite of the British Isles. Thus,
hanging in the luggage hall at Carton in 1885 was a pair of impressive *trompe
l'oeil* paintings of a dead partridge and wood snipe by Jacob Biltius.[42]

In conclusion, the catalogue to the FitzGerald family's collections is a valuable
document for a number of reasons: as a printed guide to the contents of an Irish
country house during this period it is extremely rare; it provides a link to the
provenance of paintings, silver and other objects that have resurfaced in museums
as widely dispersed as Dublin, Paris, and Texas; and it also provides an insight
into how these objects were used, where they were displayed and how their
functions changed over time; finally, it illustrates how the history of these objects
acquired meaning for the FitzGeralds in affirming their lineage, rank and status.

NOTES

1   In 1757 Emily, countess of Kildare, wrote to her husband from London in relation to Carton: 'I shall wish to have our house look *sprucish*. Every mortal's house here is so pretty, and smart, and well furnish'd, that I do long to have ours so too a little.' See Brian FitzGerald (ed.), *Correspondence of Emily, Duchess of Leinster (1731–1814)* (3 vols, Dublin, 1949–57), vol. i, p. 59.

2   Anon, *Notes on the pictures, plate, antiquities &c., at Carton, Kilkea Castle, 13, Dominick Street, Dublin, and 6, Carlton House Terrace, London* (Privately printed, 1871), revised edn 1885.

3   See Giles Waterfield, 'The origins of the early picture gallery catalogue in Europe, and its manifestation in Victorian Britain', in Susan Pearce (ed.), *Art in Museums* (London, 1995), pp 42–73.

4   A nineteenth–century printed catalogue survives for Tollymore Park, Co. Down, showing the 'hang' of the pictures on a room-by-room basis; see Anne Crookshank and Knight of Glin, *Irish Painters* (New Haven and London, 2002), p. 57.

5   The author is aware of only one surviving copy in a public library: the Gilbert Collection at Dublin City Library.

6   It is now in a private collection, illustrated in p. 131 of The Knight of Glin and James Peill, *Irish Furniture* (New Haven and London, 2007), p. 131.

7   This painting by Roberts was entitled *Bold Sir William (a Barb), an Indian Servant and French Dog in the Possession of Gerald FitzGerald Esq.* when it was shown at the Society of Artists in Ireland exhibition, Dublin, 1772. It is currently in a private collection; see William Laffan and Brendan Rooney, *Thomas Roberts: Landscape and Patronage in Eighteenth-Century Ireland* (Tralee, 2009), pp 161–9, fig. 124, and pp 364–5, no. 40. A possible source of influence for Roberts may have been the work of Aelbert Cuyp, a favourite of the dukes of Leinster. Many of Cuyp's equestrian subjects feature black pages in exotic attire; see, for example, Cuyp's *The Huntsmen Halted* in the Barber Institute, Birmingham; Stephen Reiss, *Aelbert Cuyp* (London, 1975), p. 162, no. 122.

8   Thomas Bodkin, 'New attributions to Giovanni Benedetto Castiglione', *The Burlington Magazine*, xlviii (1926), pp 264–5, plate IA.

9   See for instance Adrian Tinniswood, *A History of Country House Visiting* (Oxford, 1989).

10   John A. Walker, *Walker's Hand-Book of Ireland: An Illustrated Guide for Tourists and Travellers* (Dublin, 2nd edn) The National Library of Ireland's copy (Ir 9141g7) is annotated in pencil with the date 1872.

11   Ibid., pp 138–9.

12   William Williams, *Creating Irish Tourism: The First Century 1750–1850* (London and New York, 2010), pp 55–6.

13   In 1662, when the Duke of Ormond was conferred with the freedom of Dublin, the corporation decided that the freedom should be presented to him in a specially-made gold box. It became a regular practice to present freedom certificates in gold or silver boxes after this.

14   Significantly, the mace was not mentioned in the 1871 edition of the catalogue. The 1885 edition notes that: 'After the abolition of the corporation, the mace was bought by the Duke of Leinster, and presented to John Butler, Esq., the late sovereign of the town, in Nov. 1841. From his son Thomas it was purchased by the Duke of Leinster in Jan., 1876' and a new inscription was added to commemorate this: *Notes on the Pictures, Plate, Antiquities &C. at Carton* (London, 1885), p. 4.

15   'Valuation of mace in plate chest at Carton, 1888', Public Records of Northern Ireland (PRONI), Leinster Papers, D3078/2/10/3. Unfortunately the family did not manage to retain this piece, it was sold in 1982 and is now in the San Antonio Museum, Texas; see John Davis, *The Genius of Irish Silver: A Texas Private Collection* (San Antonio Museum of Art, 1993), p. 47.

16   *Notes on the Pictures, Plate, Antiquities &C. at Carton.* (1871), p. 4. This piece was most likely the object described as 'a very beautiful christening vase and cover' and valued at almost £480 in the late nineteenth century; see 'List and receipt for plate lodged in the Northern Bank, Dublin, 1893', PRONI, Leinster Papers, D3078/2/10/9.

17   For example, the magnificent silver gilt toilet service (1720-2) commissioned by the 19th Earl of Kildare, as a gift to his wife on the occasion of their son's birth (now in the Ulster Museum); see Elise Taylor, 'Silver for a Countess's Levee: The Kildare toilet set', *Irish Arts Review* xiv (1998), pp 115–24.

18   According to James Lomax and James Rothwell, in *Country House Silver from Dunham Massey* (National Trust, 2006), p. 64: 'Coolers reached their apogee around the early years of the eighteenth century'. The Kildare cistern dates to 1727. The Ulster Museum holds another rare example with the mark of the Dublin silversmith John Hamilton (1715).

19   Lomax and Rothwell, *Country House Silver*, p. 4.

20   *Notes on the pictures, plate, antiquities etc. at Carton* (1871), p. 3.

21   Timothy Schroder (ed.), *The Francis E. Fowler, Jr. Collection of Silver* (California, 1991), p. 31. Silver fountains were part of the wine equipage. Harold Newman describes them as 'receptacles for holding and dispensing wine', more usually located on a serving table or sideboard than suspended on a wall. The Kildare fountain has a flat base allowing for this manner of display; Harold Newman, *An Illustrated Dictionary of Silverware* (London, 2000), p. 363.

22   For example, in an undated typescript list among the family's papers it is listed as a 'Fountain 22½ inches high of fine form, semi-circular front and base engraved with coat of arms and covered top. (In Dublin Bank) £190'. See 'Duke of Leinster's estate. Copy schedule of heirlooms at Carton, Kilkea Castle &c.', PRONI, Leinster Papers, D3078/2/10/18. The marks on this piece are problematic; see Schroder, *The Francis E. Fowler*, p. 21.

23   For further information of this service see Elaine Barr, *George Wickes, Royal Goldsmith 1698-1761* (London, 1980); Charles Truman et al, *The Glory of the Goldsmith: Magnificent Gold and Silver from the Al-Tajir Collection,* (London, 1989), pp 130–1; Joseph McDonnell, 'Irish Rococo Silver', *Irish Arts Review Yearbook,* xiii (1997), pp 78–87.

24   W. Cooke, *Memoirs of Samuel Foote Esq.* (3 vols, London, 1805), vol. ii, p. 114.

25   See for instance 'List and receipt for plate lodged in the Northern Bank Dublin, 1893', PRONI, Leinster Papers, D3078/2/10/9.

26   On the collecting of paintings in eighteenth-century Ireland see Toby Barnard, *Making the Grand Figure: Lives and Possessions in Ireland, 1641–1770* (New Haven and London, 2004), pp 151–88; John Coleman, 'Evidence for the collecting and display of paintings in mid-eighteenth century Ireland', in *Bulletin of the Irish Georgian Society,* xxxvi (1994), pp 48–63; Crookshank and Knight of Glin, *Irish Painters,* pp 51–65; Alistair Laing, (ed.) *Clerics and Connoisseurs* (London, 2001); Aidan O'Boyle, 'The Milltown Collection: reconstructing an eighteenth-century picture hang', in *Irish Architectural and Decorative Studies,* xiii (2010), pp 30–60; idem, 'The assembly, display and dispersal of Irish art collections, 1700-1950' (Unpublished M.Litt. thesis, Trinity College Dublin, 2011).

27   Galleries of this nature, for the display of the most distinguished works, were typical of the eighteenth century. For a thorough description of Wyatt's Picture Gallery, see David Griffin and Caroline Pegum, *Leinster House, 1744-2000: An Architectural History* (Dublin, 2000), pp 49–51.

28   James Malton, *A Picturesque & Descriptive View of the City of Dublin* (Dublin, 1792-99).

29   The work that Malton attributed to Luca Giordano was entitled *The Triumph of Galatea* in the 1871 catalogue. The paintings that Malton suggested were by Anthony van Dyck were described in the 1871 Carton catalogue as copies after Rubens of a self-portrait and the artist's wife. These

companion pieces were sold by the Dublin auctioneers Bennett & Son on 2 Dec. 1925 (lot no. 471). The representation of dogs killing a stag was probably the 'stag hunt' by Jean–Baptiste Oudry listed in the 1871 catalogue. The painting of St Catherine of Siena was attributed to Charles Le Brun in the 1885 catalogue (the 1871 catalogue had attributed it to 'Coello'). It was sold at the Bennett sale in 1925 (lot no. 521).

30   Jacques Foucart, *Catalogue des Peintures Flamandes et Hollandaises du Musée du Louvre* (Paris, 2009), p. 174.

31   Waterfield, 'The origins of the early picture gallery catalogue', p. 47.

32   On the use of portraits as signifiers of status and lineage see Christopher Christie, *The British Country House in the Eighteenth Century* (Manchester, 2000), pp 188–99; Kate Retford, 'Patrilineal portraiture? Gender and genealogy in the eighteenth-century country house', in John Styles and Amanda Vickery (eds), *Gender, Taste, and Material Culture in Britain and North America, 1700–1830* (New Haven, 2006), pp 323–52.

33   In Dec. 1902 Maurice FitzGerald, 6th duke of Leinster, while still a student at Eton College, consented to having £800 paid from his father's estate for the purchase of 'family pictures, plate, etc from the representatives of the late Lord William FitzGerald'; 'Duke of Leinster's consent to the purchase of plate and pictures, 16 Dec., 1902', PRONI, Leinster Papers, D3078/2/10/11. Another letter dated 1 Nov. 1905, discusses the replacement of a 'very bad likeness' of his mother in the dining room at Carton with a recently acquired portrait of the 16th Earl of Kildare; 'Letter from Duke of Leinster to Frederick FitzGerald, 1 Nov. 1906', PRONI, Leinster Papers, D3078/2/10/13. His purchases of family portraits between 1894 and 1915 are listed in a separate document, 'Pictures purchased during the minority of the Duke of Leinster', PRONI, Leinster Papers, D3078/2/10/6/7.

34   The painting was sold at Christie's, Milan, on 28 June, 2008 (lot no. 148) and acquired by the French dealer Eric Turquin. See also Hella Robels, *Frans Snyders: Stilleben und Tiermaler 1579–1657* (Munich, 1989), no. A42, where the suggested attribution was 'probably Frans Ykens' and the provenance erroneously given as 'Duke of Leicester, England'.

35   If these works were acquired during the eighteenth century they reflected prevailing patterns in terms of taste.

36   Michael Kitson, Claude's earliest 'Coastal Scene with the Rape of Europa', *The Burlington Magazine* cxv (1973), pp 175–9.

37   Humphrey Wine, *Claude: The Poetic Landscape* (London, 1994).

38   For topographical views of the Carton demesne by Roberts and Ashford, see Laffan and Rooney, *Thomas Roberts: Landscape and Patronage*, pp 271–303.

39   The paintings by Cuyp were described as 'Landscape and cattle', 'Herdsmen and cattle', 'Landscape', 'Horses and groom', 'Cattle', 'Men on horseback', and another 'Men on horseback'. Only four of these can be identified today. The two paintings listed as 'Landscape and cattle' and 'Cattle' share identical dimensions and could be either the painting now in the Wernher Collection as identified by Alan Chong, 'Aelbert Cuyp and the meanings of landscape' (Unpublished Ph.D. thesis, New York University, 1992, no. 120), or a work of doubtful attribution that is presently in a private collection (Chong 1992), ibid., no. C35. 'Herdsmen and cattle' is untraced since it was disposed of at auction by the Leinster estate in 1925 (Christie's, London, lot no. 99). Chong (Chong (1992), no. B14b) questions its authenticity and regards it as a version of another work in the Frick Collection, New York. The second, 'Men on horseback' (42.5 x 58 inches), which hung in the library at Carton, was recently purchased by the National Gallery of Ireland. The author is grateful to John Loughman for information on Cuyp and on the provenance of Netherlandish paintings in the Leinster collection.

40   C. W. Ganly, *A Tribute to a Noble Life. In memoriam Gerald, Duke of Leinster* (Dublin, 1894), p. 5.

41   Alan Chong, 'Aristocratic imaginings: Aelbert Cuyp's patrons and collectors', in A. K. Wheelock (ed.), *Aelbert Cuyp* (Washington, London and Amsterdam, 2001), p. 47.

42   The paintings, dated 1668, are now in a private collection. They are illustrated in the exhibition catalogue *Im Lichte Hollands: Holländische Malerei des 17. Jahrhunderts aus den Sammlungen des Fürsten von Liechtenstein und aus Schweizer Bezit*, nos. 16 and 17.

Painting Carton
The 2nd Duke of Leinster, Thomas Roberts and William Ashford

William Laffan and Brendan Rooney

The 2009 exhibition at the National Gallery of Ireland (NGI) devoted to Thomas Roberts (1748–77) offered the first opportunity in a generation to reassemble a set of six views of Carton demesne commissioned from the artist by the 2nd duke of Leinster, two of which were executed, after Roberts's untimely death, by William Ashford (see plate section).[1] This also seems to have been the first time that all six pictures were seen together *in public* – only two of the paintings having been included in the NGI Bicentenary Exhibition in 1978, and the four views by Roberts having been separated at Christie's in 1983. Indeed, the six pictures had initially been exhibited piecemeal in 1775, 1776 and 1780 at the Society of Artists in Ireland, William Street, Dublin. Pleasingly, the Roberts quartet has, more recently, been reunited and brought home to an Irish private collection; while the two works by Ashford have found the most appropriate home of all in the drawing room at Carton. Hanging in a dedicated room at the NGI in 2009, which allowed for a close study of the set's internal dynamics, the four works by Roberts triumphantly affirmed the artist's position – acknowledged in his own day – as the leading painter of the Irish landscaped demesne, and highlighted the deliberately different approach that Ashford took when he came to paint two works to round off the set. On display, there was a very real sense that although it was the accident of Roberts's premature death that made these the last works in the exhibition, still, somehow, they offered a wholly natural climax to the exhibition – and hence to Roberts's art. The sophistication of Roberts's landscape technique seemed perfectly in tune with the subject matter to which it was applied – the great landscape demesne created by James and Emily FitzGerald, the 1st Duke and Duchess of Leinster.

Roberts came to paint at Carton around 1775, the year when he exhibited two of his paintings at the Society of Artists in Ireland. However, he had already worked for the FitzGeralds a few years earlier, painting, in 1772, an Arabian pony belonging to Gerald FitzGerald (1766–1788), son of the 1st Duke and Duchess.[2] The picture, *Bold Sir William* (see plate section), the frame of which still bears its distinctive Carton tablet, shows the pony accompanied by a sumptuously dressed East Indian page; in a watercolour of about 1800 it can be seen hanging in the drawing room at Carton.[3] It seems reasonable to suggest that Roberts's client here was Emily, 1st Duchess of Leinster. The year after Roberts painted *Bold Sir William*, however, Emily's husband died and was succeeded by William Robert FitzGerald (1749–1804), who was to be Roberts's patron for his set of demesne views.

The 2nd duke of Leinster has been overshadowed to a large degree in the story of Carton, not least by his formidable mother, but he was responsible for continuing the demesne developments begun by his parents. Perhaps, however, William's greatest achievement in this regard was the commissioning of Roberts's views of the demesne. Roberts must have been an obvious candidate for this prestigious commission, having already worked for the family as well as painting landscapes for the new duke's friends including Lord Charlemont, the Powerscourts, and the Milltowns of Russborough. Furthermore, immediately before working at Carton, Roberts had completed a high-profile commission in London for Sir Watkin Williams-Wynn, a friend of the 2nd duke who had travelled with him on his Grand Tour. Moreover, Roberts had already clearly demonstrated his suitability for the task with his depictions of Lucan, a nearby estate well known to the FitzGeralds.[4] Just how small the circles of patronage in which Roberts operated were is evident from the correspondence to and from William's mother, Emily. In 1775 for example, as Roberts was working on the commission, a letter to the dowager duchess from her sister Louisa Conolly includes news and gossip on a number of individuals who had also commissioned work from Roberts: Lord Harcourt, Lord Ross and the Veseys (who were spending time in England while Lucan was being rebuilt).[5] Though young, Roberts was far from an unknown quantity in fashionable society.

While Roberts's *Bold Sir William* was on display at Carton (see plate section), the set of paintings of the demesne seems, in accordance with standard practice, to have been hung in the family's town house. The first record of the Carton pictures is in *Notes on the Pictures, Plate, Antiquities, &C. at Carton, Kilkea Castle, 13, Dominick Street, Dublin and 6, Carlton House Terrace, London*. This catalogue from 1871 records the set as hanging in the dining room of their town house at 13 Dominick Street, Dublin, where many of the family's pictures appear to have been moved after the sale of Leinster House in 1815. Leinster House was very likely the original location for Roberts's commission; in 1775, his patron, the 2nd duke, was turning his attention to the decoration of the house's picture gallery – now the chamber of Seanad Éireann – for which task he employed James Wyatt. According to the revised edition of the Leinster catalogue in 1885, three other works by Roberts were also hanging in Dominick Street.

These were views of Tinnehinch and Clonskeagh, and one simply described as a landscape.[6] While it is, of course, possible that they were acquired by a subsequent generation of the FitzGerald family, it seems much more likely that these too were purchased directly from the artist. If this is indeed the case, it would indicate that the ducal Leinsters, as owners of a total of eight works by the artist, were among Roberts's most significant patrons – as indeed Anthony Pasquin had already suggested in the eighteenth century.[7]

If not the picture gallery, then another prominent location within Leinster House seems the most likely intended setting for Roberts's set. Given the size and number of the paintings some thought must have been given when they were commissioned to their eventual destination. The FitzGeralds owned works by the most revered of the Old Masters, but they also commissioned and supported young Irish talent, notably Roberts, but also the slightly older Hugh Douglas Hamilton who received patronage from successive generations of the family. The fact that Roberts and the 2nd duke of Leinster were almost exactly the same age may have encouraged an easy familiarity between artist and patron. More generally, the young duke's patriotic support of all things Irish – which extended to a fancy dress ball at Leinster House in which guests were required to wear garments of native manufacture, 'down to the petticoats and shoes of the ladies' – may have encouraged him to complement his inherited pictures by the great masters with those of a young Irish artist.[8] Even if Carton's park was largely the creation of his English mother and her English gardeners, it was resolutely viewed as an Irish demesne. The duke was emerging as the leader of the Patriot party, and subsequently of the Volunteer movement in whose uniform he is shown in a fine pastel by Hamilton (private collection). The duke also involved himself in the politics of the Dublin art scene, even down to the level of lobbying for his favoured candidate to replace James Mannin as head of the Dublin Society Schools. As the leading peer of the realm, it was politically expedient for the duke to be seen to support Irish artists but, as with Lord Charlemont, this was also undoubtedly a sincerely-held tenet. Significantly, Roberts added the word 'Ireland' to his signature on one of the Carton views, presumably as a patriotic affirmation of himself as an Irish artist and one which would have accorded well with his patron's principles. In the previous decade Robert Carver had bemoaned the preference of Irish patrons for imported art, the work of 'Signor Sombodini', rather than his own.[9] In the milieu of the young duke of Leinster, by contrast, Irish painting was celebrated for its native qualities and hung proudly in the same space as works by the likes of Claude.

By 1776, the date of at least one of the Carton pictures, Roberts was seriously ill and had sought a cure in Bath, where his cadaverous state was noted in a letter from his friend, John Warren.[10] In November he posted an advertisement in *Faulkner's Dublin Journal* to 'inform his friends who have honoured him with their Commands, that he intends spending the Winter in Lisbon, which he hopes, will enable him to execute all commissions, to the general satisfaction'.[11] Among these unfinished commissions were the Carton pictures, but Roberts's optimism regarding his recovery proved misplaced and he died in Lisbon in March of the following year. At some point thereafter, William Ashford was commissioned to paint two further pictures to complete the set and these were exhibited at the Society of Artists in 1780. This may have been the reason for confusion in relation to the attribution of the entire set – in the 1871 catalogue the six Carton pictures displayed in Dominick Street were all attributed to William Ashford. The two surviving Ashford views of the demesne are both quite prominently signed and dated 1779, but it seems that the compiler of the 1871 inventory mistakenly presumed that the remaining four pictures were also by Ashford (despite the fact that one of them is clearly signed and dated by Roberts).

A set of six demesne views would have been unusual for the time, the usual convention being four. However, at an earlier point in his career, Roberts had painted six views of Dawson Grove, County Monaghan, while Jonathan Fisher had also painted a set of six pictures of Castle Ward, County Down. There is strong circumstantial evidence that six works were envisaged from the start: the fact that so soon after Roberts's death Ashford painted additional views of the same size, and that all six were hung together. In addition, compositional oddities within Roberts's Carton pictures strongly suggest that he had made plans for two further works, and perhaps even that he had either sketched them out or had, at least, determined their essential format. Somehow, too, the ambition of the existing set of four pictures – their scale and the effort evidently expended on their execution – seems almost programmatic. It is as if Roberts and his patron were setting out to excel, and to produce the finest set of demesne paintings yet completed in Ireland. Perhaps, the status of the duke and his recent marriage and inheritance of Carton invited extravagance and the decision by Roberts, or the duke, to expand the conventional format from four to six views may have seemed appropriate.

The circumstances of the 2nd duke's inheritance were not altogether propitious. As the second son, William came to the title on the death of his older brother George (1748–65). A 'plump and hesitant man whose lack of aptitudes and ambition were unfavourably compared with the shining talents of his cousin Charles Fox', William was also saddled with debts of some £148,000 and the scandal of his mother's second marriage to her children's tutor, William Ogilvie.[12] The 1st duke's will had given his widow a lifetime interest in Carton, provided she did not remarry. Emily, however, gave up Carton in exchange for Frescati, the seaside villa in Blackrock, south Dublin, and a large cash payment, and eloped to France with Ogilvie. With his mother's departure, William took possession of an estate commensurate with his ducal standing. It is this awareness of new-found status, and the pride of ownership that it entailed, that seems to account for the commissioning of such a large and ambitious set of views of Carton so soon after gaining possession of the demesne.

If the paintings celebrate the contemporary wealth, status and refinement of taste of the FitzGeralds, equally important were more personal factors such as the feeling of home and attachment to ancestral lands. The manor of Maynooth had been granted to Maurice FitzGerald in the twelfth century and the ruins of the old FitzGerald castle in the town bore testament to the family's longevity (if not continuity of residence) in the area. The fondness that Carton, William's childhood home, inspired in him is manifest in his letters. Writing home from his Grand Tour, his longing for it becomes something of a leitmotif: 'To be sure I envy you dining at Waterstone [the cottage ornée in the demesne]'; 'I can assure you I often think with pleasure how happy we shall be at Carton'.[13] There was, of course, an element of simple homesickness here, but a letter from the duke's aunt, Louisa Conolly, to his mother also testifies to the feelings that Carton engendered in its occupants. Written as Roberts was working on his landscapes, and rather poignantly signalling the passing of the generations, Louisa indicated the pleasure in ownership that led the 2nd duke to commission the set of landscapes:

> to confess the honest truth, poor dear Carton does not go down with me. I cannot feel pleasant there and do not love to go there, though I love it, am happy to think that dear William enjoys it as he does, and should be miserable to have it neglected.[14]

A further personal emotion which the commissioning of Roberts's works was related to perhaps underlaid the duke's marriage. The first two of Roberts's pictures were exhibited in 1775, the year after William had married Emilia St George (*c.*1753–98), the only child of Lord St George of Headford Castle, County Galway. The duke and duchess appeared walking the grounds in three of Roberts's pictures, and it seems highly likely that the set was commissioned, in part at least, to commemorate the wedding. While the marriage was to a degree dynastic – and Emilia's dowry of £68,000 clearly helped the strained family finances – there was also great fondness between the young husband and wife.[15] In another letter to the dowager duchess, again written while Roberts was at work on the commission, Louisa Conolly recounts: 'The duke and duchess of Leinster are making such a noise with kissing and bustling at the end of the gallery, that it is impossible to write a regular letter'.[16] The happiness enjoyed by the young married couple is also clearly communicated in Roberts's depiction of them advancing towards a boat in *Sheet of Water*. Irish demesne landscapes have sometimes been interpreted over-reductively, as images of power enjoyed and control exerted, and while on occasion such an analysis may be fruitful, indeed inevitable, its rigid application can result in the neglect of more human emotions such as pride in inheritance and marriage, the fondness for home, or young love that may also account for the commissioning of such paintings and explain the form they took.

Taking the viewer on a virtual tour of the demesne, Roberts's Carton quartet is organised according to clearly considered compositional dynamics. While two of the views are evidently conceived as a pair to be hung side by side, or at least in a way that allowed their matching rhythm to be appreciated, the other two are related formally, but in an overlapping rather than complementary fashion, and were probably each conceived with matching pendants in mind – these were the two pictures which the artist's death prevented him from executing. Roberts depicts the Carton estate at different times of day, so affording himself the opportunity to introduce a temporal progression between the individual pictures, while at the same time demonstrating his unusual skill in capturing the effects of nature. In addition to these distinctive structural and atmospheric qualities, a feeling of movement through the landscape animates the set. In all but one of the four paintings the viewer shadows the duke and duchess as they wander through their grounds. All of these elements – structural, temporal and mobile (or progressive) – which run from picture to picture, demand that the set is treated as an entire series, rather than as the sum of its individual works – hence the interest in seeing the works hung together in the NGI in 2009. Even if these are purely formal elements, they nevertheless combine to give the impression of a timeless sense of order, and of the status quo being ordained. The focus on the time of day evokes the unchanging pattern of the natural world around which a day for the duke and duchess and their staff was organised. The neat pattern of nature reshaped suggests that everything – and everyone – was in its place. The estate was shown both as a productive farm, through scenes of haymaking and sheep-rearing, and as elegant pleasure grounds that testified to the refined good taste, and beneficent rule, of its owners.

The series opens with a tranquil, early morning scene, *The Bridge in the Park* (see plate section). Appropriately, this is the only view in which the duke and duchess do not feature, as – we may presume – they are yet to rise. Instead, the foreground is dominated by a scene of labour, with farm workers hauling a boat laden with logs and sacks to the bank of the Rye Water. This is also the only view in which Carton House itself appears, although tucked so discreetly into the left-hand corner as to be easily missed. Such an elliptical reference to the mansion around which the estate was developed is typical of Roberts, but differs radically from the approach taken by Irish landscapists of a slightly older generation including William van der Hagen. By miniaturising the house in this way, Roberts proclaims that Carton's setting – the landscape or demesne – is the actual subject of his series. The view is taken from close to the demesne wall, downstream from the stone bridge built in 1772 by Thomas Ivory, over which diminutive figures make their way to the house. The viewpoint clearly shows how the river has been widened and an artificial island created in accordance with Brownian principles of landscape design.[17] 'Capability' Brown, it should be remembered, had rebuffed the 1st duke's attempts to employ him at Carton, yet the park landscape, particularly in this section of the estate, was created very much in his idiom. Roberts's own composition was itself informed by Brownian concerns, including the principle that the house should be approached from an oblique angle rather than along a straight avenue. Similarly, like any good landscape gardener, Roberts enjoyed manipulating scale, toying with the relative heights of trees to exaggerate the sense of distance, and affording buildings Lilliputian proportions compared to the surrounding foliage.

The next work, *The Ivory Bridge* (see plate section), is one of three of the series in which the distant Tyrconnell (or Prospect) tower helps to orientate the viewer. In the middleground, the duke and duchess disembark from a boat to be met by grooms and horses that have come from the house. Of all the Carton pictures, it is here that Roberts's miniaturist technique is most dazzling. His extraordinary attention to detail is exemplified by the tiny head of a horse that can just be seen through a fork in a tree. Despite this meticulous approach to surface detail, the picture is surprisingly monumental in feel, brightly lit and dominated by a majestically painted midday sky. In the interest of detail and expanse, Roberts conflates two viewpoints: one from a rise in the land between the bridge and the estate wall, the other a more square-on view of the bridge. This manipulation of viewpoint has the pleasing effect of making the river meander from the bottom left corner of the picture until it disappears in the distance – in reality this could not be seen from any single viewpoint. The bridge which forms the focal point of this view, built to designs inspired by Isaac Ware, was a handsome, and long-anticipated, addition to the park. Roberts was rather partial to the inclusion of bridges as a compositional feature in his landscapes, and it is perhaps no surprise to find the Carton views linked by the motif. Here Thomas Ivory's pristine bridge acts as a symbol for the taming and crossing of the remodelled landscape, though this is no more than an elegant conceit as, in truth, the modest river hardly required so elaborate a structure.

In *A View in the Park with Haymakers* (see plate section), the duke and duchess have now crossed the river and appear on a pathway followed by a third figure, perhaps a lady-in-waiting. The duke has his arm outstretched as if pointing out features of the demesne to his new wife. The Tyrconnell Tower again helps to orientate the viewer, but the cottage at Waterstone – one of William's favourite spots on the demesne – is conspicuously absent. A steeple breaking the line of the trees in the distance represents the village of Maynooth synecdochically. Here Roberts liberally deploys artistic license, assuming an elevated vantage point and exaggerating the panorama afforded from this spot, and, again in empathy with the landscape gardener, overstating the ruggedness of the land in contradistinction to other areas of the demesne. The estate workers shown loading hay into a wagon may have evoked nostalgic associations of childhood for the 2nd duke; his mother had noted how William 'lives with the haymakers and sheepshearers' and later, in 1762, wrote: 'If William has a turn to anything I think it is farming'.[18] For children at least, the lines of social demarcation surrounding the house were not as strictly enforced at this date as they would become in the following century. Taken as a whole, Roberts's series suggests a certain – and paradoxical – communality of life on the estate; gardeners, labourers, boatmen and haymakers share the same space and are given prominence equal to that of the duke and duchess. Carton is portrayed here as a microcosm of a well-ordered world; the estate is self-sufficient and the social hierarchy is ordained or God-given.

Roberts's final work (see plate section) depicts an area on the other side of the house from the first three, focusing on a feature that had been added to the Carton landscape less than 20 years previously. The demesne's terrain did not lend itself to the substantial lake that was such an important element of contemporary landscape design – and of the sort that William's mother had famously admired at Ballyfin – but by 1762 a narrow feeder channel to the reservoir was widened to create a 'new river', titled, rather grandly, the 'Sheet of water' (see chapter 6). Roberts manipulates the scene by introducing three tiny figures on the shore to draw the viewer's attention to the island within the lake, which has the effect of exaggerating the size and length of the Sheet itself. With its polished sheen, its sinuous contours, and the high finish of the foliage, this picture can be seen, retrospectively, as Roberts bringing the genre of demesne painting to its logical conclusion of exaggerated sensibility. Indeed, it is wholly appropriate that it is into this landscape that the duke and duchess finally emerge as large-scale and recognisable characters rather than as diminutive figures in the distance. They approach a boat, crewed by a smartly-liveried servant, as if to make a journey down the river, albeit one that, given the distances involved, would have been very short, if not altogether pointless. Here Roberts exploits the ready-made iconography of the 'landscape marriage portrait', or 'promenade portrait' utilised most famously by Thomas Gainsborough in *The Morning Walk* (1785).[19] He choreographs a deliberate contrast through the contiguity of the posed aristocrats with the two gardeners straining as they pull a heavy roller along the path. While the duke and duchess's refinement of costume and carriage complements the manicured elegance that was the defining characteristic of this area of the estate, their juxtaposition with the toiling estate workers emphasises that the demesne's appearance is man-made and requires constant maintenance to preserve its perfection. However, such is the totality of artifice Roberts conjures up here that these figures only add to the exquisitely pitched feeling of heightened sensibility.

Roberts crafted his group of Carton pictures very carefully so that they relate one to another. All share certain formal characteristics, including an elevated viewpoint, an area of shadow in the foreground, and a stretch of water extending through the composition into the distance. The mirrored compositions of *The Ivory Bridge* and *The View in the Park with Haymakers* suggest that these works were designed to be hung side-by-side, with the former on the left. *The Sheet of Water* and the *Bridge in the Park*, meanwhile, seem to relate not to one another but each to a missing pendant – presumably the two pictures that were never completed. However, when William Ashford took over the commission after Roberts's death he completely disregarded the organisational structure and, instead of painting Carton's mild and gentle slopes, sought out the more enclosed landscape of the lower Rye Water valley, which was 'considered wilder and more natural than the landscape further upstream'.[20] In addition to better suiting Ashford's talents, the decision to depict this area may have come from his patron's desire to round off Roberts's views with the further flung areas of the demesne which had only recently been developed.

Ashford's first view (see plate section) shows an angler by the Rye Water with a gamekeeper approaching along a path. The figure of the gamekeeper is repeated almost exactly, though shown more fully, from a painting by Ashford of the Powerscourt demesne, a work which was certainly known to Roberts.[21] However, just as this was one detail that Roberts chose not to repeat in his own depiction of the Powerscourt deerpark, it was also alien to Roberts's more rarefied vision of Carton.[22] Meanwhile, Ashford's second picture (see plate section) does owe something to Roberts's model, as it too features the duke and duchess touring the demesne, in this instance in a smart, horse-drawn carriage. However, while Roberts focuses on the landscape created by William's parents, Ashford records the part of the demesne cultivated by the 2nd duke himself. His looser technique complements William's aim to 'make the banks more pasture & the heads more rustick so as to match the rocks'.[23] Ashford's views of Carton are undoubtedly accomplished and distinctive, but perhaps fail to equal the compositional subtleties and majestic grandeur of vision that Roberts achieves. Their respective Carton pictures evince the fundamentally different artistic approaches to landscape; in essence, Roberts's work is as ethereal as Ashford's is anecdotal.

These questions of different artistic personalities, however, combine with larger issues: the shift in generation from Emily, 1st duchess of Leinster, to her son, and even more fundamentally the move from enjoyment of Brownian parkland to an incipient interest in the picturesque, which Ashford's views clearly demonstrate. Indeed, the contrasts as much as the congruencies within the combined set were dynamically apparent when the six views by the two artists were put on display together in 2009. It is nevertheless apparent, and appropriate, that Roberts reserved his most virtuoso set of demesne landscapes for his depiction of the home of Ireland's premier peer and only duke. Just as estates like Carton came to epitomise the refined ideal of ascendancy living, Roberts's pictures, an unashamed celebration of life behind the walls of an enclosed demesne, represent the apex of the subject's portrayal in Irish art.

NOTES

1   *Thomas Roberts, 1748–1777*, National Gallery of Ireland (NGI), 2009. For a fuller discussion of the subject see William Laffan and Brendan Rooney, *Thomas Roberts, Landscape and Patronage in Eighteenth-Century Ireland* (Tralee, 2009), pp 270–303. The 2009 publication catalogued 64 works by the artist. It is pleasing to note that Roberts's extant oeuvre can now be increased to 67 as three further works have now been identified, two of these are discussed in William Laffan and Brendan Rooney, 'Two new works by Thomas Roberts (1748–1777)', *Irish Architectural and Decorative Studies*, xv, (2012).

2   Private collection.

3   Private collection.

4   *Lucan House and Demesne with Figures quarrying Stone* (NGI 4463); *The River Liffey in Lucan House Demesne* (NGI. 4464); *The Weir in Lucan House Demesne* (NGI. 4465); *A View in Lucan House Demesne* (NGI. 4466).

5   Brian FitzGerald (ed.), *Correspondence of Emily, Duchess of Leinster (1731–1814)* (3 vols, Dublin 1949–57), vol. iii, pp 140–1.

6   The two topographical views are presumably the surviving works of the same subjects, now in a private collection and the NGI respectively; Laffan and Rooney, *Thomas Roberts*, Cats 6 & 9.

7   Anthony Pasquin [John Williams], *An Authentic History of the Arts in Ireland* (London, 1796), p. 8.

8   Elizabeth FitzGerald, *Lord Kildare's Grand Tour, 1766–1769* (Wilton, 2000), p. 146.

9   John Thomas Gilbert, *A History of the City of Dublin* (3 vols, Dublin, 1854–59), vol. iii, p. 347.

10   Philip McEvansoneya, 'An Irish artist goes to Bath: Letters from John Warren to Andrew Caldwell, 1776–84', in *Irish Architectural and Decorative Studies*, ii (1999), p. 160.

11   *Faulkner's Dublin Journal*, 26–28 Nov. 1776.

12   Stella Tillyard, *Aristocrats: Caroline, Emily, Louisa and Sarah Lennox, 1740–1832* (London, 1994), p. 251.

13   William, Lord Offaly to Emily, Marchionness of Kildare, 19 Oct. 1766, and same to same (though by now William, Marquis of Kildare, to Emily, Duchess of Leinster), 13 Mar. 1769, in FitzGerald (ed.), *Correspondence of Emily*, vol. iii, p. 431, 558.

14   Lady Louisa Conolly to Emily, Duchess of Leinster, 7 Dec. 1775, ibid., pp 167–8.

15   Anthony Malcomson, *The Pursuit of the Heiress, Aristocratic Marriage in Ireland, 1740–1840* (Belfast, 2006), p. 42.

16   FitzGerald, *Correspondence of Emily*, p. 169.

17   Finola O'Kane, *Landscape Design in Eighteenth-Century Ireland: Mixing Foreign Trees with the Natives* (Cork 1994), p. 104; and generally pp 89–129.

18   Emily, Countess of Leinster to James, Marquis of Kildare, 17 June 1757 and same to same 23 Dec 1762. FitzGerald, *Correspondence of Emily*, vol. i, p. 48, 162.

19   National Gallery, London.

20   O'Kane, *Landscape Design*, p. 116.

21   Laffan and Rooney, *Thomas Roberts*, fig. 156 and pp 190–213.

22   Ibid., Cat. 56.

23   O'Kane, *Landscape Design*, pp 171–2.

The 2nd Duke of Leinster
and the Establishment of St Patrick's
College, Maynooth

Cormac Begadon

St Patrick's College occupies a prominent location in the village of Maynooth, sitting at one end of Leinster Street, on a site bordering the twelfth-century Geraldine castle. Founded in 1795 as the Royal Catholic College of St Patrick, it remains the most recognisable symbol of the Catholic Church in Ireland to this day. Established by an act of parliament, it was one of the earliest concessions granted by government to Catholics, and coincided with the commencement of a programme of renewal and reform for the Catholic Church in Ireland. The story of the College's founding has been well documented by a number of historians.[1] The aim of this chapter is not solely to retell this story, but rather to bring to light the often underplayed contribution of the 2nd Duke of Leinster, William Robert FitzGerald (1749–1804), to the establishment of the College.

Born in London and educated at Eton, William only became the heir apparent to his father's title upon the death of his elder brother in 1765, after which he received the honorary title of marquis of Kildare and embarked upon his Grand Tour. After returning to Ireland, he was elected as MP for Dublin in 1767, taking his seat in 1769 and assuming the title of duke of Leinster upon the death of his father in 1773. He soon showed a determined resolve to establish himself as one of the country's leading political figures. In his early political career he gave his support for the campaign for free trade, but stopped shy of calling for Irish legislative independence. For much of the 1780s he gave his support to the Whig opposition. However, he was never exclusive in his support for the Whigs, often demonstrating a pragmatic streak by supporting the government when his interests were better served. His determination to assert himself as a leading political and social figure stretched beyond his parliamentary interests. During his Grand Tour he had joined the Freemasons in Naples, and was subsequently appointed grand master in Ireland. He was also a pivotal player in the early years of the Irish Volunteers, serving as colonel in the Dublin regiment from its inception in 1778. Both of these experiences undoubtedly exposed him to certain Enlightenment principles.

In terms of religious toleration and Catholic relief, William was broadly supportive from the outset of his political career. He publicly declared support for the earlier Catholic relief measures, but in 1792 he withdrew his support for outright emancipation. He later voted against two further relief measures that were brought before parliament. Nevertheless, with the passing of the 1795 act of parliament for the establishment of a Catholic college, William was to assume a central role in the establishment and location of the new college at Maynooth. The founding of a national seminary was a watershed moment for the Catholic Church in Ireland. Following the successes of the Protestant Reformation across Europe, the Catholic Church had been forced to become increasingly concerned with the education of its clergy; at the great Counter-Reformation's Council of Trent the establishment of seminaries in all countries had been recommended. However, the increasing authority of the Protestant state in Ireland had severely hampered efforts to establish Catholic secondary schools and seminaries. When Trinity College Dublin was founded by royal decree in 1592, it proved uncongenial to Catholic interests. The only alternative, therefore, was to establish a system of clerical education on the continent to form priests for ministering in Ireland. From the later decades of the sixteenth century, Irish colleges slowly began to spring up across Catholic Europe. At first the number of places available to Irish students was small, but by the middle of the eighteenth century large numbers of Irish priests were receiving at least part of their formation abroad.

Indeed, the establishment of a network of Irish colleges on the continent has been described as 'the most outstanding feature of the exiled Church in Europe'.[2] Thus the Irish Catholic Church possessed a vast, sophisticated, and well-endowed educational network stretching across Europe, with colleges in Rome, the Iberian Peninsula, the Austrian Netherlands and France. By the later decades of the eighteenth century, however, some Irish bishops were expressing serious concerns over the spread of radical ideas and irreligion, especially in France, where the greatest numbers of colleges were located. Both the Irish Catholic clergy and the British government perceived the dangers of facilitating the exposure of Irish priests to what the Archbishop of Dublin, John Thomas Troy, famously described as the 'French disease'. In his Lenten pastoral of 1792, he painted a bleak picture for the future of the Irish Catholic Church if Irish priests continued to receive a continental education, lamenting what he thought was the very real possibility of the Irish laity becoming imbued with the 'Poison of the affected Liberality' by their own clergy.[3] The death knell for Irish colleges on the continent was effectively sounded with the advent of the French Revolution, and the subsequent spread of revolutionary ideologies. The college network, as it had existed in its pre-revolution form, was effectively destroyed by the closure of the colleges in the 1790s.[4]

While the situation for Catholic education on the continent was rapidly worsening, it was becoming gradually more favourable in Ireland. The Relief Acts of 1782 and 1792 relaxed the restrictions on Catholic education and allowed for the establishment of Catholic schools under certain conditions. By removing the need to acquire permission from the local Protestant bishop, the Relief Act of 1792 also effectively allowed for the setting-up of the first post-Reformation Catholic seminaries at Carlow and Kilkenny. The success of these colleges was, however, limited as they were unable to receive endowments, either from government or from private donors, and it has been suggested, they were totally reliant on tuition fees paid by students.[5] Although they were welcome improvements to Catholic education, the seminaries were not the solution sought by bishops for the impending loss of the continental colleges. In the wake of the 1792 Relief Act, Archbishop Troy implored the government to establish a national seminary, fearing that

> the later restoration of the elective franchise to the Roman Catholics of Ireland places them in a novel situation, which, if not under the guidance of religion, may operate against the peace and obedience to the laws, which the Roman Catholic clergy have endeavoured to promote.[6]

In the same year he wrote to the Archbishop of Cashel, James Butler, recommending that all sixth-year students at the Collège des Lombards in Paris 'ought to be called home', as the 'situation in France is becoming alarming'.[7]

In light of this the Irish bishops joined forces – assuming a relatively novel corporate attitude – to forward their case for a national seminary. To help further their cause they approached Edmund Burke, who in turn enlisted the services of his son, Richard, and Thomas Hussey, a Catholic priest with diplomatic connections in London and Spain. (Hussey was later appointed as first president of Maynooth College (1795–97) and subsequently as bishop of Waterford and Lismore.) In 1793 a delegation of leading Catholic bishops met the lord lieutenant, the earl of Westmoreland, presenting him with a petition of loyalty intended for the king. This meeting proved to be a watershed in relations between the government and the Catholic hierarchy – it was the first such meeting in over a century, and signalled the beginning of better relations between both parties.[8] The goal of the bishops was the attainment of an exclusively Catholic establishment, with an overriding clerical nature; this was in stark contrast with the more egalitarian wishes of a radical 'sub-committee' of lay Catholics. This group, formed to forward Catholic educational claims and consisting of many who would go on to become United Irishmen, advocated that the new college accommodate not only Catholics, but also Protestants and Dissenters. Their college would resemble a university more than a Catholic seminary. By contrast, the bishops' petition to the lord lieutenant played on the role that an educated, orthodox, conservative Catholic clergy would play in the fight against the spread of French radicalism in Ireland.

At the same time as the bishops were advancing their case for a Catholic college, a Catholic relief bill was being debated in parliament. This bill, which allowed Catholics access to the municipal and parliamentary franchise as well as to attend universities, stopped shy of providing for a Catholic college. Although this represented a serious setback, Catholic hopes were raised upon the appointment of Earl Fitzwilliam as lord lieutenant in late 1794. Fitzwilliam was known to be inclined towards further concessions to Catholics, and Catholic hopes were heightened when upon his arrival he made a number of sweeping changes, removing both John Beresford, the chief revenue commissioner, and Arthur Wolfe, the attorney general, from their positions. Both of these men had been seen as barriers to further reform. The Catholic bishops took Fitzwilliam's appointment as a positive sign of things to come and wasted no time courting his support, setting about arranging another submission. The leader of the opposition in the Irish House of Commons, Henry Grattan, then introduced to parliament a bill calling for emancipation on 12 February 1795 – it was defeated. It had proved to be a step too far too soon. In its wake the Fitzwilliam administration collapsed almost immediately, with the lord lieutenant himself being recalled to London. The bishops now feared the worst for the future of a Catholic college.

However, Fitzwilliam's successor, Earl Camden, was requested by the London home secretary, the duke of Portland, to proceed with plans for the establishment of a new college. It was widely accepted that both the Irish and English governments viewed the establishment of a Catholic college as a final concession which would suffocate further calls for complete Catholic emancipation. Thus, on 24 April 1795, a bill introduced to the House of Commons was easily carried. Compromise was also reached on the governance of the new college; the bishops had sought exclusive clerical control while opponents desired an element of government supervision. In the end the bishops agreed to meet the government halfway: the new college was to be governed by a board of trustees, including the lord chancellor, three high court justices, six leading Catholic laymen, as well as ten Catholic bishops. Having the three Protestant judges on the board was not ideal to the Catholic hierarchy, but the bishops were sufficiently content that the internal affairs of the college would be entirely in their own hands, free from outside interference.

Finding a suitable site for the new college was the next task, but it was not a straightforward one. The 2nd duke of Leinster had proposed the recently built home of one of his employees, John Stoyte, in Maynooth as an appropriate location (see chapter 8). The duke had a long and favourable association with the Catholic community in his role as a landowner and as a leading peer and politician. Like many other landowners, the FitzGeralds had donated sites for new Catholic chapels: James, the 1st duke of Leinster, for example, famously granted a site for a chapel in Kildare town, and was credited by a Dublin newspaper with being 'the first Protestant gentleman who set the noble example in this kingdom of accommodating the Roman Catholics with a proper place of worship'.[9] It was no surprise then that when his son, William Robert, offered a site at Maynooth, Troy and the other bishops were eager to display their gratitude to the duke and the family. Troy forwarded a letter to the duke in June 1795 thanking him, but stating that although the 'vicinity of Mr. Stoyte's house to Carton' would be deemed favourable by the trustees, he feared that its distance from Dublin might be an issue and suggested that a closer alternative 'may be deemed more eligible'.[10] Initially there were, it seems, three proposed sites closer to Dublin city: Glasnevin House, Barry House in Donnybrook, and Stillorgan House.[11]

These options were well-known to the public and, on 2 July 1795, the *Dublin Evening Post* informed its readers that the

> trustees of the Catholic College have not yet been accommodated with a situation to their liking for the establishment of their seminary. Several situations have been mentioned for their choice; and amongst them Stillorgan house and demesne, the house of Mr. Mitchell, near Glasnevin, the house and concerns of the late Judge Helen at Mespil Bank, corner of Donnybrook road.[12]

However, the account contained no mention of a site at Maynooth. In fact, it seems that negotiations for the site at Stillorgan were quite advanced, so much so that the owner displayed considerable grievance when he learned that the Maynooth site had been chosen, even threatening to initiate legal proceedings against the trustees.[13] Stoyte's house, however, had been 'unanimously preferred to all others' and chosen at a meeting of the trustees held in the lord chancellor's chambers in the House of Lords. Present at this meeting were: John Fitzgibbon, 1st Earl of Clare; John Henry Scott, 1st Earl of Clonmel; Barry Yelverton, 1st Viscount Avonmore; Jenico Preston, 12th Viscount Gormanstown; Patrick Joseph Plunkett, Bishop of Meath and, of course, Archbishop Troy.[14]

The choice of the Maynooth site was, as Patrick Corish suggests, unquestionably due to 'the active goodwill of Ireland's premier nobleman, the duke of Leinster'.[15] Indeed, Troy wrote to the dowager duchess and her sister, Lady Louisa Conolly of Castletown, to thank them for 'their attention to us, and [we] received a very polite reply from each'.[16] The duke enjoyed a relatively cordial relationship with both Troy and the college president, Thomas Hussey, as is evidenced in their correspondence. For the duke, the establishment of a national Catholic college in the burgeoning town of Maynooth must have been a very attractive proposition. He was a major investor in the recently constructed Royal Canal, and the location of the new college was undoubtedly beneficial in economic terms and added further prestige to 'his' town. From the Catholic Church's point of view, Maynooth's more secluded setting may also have had advantages over any site nearer to Dublin city.

Since the establishment of the Irish colleges on the continent, the formation of Irish priests had taken place in an almost exclusively urban setting. As we have seen, this had worked well until the later decades of the eighteenth century when many European cities which hosted Irish clerical students, most especially in France, became centres of impiety and radicalism. In Bordeaux, for instance, the college superior lamented the pitiful situation that Irish students were forced to endure and wrote: 'The sad necessity is that they are scattered through the streets and squares of the city mingling with a low crowd that insults and reviles them'.[17] Mindful of the rising levels of impiety and 'insults' to which Irish students were exposed, the bishops were always likely to look for a more morally acceptable location for the college. This was certainly the view of the English Catholic writer, Francis Plowden (1749–1819), who wrote some years later that it was 'well known, that a principal inducement to establish the Catholic College at Maynooth, was to prevent the mischief of young men destined for the gospel ministry being sent abroad for that education'.[18] This was a view shared by Bartholomew Crotty, president of the college from 1813 to 1832, who considered the college's association with the 2nd duke of Leinster, and the proximity to his home at Carton, as morally edifying for the students.[19]

Another little-known proposition regarding the establishment of the College came from one of the trustees, Richard Strange, a 'leading Catholic', a County Louth landowner of some note, and a former member of the recently defunct radical committee of lay Catholics. In a letter to the 2nd duke dated 5 August 1795, Strange boldly suggested that the president and members of the college 'board' should 'have municipal power not only over the grounds belonging to the College, but also over the village of Maynooth'.[20] He proposed that such an unusual state of affairs was 'necessary to protect the morals of the students' and to 'promote this institution & to give it ... reputation'.[21] Strange had evidently discussed his proposal with one of the 'high judge' trustees, Lord Clonmel, who advised him that 'with respect to the actual municipal jurisdiction within the precinct of Maynooth, Your Grace certainly cannot grant to thy member of the college nor is thy decree necessary for the well being of the jurisdiction'.[22] Unfortunately there is no record of the duke's reaction to Strange's proposal; nothing ever came of it and municipal jurisdiction was never granted to the college; indeed, it would seem unlikely that the duke would have seriously considered Strange's request. Nonetheless, it was a sign of how far Catholic confidence had come in that they felt sufficiently at ease to petition Ireland's premier peer to hand over municipal control of what was, in effect, his town to the college.

The belief that the setting of the college would help to promote piety and morality amongst the students was clearly an important consideration in its foundation at Maynooth. Propaganda Fide, the Roman congregation with overall responsibility for the Irish Church, informed the Irish bishops that while it was happy with the establishment of the college it encouraged them to introduce a system of strict morality and discipline and, more significantly, to promote loyalty to 'temporal rulers'.[23] Maynooth, in their eyes, was to be everything that revolutionary Europe was not: it was to be moral, orthodox, and above all, loyal to its lawful national government and monarch. Similarly, Lord Clonmel, one of the four Protestant high judges appointed as trustees, expressed his approval at the choice of Maynooth, commenting: 'I am extremely glad to find that the site for the Roman Catholics is fixed at Maynooth. There cannot be a more eligible situation for it, and with Your Grace's patronage and protection, it will I make no doubt flourish'.[24] Troy himself, the de facto leader of the Irish Church, was always ready to stress the Church's gratitude to both the government and the duke for the foundation at Maynooth and for his paternal protection.

The College did not purchase the house and land but, rather, paid rent to the Stoyte family.[25] The trustees also endeavoured to secure the adjoining land of Stoyte's neighbour, Mr Chamberlain: 'The sooner a bargain can be closed with Chamberlain' Troy informed the 2nd duke of Leinster, 'the better, as no plan for additional buildings can be formed until the ground is surveyed & described.'[26] The site was duly acquired, bringing the total area of the College grounds to roughly 60 acres. Troy wrote to the Archbishop of Cashel, Dr Thomas Bray, that the duke had 'promised to grant a lease forever on moderate terms, not to exceed a guinea an acre.'[27] The trustees eventually received possession of the land in September 1795, and the college officially opened its doors to its first 50 students. In the beginning the college was limited to Stoyte House, although a separate lodging house was erected in 1796, and Riverstown Lodge (which now houses the offices of the president of the National University of Ireland Maynooth) was acquired in 1802.[28]

Apart from his role as landowner and patron, relatively little has been written, or indeed is known, about the duke's relationship with the college. Unfortunately there is a very real scarcity of sources to allow for a detailed examination. What evidence there is suggests that he took a genuine interest in the life of the college until his death in 1804. An interesting, if albeit fleeting, insight into the 2nd duke's good relations with the college and its students can be found in the correspondence of Eugene Conwell, a clerical student from the diocese of Derry.[29] Writing to his uncle in 1798 he lauded the duke saying, the 'duke of Leinster often visits us here. He is the most agreeable and affable gentleman I ever saw. Every Wednesday we visit his demesne which is most spacious and beautiful, and of endless variety.'[30] Conwell's high esteem for the duke may have been encouraged by the provision of free postage (his letters certainly imply that the duke shared his franking privileges with Maynooth students). The duke also appears to have been ever present when the trustees visited the college and at official functions; in April 1796, for example, he accompanied the lord lieutenant and visiting dignitaries at the laying of the foundation stone for new buildings, and attended a related event held at Dublin Castle.[31] The Bishop of Meath, Dr Plunkett, recalled happily that the 'duke of Leinster, on whose estate the college is situated, assisted with delight at the ceremony of the laying of the first stone ... His Grace behaved towards us with marked civility and kindness'.[32] The duke also presented to the college 'a capital of Portland stone, four feet high, to serve and stand for a horizontal sun dial', which was designed by the Dublin architect, Thomas Saunders.[33] Similar visits and occasional bequests followed.

After 1798 the involvement of the 2nd duke of Leinster in the life of the fledgling college waned, he retreated from public life and politics after the deaths of his wife, Emilia, and his younger brother, Lord Edward (in the 1798 rebellion). In 1800 however, he was forced to defend the existence of a lay college at Maynooth; upon an official visitation, led by Arthur Wolfe and Lord Kilwarden, it was put to the trustees that, under the terms of the 1795 Act, the new college should be exclusively for clerical education.[34] The duke's intervention probably ensured a lay college at Maynooth until 1817, a date which suggests that the 2nd duke's concern for the general education of Catholics was also shared by his son and heir, Augustus (1791–1874) who had succeeded in 1804. Upon its eventual closure, the lay college was superseded by the recently founded college at nearby Clongowes. There the 3rd duke of Leinster continued to offer patronage and support accompanying professors from Maynooth at the yearly 'academics', at which young scholars were formally examined in the Classics.[35] The duke was apparently very satisfied with the education system, telling a committee of the House of Lords that it was 'the most curious establishment' he ever saw 'as the boys are brought up well. A public examination is held every year and the Fellows of Trinity College are invited to go down: the Fellows are given a list of what Classics they are to examine in, and the answer is wonderful'.[36]

The college at Maynooth stands today as a symbol of the evolving fortunes of the Catholic community in Ireland. Crippled by an infrastructural poverty, the Catholic Church in Ireland had a precarious existence for the majority of the eighteenth century, its pastoral mission greatly restricted. It resembled nothing of the great 'national churches' of Catholic Europe and, despite the ties with the Catholic communities of France and Spain, had far more in common with co-religionists in England. But, after decades of endurance there came emergence and, by the 1790s, the fortunes of the Church and its community were improving steadily. The Catholic Church could now embark more freely on its much-needed programme of chapel building, catechesis and poor-relief. Its continued presence in the town is a constant reminder of the patronage and support extended to that programme by the 2nd duke of Leinster and his family.

NOTES

1   See Patrick Corish, *Maynooth College, 1795–1995* (Dublin, 1995); John Healy, *Maynooth College: Its Centenary History, 1795–1895* (Dublin, 1895); Dáire Keogh, *The French Disease: The Catholic Church and Radicalism, 1790–1800* (Dublin, 1993).

2   Cathaldus Giblin, 'Irish exiles in Catholic Europe', in Patrick Corish (ed.), *A History of Irish Catholicism*, iv, no. 2 (Dublin, 1971), p. 3.

3   Lenten pastoral letter, 20 Feb. 1792, Dublin Diocesan Archives (DDA), Troy Papers, AB2/116/5(85).

4   The colleges at Lisbon, Salamanca, Paris, and Rome were reopened subsequently in the nineteenth century. However, the numbers attending the colleges paled in comparison with those before revolution.

5   See Peadar Mac Suibhne, 'The early history of Carlow College', in *Irish Ecclesiastical Record*, lxii (1943), pp 230–48.

6   Troy to Chief Secretary Hobart, 29 Nov. 1793, cited in Vincent McNally, 'John Thomas Troy, Archbishop of Dublin, and the establishment of Saint Patrick's College, Maynooth, 1791–1795', in *Catholic Historical Review*, lxvii (1981), p. 571.

7   Troy to Butler, 5 May 1793, cited in Mark Tierney (ed.), 'A short title calendar of the papers of Archbishop James Butler II in Archbishop's Houses, Thurles, part 2', in *Collectanea Hibernica*, no. 20 (1978), p. 102.

8   Dáire Keogh, 'A Catholic seminary in a Protestant State', in *History Ireland*, iii:3 (Autumn, 1995), p. 44.

9   'Hoey's Journal', 10 Nov. 1794 in John Brady (ed.), *Catholics and Catholicism in the Eighteenth-Century Press* (Maynooth, 1965), p. 293.

10   Troy to Leinster, 6 Jun. 1795, DDA, AB2/116/6(78).

11   Corish, *Maynooth College*, p. 13.

12   *Dublin Evening Post*, 2 July 1795, cited in Jeremiah Newman, *Maynooth and Georgian Ireland* (Galway, 1979), p. 28.

13   See ibid., p. 31.

14   Troy to Bray, 28 July 1795, DDA, AB2/29/5/8(1).

15   Corish, *Maynooth College*, p. 13.

16   Troy to Bray, 28 July 1795, DDA, AB2/29/5/8(1).

17   Martin Glynn to Charles Kelly, 1774, cited in T. J. Walsh, *The Irish Continental Colleges Movement: The Colleges at Bordeaux, Toulouse and Lille* (Dublin, 1973), p. 111.

18   Francis Plowden, cited in Newman, *Maynooth and Georgian Ireland*, p. 10.

19   Newman, *Maynooth and Georgian Ireland*, p. 31.

20   Strange to Leinster, 5 Aug. 1795, National Library of Ireland (NLI), MS 41,552/40.

21   Ibid.

22   Clonmel to Leinster, 27 Aug. 1795, ibid.

23   Propaganda Fide to the Irish bishops, 9 July 1796, DDA, AB2/116/6(78).

24   Clonmel to Leinster, 27 Aug. 1795, NLI, MS 41,552/40.

25   The Stoyte family was still receiving rent from the college in the late nineteenth century.

26   Troy to Leinster, 31 July 1795, NLI, MS 41,552/40.

27   Troy to Bray, 28 July 1795, DDA, AB2/29/5/8(1).

28   Corish, *Maynooth College*, p. 16.

29   Luke (ed.), 'Calendar of the letters of Eugene Conwell, C. C., Collon', in *Journal of the County*

Louth Archaeological Society, ix:4 (1940), pp 290–377. [In this case, the author, 'Luke', has no given surname as he was a religious brother].

30   Eugene Conwell to Henry Conwell, 28 Oct. 1798 in 'Calendar of the letters of Eugene Conwell', p. 304.

31   Corish, *Maynooth College*, p. 17.

32   Cited in ibid., p. 18.

33   *Dublin Evening Post*, 28 Jan. 1797, cited in Brady, *Catholics and Catholicism in the Eighteenth-Century Press*, p. 301.

34   See Corish, *Maynooth College*, p. 40.

35   Thomas Morrissey, *As One Sent: Peter Kenney S. J., 1779–1841* (Dublin, 1996), p. 122.

36   Cited in ibid.

CHAPTER 12

Family Politics and Revolutionary Convictions
The Career of Edward FitzGerald
(1763–98)

Liam Chambers

Thomas Moore (1779–1852) opened his influential work *The Life and Death of Lord Edward FitzGerald* by observing: 'There is, perhaps, no name, in the ranks of the Irish peerage, that has been so frequently and prominently connected with the political destinies of Ireland as that of the illustrious race to which the subject of the following memoir belonged.' He went on to comment that in the story of the FitzGeralds from their arrival in Ireland in the late twelfth century to the death of Lord Edward FitzGerald in 1798: 'a complete history of the fatal policy of England towards Ireland, through a lapse of more than six centuries, may be found epitomized and illustrated.'[1] One might dismiss Moore's exaggeration regarding the family, but his contention that Edward FitzGerald (1763–98) occupied an important place in Irish history has endured. Edward was born on 15 October 1763, the twelfth child of James FitzGerald, 1st Duke of Leinster, and his wife Emily. His early career followed the kind of path typically pursued by an aristocratic younger son: a military profession coupled with an Irish parliamentary seat on the family interest. In the 1790s Edward emerged as a convinced radical, enthusiastically embracing the French Revolution. He joined the Society of United Irishmen and played an important role in organising the 1798 rebellion. He was arrested only days before the rebellion broke out and died of wounds inflicted during his capture, on 4 June 1798.

Edward's dramatic story has been re-told frequently by biographers, historians and novelists. The classic biography was Moore's *Life and Death*, a sympathetic account which painted its subject as a romantic nationalist pushed to revolution by a repressive government, his own passionate nature and a character easily influenced by external forces. In this way Moore produced a sensitive account of one of the chief architects of the 1798 rebellion, despite the fact that it had been thoroughly associated with indiscriminate sectarian slaughter in the minds of the Irish and English establishment, thanks in large part to the work of Richard Musgrave.[2] Moore effectively distanced his subject from violence and specifically rejected parallels between revolutionary Ireland in 1798 and revolutionary Europe in 1830.[3] Moore's careful politics, combined with an exhilarating account of an exciting character, cast a shadow over almost every other attempt to tell Edward's story in the nineteenth and twentieth centuries. While the historian, R. R. Madden, presented a more single-minded, militant and revolutionary profile in the 1840s, it was the influence of Moore which persisted into the less well known versions penned by Bodkin, Taylor, Tynan, Molony, Lindsey, Byrne and Hagan.[4] The latest full biography, Stella Tillyard's *Citizen Lord: Edward FitzGerald*, 1763–98, made a conscious break from Moore's influence, but while her account recognised FitzGerald's revolutionary militancy it retained a sense of his alleged political naivety.[5]

Moore's historiographical legacy was only one problem facing biographers. The other was lack of access to primary sources. Moore had been prompted to work on Edward's story by members of the FitzGerald family, though not all of them were enthusiastic. As a result he had access to private family papers in England, to which he added research in Ireland. Private family papers also formed the basis for two later works, which quoted extensively from them. The little-known second addenda (effectively the third volume) of Charles William FitzGerald's *The Earls of Kildare and their Ancestors*, which appeared in 1872, published dozens of hitherto unknown family papers for the first time. Further family papers appeared in Gerald Campbell's *Edward and Pamela FitzGerald*.[6] So, while later historians therefore knew about the existence of an extensive paper trail relating to Edward FitzGerald, they were generally unable to consult the sources themselves and had to rely instead on the selections and editions presented by Moore, FitzGerald and Campbell. Since the late 1990s this situation has changed dramatically, and in recent years the National Library of Ireland has acquired thousands of manuscripts relating to Edward FitzGerald and his family.[7] Many of these had been consulted and cited by Moore, FitzGerald and Campbell, so that their contents were already known to historians. However, the opportunity to read the originals and to examine how Moore, FitzGerald and Campbell had selected, edited and presented material is an exciting one to which historians are responding.[8] The 'new' material allows for a more nuanced and elaborated understanding of Edward's life and career. It underlines two particularly significant aspects of his biography, both highlighted in the present essay. First, the papers demonstrate how Edward's positions developed, in part at least, out of his involvement in his family's complex political world. Indeed, they suggest that his political relationship with his elder brother, William Robert, the 2nd Duke of Leinster, was more significant than usually appreciated. Secondly, the papers offer some further evidence that Edward became a committed revolutionary in his own right. A short essay cannot hope to answer conclusively the central question of Edward's biography: how did a son of Ireland's most senior aristocratic family become a dedicated, republican revolutionary? However, it can suggest that the answer must take more account of both FitzGerald family politics and the subject's revolutionary convictions.

Edward's early life, much of which was spent under the tutelage of William Ogilvie at his home, Frescati, in Blackrock, south Dublin, and then with his mother and Ogilvie (by now his step-father) at Aubigny in France, is reasonably well documented. While Thomas Moore skipped quickly over his early years, subsequent authors commented on them extensively and a number of biographers have placed particular emphasis on his relationship with his mother. In 1779, Edward finally embarked on a military career under the guidance of his uncle, Charles Lennox, 3rd Duke of Richmond. Despite his many advantages, Edward was a younger son in a very large family which did not really have the finances to match its social position. Edward's brother, William Robert, the 2nd Duke of Leinster, had inherited massive debts from their father, and the generous settlement afforded to their mother, along with the need to provide for a wide family network was almost too much for him. An advantageous marriage eased the problem, but did not solve it.[9] For Edward, connections were insufficient to advance a military career – but experience counted for something, as did money. The American War of Independence offered the possibility of experience, and Edward belatedly fought in the conflict, where he was wounded at Eutaw Springs in 1781. Money was a more intractable problem. In late 1782 Edward pushed for promotion. In response, his uncle, the Duke of Richmond, wrote to the duke of Leinster informing him that promotion was only possible by purchase and that the price would be at least 1,700 guineas, at most 3,500.[10] This seems to have effectively ruled it out, despite Edward continuing to raise the subject in letters to his mother the following year. On his return from America in 1783, Edward discovered that he had been elected MP for Athy Borough on the interest of his brother, William, the duke. Over the next decade he found that a parliamentary seat on the opposition benches created another obstacle to military advance.

Edward's oppositional political outlook developed during the 1780s and was heavily influenced by his cousin, Charles James Fox. Indeed, Edward acted as an important conduit between his family in Ireland and Fox in England. In a letter to William, written in July 1786, Edward explained how he had met Fox at William's request to explain that the duke's continued opposition could not be taken for granted.[11] The price was William's place 'at the head of affairs' in Ireland when Fox came to power in England. Fox wanted the duke to persevere, and agreed that everything would be made up to him. Edward agreed fully with Fox and his frank comments on the meeting are interesting. Opposition, he argued, was

... the only method of getting the government out of the hands of that vile set of jobbers who think of nothing but plundering it and enriching themselves; I own, if you consider only your own private interest, it is playing a deep game but as the French proverb says *il faut reculer pour mieux sauter* [one must move back to jump better].

A month later William commented to another brother, Charles, that he was happy that Edward agreed with his political line.[12] When William did enter government – largely for family-financial reasons – during the lord lieutenancy of the marquis of Buckingham in late 1787, he wrote to a disapproving Edward (at length) to explain his decision.[13] The spell in government did not last long: William backed the case for making the Prince of Wales, George (1762–1830), Irish regent during the temporary insanity of his father, George III, in the late 1780s. When the king suddenly recovered, the Irish supporters of the prince were left politically stranded. The upshot was the formation of an Irish Whig Club, with the duke of Leinster as a leading member. Through William's political rough ride from opposition to government and back to opposition, Edward's military career prospects (of promotion to lieutenant colonel) made no progress. Indeed, Edward's attitude to promotion changed dramatically in the course of the 1780s. Initially willing to engage his impressive family connections to ensure promotion, Edward later became unwilling to renounce his Foxite opposition in return for advancement. In 1788 he expressed grudging support to his uncle, Richmond, for his brother entering government, though he rejected Richmond's attempts to secure promotion for himself while he was an MP. Fox's plans for Edward's promotion under the Regency came to nothing; and in 1790, a promotion arranged by Richmond floundered when Edward discovered that he was now MP for County Kildare – and just as unwilling to support the government. By the early 1790s Edward had become more firmly convinced than ever that he could only accept promotion on merit as a point of principle, and not through influence or purchase.[14] Of course, his unfaltering Foxite sympathies were not surprising; Fox was his cousin, and for the FitzGeralds, the fissures of Irish and English high politics were deeply intertwined with familial relationships.

During the late 1780s Edward undertook lengthy journeys in continental Europe and North America. Much has been made of his experience of settler and native societies in America between 1788 and 1790. Indeed, some biographers have traced his radicalism to this American sojourn. These travels were undoubtedly formative and, as Kevin Whelan has shown, placed Edward firmly within the compass of Enlightenment cosmopolitanism, but there is no clear evidence that he arrived back in Europe a convinced republican.[15] The evidence points more strongly to the French Revolution, which impacted so significantly on Ireland, as the pivotal political event of Edward's life. Back in

London, during the early 1790s he was drawn to reforming and radical political networks. He joined the Friends of the People on their inauguration in April 1792.[16] This society, which took a more radical position on parliamentary reform than the Whig Club, provided an important model for the duke of Leinster's Association of the Friends of the Constitution, Liberty and Peace, founded in Ireland later the same year. Edward also associated with more radical activists, particularly those gathered around Thomas Paine. His obvious political positioning ensured that his military advancement had come to a complete standstill. In April 1792, a few days before he attended the first meeting of the Friends of the People, he informed his brother that he had again been passed over for promotion:

> I hope you will agree with me that after this I should not stay in the service. When things come to that pass, that independence of conduct and attachment to one's family interest are made a crime of in one's profession, it is time to leave that profession. I have a long time since seen there is but one way of getting on in the army, that is being a courtier, and that I never can be to any thing, it is so totally repugnant to all my principles. In addition to these reasons the restraint that my attendance to the Reg[imen]t would put me under, have determined to sell out. I am then totally out of the power of the crown and can do as I please without suffering for it. I can attend to my duty in Parl[iamen]t, can see my friends in England, go abroad, in short do as I like ...[17]

William could not have missed the clear signals in this letter: his 'friends' meant his radical friends; and 'abroad' could only mean France. The practical purpose of the letter was to instruct the duke to sell the position, but whether that happened is not apparent, for when Edward turned up in Paris in October 1792 and famously renounced his honorary aristocratic title, he was promptly dismissed.

Edward's visit to France in the autumn of 1792 was the turning point in his life. His radicalism was well established before his journey, but his visit was an unambiguous public pronouncement of his allegiances. He arrived in a France that had recently been declared a republic, imprisoned Louis XVI and brutally massacred prisoners and other perceived enemies of the revolution. Edward, for his part, enthusiastically embraced the radical turn.[18] His marriage to Pamela de Genlis, adopted (or natural) daughter of Philippe Égalité (formerly the Duke of Orléans) confirmed his political views – and there is abundant evidence that his family was well aware of them. The couple's return from France to Ireland, via England, was a source of apprehension. On 2 January 1793, Edward's step-father, William Ogilvie, expressed his concerns to the duke of Leinster:

> I acknowledge that I dread Edward and I think it will require all your temper and moderation to keep him quiet for I fear he has taken up strong notions of Republicanism, which I totally differ from him in; but tho I cannot bring him to think as

I do, I hope we shall prevail on him to be quiet. We expect him in about a week with his woman as he calls her [Pamela]. Many people here who know her talk of her as a prodigy for accomplishments and uncommonly beautiful. I wish she had a little more money. She has an annuity of 7,000 livres, near £300 a year. I suppose they will not stay long in London.[19]

The end of his military career meant, as he had judged, that Edward was able to attend the Irish parliament. Since late 1792 his brother had emerged as one of the country's pre-eminent proponents of Catholic Relief and Parliamentary Reform.[20] Back in Dublin in 1793 Edward went further, causing uproar in the House of Commons when he denounced the lord lieutenant and 'the majority of this House' as 'the worst subjects the king has'.[21] This has sometimes been attributed to procedural naivety, but it is more likely that it was a calculated statement of political principle given that he had sufficient parliamentary experience in the 1780s to know the likely reaction. The family was increasingly worried by Edward's activities as war with France broke out. In March Ogilvie again wrote to William 'to beg of him [Edward] to avoid talking as a Republican to any body. It can do no good and is doing a great deal of harm by exciting great violence against him here.'[22] As for parliament, Edward quickly became disillusioned with the moderation of the opposition and, while he continued to view his brother in a positive light, he wrote to his mother in early 1794: 'It is in vain to look to that quarter for anything; and if the people don't help themselves, why, they must suffer.'[23]

During 1793 and 1794 Edward and his wife Pamela visited Carton regularly and their first child, also named Edward, was christened there, with the duke of Leinster and (in his absence) Charles James Fox as godfathers.[24] From 1794 Edward turned increasingly to 'out-of-door' politics and he settled, with his family, in Kildare town. He remained supportive of his brother's willingness to pursue an oppositional stance, but he was also developing a more independent political line. In July 1794 he commented to his mother that he would not follow William on to the government benches should he choose that route, arguing that 'these two countries must see very strong changes, and cannot come to good, unless they do.'[25] From his Kildare base, Edward began to assess political disaffection among the local population. The diary of his sister Lucy (1771–1851), who visited Ireland from London in 1796–7, makes it clear that her brother's home was a centre of radical politics, attracting locals like the Kildare town apothecary, George Cummins, national organisers like FitzGerald's close friend, Arthur O'Connor, as well as family members like Lucy and Pamela.[26] The tightly-knit relationship between Edward, Pamela and Lucy also emerges from the correspondence between them during this period.[27] This would later lead to suspicions and accusations about Pamela and Lucy's political involvement. Indeed, in August 1798 Edward's aunt, Louisa Conolly, wrote to the duke of Leinster asking for information on Lucy and Pamela's participation in radical activity: 'The answer to these questions must not come by post', she noted gravely, 'but pray let me have them by private hand'.[28]

During 1796 Edward committed himself fully to a French-style revolution in Ireland. With Arthur O'Connor he travelled to the continent to negotiate a French invasion of Ireland; by the end of the year he had joined the Society of United Irishmen which was, by this stage, organising for an insurrection to establish an Irish republic. Though his family may have been less clear about his activities throughout this period, Edward remained close to them. The newly accessible family papers reveal that in January 1796, for example, Edward wrote to his brother requesting money to repay sums borrowed from the La Touche banking family on the strength of an annuity, mentioned in an earlier letter by Ogilvie, expected from France (presumably Pamela's family) which never materialised.[29] In general, however, there are fewer surviving letters written by Edward for the period from 1794 onwards. Of those which have survived a few continued to discuss politics. In a letter to his mother written in February 1797 he denounced 'the violent measures of our Irish tyrants'.[30] During the same year the moderate political ground in Ireland effectively disappeared, despite the final efforts of Whig politicians like the duke of Leinster and radicals like Edward and O'Connor.[31] For Edward, parliament had become, as he put it in a letter to his brother, 'no parl[iamen]t'. 'An election is a farce', he wrote, explaining his decision not to stand for his Kildare seat in the general election.[32]

The available evidence also suggests that between 1796 and 1798 Edward was on the more militant side of the expanding United Irishmen. He was a leading figure on the executive of the organisation, and the main figure on the military committee.[33] The arrest of much of the more moderate leadership in Leinster in March 1798 ensured that Edward became even more important as the United Irishmen resigned themselves to rebellion without immediate French assistance and made the necessary preparations. His own arrest before the rebellion was therefore a major blow to the United Irishmen. Edward died in prison as a result of wounds sustained during his capture on 4 June 1798. Despite their knowledge of his revolutionary activities, his arrest came as a profound shock to his family. In the months before, he had lived in hiding in Dublin and the family seem to have had limited information on his whereabouts. William Ogilvie's comment to the duke of Leinster on 23 April 1798 that Edward was in Hamburg may have been deliberate dissembling in the knowledge that their post was monitored.[34] Initially fearful of a trial, the family despaired at Edward's death and raged against the subsequent attainder of his property. Indeed, a great deal of the surviving papers relate specifically to the family's battle to prevent the attainder. From a very early stage they sought to shift the blame away from Edward. As Louisa Conolly put it in a letter to Ogilvie on 4 June: 'The friends that he was entangled with pushed his destruction forward, screening themselves behind his valuable character.'[35] Despite the family's efforts, the scale of the 1798 rebellion ensured that there was no prospect of avoiding the embarrassment of attainder. On 6 August the duke of Leinster wrote to Cornwallis to make the case against attainder, stressing the impact on his brother's wife and children and denouncing loudly the informer, Thomas Reynolds.[36] Cornwallis replied in unequivocal terms, cutting through the family's own sense of injustice:

> Knowing as I do with the utmost certainty that Lord Edward was the great author and contriver of all the mischief and treason which has already cost so many lives and which had nearly reduced to ruin and begging the lives and families of every man of property, and deluged the island with blood, can I say to the most injured people of this country, you must not mark the man who has been the cause of all your suffering, but tamely allow him to be recorded as the innocent martyr of your violence and persecution?[37]

The family persisted in their sense of grievance, but they quietly drew a veil over Lord Edward's life and death. In effect, they accepted the advice offered by the duke of Richmond on 9 June: 'I do think the best friends to poor Edward's memory must wish to have as little said of the past as possible.'[38]

Edward FitzGerald's colourful and cosmopolitan life leaves it open to multiple interpretations, which helps to explain his continuing fascination to historians and the seemingly endless debate about his motivations. However, on Edward as 'the great author and contriver', Cornwallis was essentially correct; he was neither the pawn of malevolent radicals nor the innocent victim of circumstances. He had a political mind of his own. In the 1780s he was already developing independent political positions; this accelerated as the rough political unity of his family broke down during the following decade under the strain of the Regency Crisis, the French Revolution and the war. The 2nd duke of Leinster attempted – hesitatingly and sometimes ineffectively – to articulate a new political space somewhere between the cautious Irish Whig Club and the radical United Irishmen; he ultimately failed. Despite this failure, the 2nd duke has too often been dismissed by historians; he deserves closer attention and a full study based on the papers now available. His political views were unsurprisingly paternalistic, and he certainly did not share his brother's republicanism, but Edward and William appear to have had a closer relationship than is usually appreciated. While Edward's other brothers, Charles and Robert, rowed in behind Pitt, and Henry and William attempted to follow a moderate path, he emerged as a convinced radical, an enthusiastic republican and, ultimately, a militant revolutionary. A full study of FitzGerald family politics from the 1770s to the 1790s, coupled with a clear appreciation of Edward FitzGerald's revolutionary turn, will create an authoritative biography of this fascinating figure in Irish history.

NOTES

1   Thomas Moore, *The Life and Death of Lord Edward FitzGerald* (2 vols, London, 1831, 2nd edn), vol. i, pp 1–2.

2   For Musgrave's influence see: Stuart Andrews, *Irish Rebellion: Protestant Polemic, 1798–1900* (Basingstoke, 2006); James Kelly, *Sir Richard Musgrave, 1746–1818: Ultra-Protestant Ideologue* (Dublin, 2009).

3   Moore, *Life and Death*, vol. i, pp vii–xi. See also Ronan Kelly, *Bard of Erin: The Life of Thomas Moore* (Dublin, 2008), pp 484–5.

4   R. R. Madden, *The United Irishmen: Their Lives and Times* (7 vols, Dublin, 1842–6); Matthias McDonnell Bodkin, *Lord Edward FitzGerald: A Historical Romance* (London, 1896); Ida A. Taylor, *The Life of Lord Edward FitzGerald, 1763–1798* (London, 1903); Katherine Tynan, *Lord Edward FitzGerald: A Study in Romance* (n.p., 1916); Charles Molony, *Ireland's Tragic Comedians* (London, 1934); John Lindsey, *The Shining Life and Death of Lord Edward FitzGerald* (London, 1949); Patrick Byrne, *Lord Edward FitzGerald* (Dublin, 1955); Stella Fitzthomas Hagan, *The Green Cravat* (London, 1959). The author expresses thanks to Hazel Curran for insights on FitzGerald's historiography. On images of Fitz-Gerald see: Fintan Cullen, 'Lord Edward FitzGerald: the creation of an icon' in *History Ireland*, 6:4 (1999), pp 17–20; Fintan Cullen, 'Radicals and reactionaries: portraits of the 1790s in Ireland', in Jim Smyth (ed.), *Revolution, Counter-Revolution and Union: Ireland in the 1790s* (Cambridge, 2000), pp 161–94.

5   Stella Tillyard, *Citizen Lord: Edward FitzGerald, 1763–98* (London, 1997).

6   Charles William FitzGerald, the fourth Duke of Leinster, *The Earls of Kildare and their Ancestors, from 1057 to 1804, Second Addenda* (Dublin, 1872); Gerald Campbell, *Edward and Pamela FitzGerald* (London, 1904).

7   National Library of Ireland (NLI), Leinster Papers, MSS 41,552/1–73; Lennox/FitzGerald/Campbell Papers, MSS 35,001–35,027.

8   Kevin Whelan, 'New light on Lord Edward FitzGerald', in *History Ireland*, vii, no 4 (1998), pp 40–4; Richard J. Aylmer, 'The Duke of Leinster withdraws from Ireland: Oct. 1797', in *Journal of the County Kildare Archaeological Society* (hereafter *JCKAS*), xix:1 (2000–1), pp 151–83; Daniel Gahan, '"Journey after my own heart": Lord Edward FitzGerald in America, 1788–90', in *New Hibernia Review*, viii:2 (2004), pp 85–105; Kevin Whelan, 'Lord Edward FitzGerald', in James McGuire and James Quinn (eds), *Dictionary of Irish Biography* (hereafter *DIB*) (9 vols, Cambridge, 2009), vol. iii, pp 825–31.

9   A. P. W. Malcomson, *The Pursuit of an Heiress: Aristocratic Marriage in Ireland, 1740–1840* (Belfast, 2006), pp 41–3.

10   Duke of Richmond to the Duke of Leinster, 28 Nov., 23 Dec. 1782, NLI, Leinster Papers, MS 41,552/21.

11   Edward FitzGerald to the Duke of Leinster, 12 Jul. 1786, NLI, MS 41,791. This letter was acquired by the NLI as recently as 2007.

12   Duke of Leinster to Charles FitzGerald, 15 Aug. 1786, NLI, Leinster Papers, MS 41,552/25.

13   Duke of Leinster to Edward FitzGerald, Dec. 1787, NLI, Leinster Papers, MS 41,552/26.

14   Moore, *Life and Death*, vol. i, pp 107–19, 134–5, 160–4.

15   Cf Gahan, '"Journey after my own heart": Lord Edward FitzGerald in America, 1788–90' and Whelan, 'Lord Edward FitzGerald'.

16   Danny Mansergh, *Grattan's Failure: Parliamentary Opposition and the People in Ireland, 1779–1800* (Dublin, 2005), p. 121.

17   Edward FitzGerald to the Duke of Leinster, 7 Apr. 1792, NLI, Leinster Papers, MS 41,552/33.

18   FitzGerald was by no means alone; there was a sizeable community of pro-revolutionary Irish, English and Scottish visitors and residents in France during autumn 1792; see J. G. Alger, 'The British Colony in Paris, 1792–93', in *English Historical Review*, xiii:52 (1898), pp 672–94.

19   William Ogilvie to the Duke of Leinster, 2 Jan. 1793, NLI, Leinster Papers, MS 41,552/33.

20   Despite a wobble in early 1792, the duke warmly supported the Catholic Relief Acts of 1792 and 1793; see James Kelly (ed.), *The Proceedings of the Irish House of Lords, 1771–1800* (3 vols, Dublin, 2008), vol. ii, pp 260–7, 302, 396–410.

21   For the quotation and basic context see Moore, *Life and Death*, vol. i, pp 212–13.

22   William Ogilvie to the Duke of Leinster, 5 Mar. 1793, NLI, Leinster Papers, MS 41,552/33.

23   Cited in Moore, *Life and Death*, vol. i, p. 235.

24   Campbell, *Edward and Pamela FitzGerald*, p. 74.

25   Ibid., p. 87.

26   Excerpts from the diary were published in ibid., pp 110–14, 117–19, 140–5. The diary does not form part of the recent NLI acquisitions and is therefore, presumably, still in private hands.

27   See the letters from Emily, dowager duchess of Leinster, and Pamela FitzGerald to Lucy FitzGerald, written in 1796 and 1797, NLI, Lennox/FitzGerald/Campbell Papers, MSS 35,005 (1), (2), (4) and (5).

28   Louisa Conolly to the Duke of Leinster, 1 Aug. 1798, NLI, Leinster Papers, MS 41,552/48.

29   Edward FitzGerald to the Duke of Leinster, 21 Jan. 1796, NLI, Leinster Papers, MS 41,552/41.

30   Edward FitzGerald to Emily, dowager duchess of Leinster, 20 Feb. 1797, NLI, Lennox/ FitzGerald/Campbell Papers, MS 35,011.

31   For a recent discussion see, Mansergh, *Grattan's Failure*, pp 191–241.

32   Edward FitzGerald to the Duke of Leinster, 17 Jul. 1797, NLI, MS 41,791/2. Like the letter cited at note 11 above, this letter was also acquired by the NLI in 2007.

33   For an appraisal of the military committee, see: Ruan O'Donnell, 'The Military Committee and the United Irishmen, 1798–1803', in Michael T. Davis and Paul A. Pickering (eds), *Unrespectable Radicals? Popular Politics in the Age of Reform* (Aldershot, 2008), pp 125–46.

34   William Ogilvie to the Duke of Leinster, 23 Apr. 1798, NLI, Leinster Papers, MS 41,552/47.

35   Louisa Conolly to William Ogilvie, 4 Jun. 1798, NLI, Lennox/FitzGerald/Campbell Papers, MS 35,002 (5).

36   Charles William FitzGerald, *The Earls of Kildare and their Ancestors*, pp 321–4.

37   Marquis of Cornwallis to the Duke of Leinster, 11 Aug. 1798, NLI, Leinster Papers, MS 41,552/49; there is also a copy in the NLI, Lennox/FitzGerald/Campbell Papers, MS 35,008 (1).

38   Duke of Richmond to William Ogilvie, 9 Jun. 1798, NLI, Lennox/FitzGerald/Campbell Papers, MS 35,002 (5).

CHAPTER 13

In the Shadow of the FitzGeralds
Maynooth *c*.1700 to *c*.1900

Arnold Horner

Over the long period during which the great house and park at Carton were created and then flourished, the nearby village of Maynooth, part of the broader estate of the FitzGeralds, was also transformed. Acting as a local service centre for both Carton and, after its foundation in 1795, the newly-created St Patrick's College, much of Maynooth was redeveloped and laid out to a new regular plan during the second half of the eighteenth century. Over the 200 years from the early 1700s, the role played by the FitzGeralds in the fortunes of Maynooth varied considerably, their greatest impact being between the late 1740s and the late 1790s.

In the 1630s, the prospects of the village of Maynooth were on the rise. The great medieval castle had been significantly damaged when besieged a century earlier during the rebellion of Silken Thomas. Now, under the direction of Richard Boyle, the 'Great Earl' of Cork and father-in-law of the 16th Earl of Kildare, the castle was being re-built and extended, with new buildings flanking the medieval keep on three sides of an interior courtyard. A palatial new complex appears to have been created, set within an extensive walled court and green that also took in a mill and the re-built church.[1] But this development had a short life, as the castle was attacked and subsequently dismantled during the prolonged strife of the 1640s. Estimated to have been worth £3,000 in 1640 (the highest value attached to any building in County Kildare), it was valued at £500 in the mid-1650s when only the walls were left standing.

Thereafter the village co-existed in the shadow of the great ruined castle. Some attempt may have been made to revive the village during the 1650s, when several leases were granted for houses 'whited and glazed in the English style'. Tellingly, the new occupants were also given the right to take timber from the woods apparently still in existence nearby. But no immediate attempt was made to restore the castle, and a 1680s description could refer to Maynooth 'where is to be seen the remains of an ancient pile, venerable in its ruins, and which did partake of the hottest, and felt the fiercest malice of a revengeful enemy in the last rebellion.'[2]

Over 30 years after the end of Maynooth Castle, however, there is evidence that the village of Maynooth had become a small service centre and that it was adapting to the slowly-growing traffic along the 'Great Connaught Road'. A weekly market and two annual fairs are confirmed in 1678, and a 1684 rent roll lists 24 houses, six or more cabins, a mill, a tan-house, a new shop, a slaughter house and a 'cabin employed for a schoolhouse'. When the traveller John Dunton visited Maynooth in the 1690s he wrote of a 'tolerable village with one or two good inns where meat is well dressed and good liquors be had'. Later, as traffic expanded, the Dublin to Kinnegad coach rolled through the village twice weekly from 1717.[3] In the 1730s Maynooth, by now on the new Dublin to Mullingar turnpike road, became a post town.

In the late seventeenth and early eighteenth centuries the involvement of the FitzGeralds in the Maynooth and Carton areas was very limited. Members of the Kildare branch of the family lived either in England or at Kilkea Castle in south Kildare. Large tracts in and around the village had been leased to James McManus, a merchant who made the medieval Council House near the old castle his home. Nearby Carton, initially the residence of the Talbot family, had been developed with formal avenues by Richard Talbot, Duke of Tyrconnell, whose fortunes had nosedived with the flight of James II. One of the forfeited estates, Carton was in 1703 sold to the Ingoldsby family.

The FitzGerald interest in the Maynooth area only re-surfaced in the late 1730s when Robert, the 19th Earl of Kildare, appears to have considered redeveloping the old castle before settling on making Carton his principal country seat. By this time, the restricted castle area may have seemed an inauspicious site for a major residential initiative. The long lease confirmed to the McManus family in 1727 may also have been an impediment to any redevelopment around the castle. Instead, as discussed in chapter 6, the earl opted to purchase Carton from the Ingoldsbys and then to expand his holding over the following decade by purchase and exchange of additional lands. As a result the architect Richard Castle was given the opportunity to create a great country house in a great setting. As the house was completed, the focus shifted. In partnership with his wife, Emily, Robert's son, James, oversaw the landscaping and enclosing of the great deer-park demesne around the big house. A parallel, less personal project was the improvement of the village of Maynooth.

For the FitzGeralds, as for many Irish landlords of the period, village improvement encompassed the creation of an orderly appearance alongside, where possible, the enhancement of basic services and, on occasion, the promotion of a loyal, dependent and sometimes Protestant population. Such objectives might meet with mixed success, proving much more difficult to implement than to project. In the case of Maynooth, the village of the 1740s and 1750s is shown on contemporary maps as having a chaotic layout with the principal street irregular in both its direction and width. This street served also as part of the main road west from Dublin, exiting the village through the castle ruins. The huddle of houses and cabins around the castle are still evident in the views of that area painted around 1780 and later engraved for Alexander Taylor's 1783 map of County Kildare (Fig. 1a). In a map drawn a generation earlier in 1757 (Fig. 1b), John Rocque portrays the whole village and its environs. The village comprised about 40 houses and 80 cabins, suggesting that its population may have been around 500–700. Other buildings shown on this map include a mill, the (Protestant) church, a Catholic chapel, and an essential service point for travellers, the Kildare Arms Inn. Occupying vaults amongst the castle ruins were several small distilleries. Only much to the east, at the opposite end of the village, were there any signs of the redevelopment initiatives that would ultimately extend to much of Maynooth over a 60-year period.

FIGURE 1a
Part of Maynooth village as it appears in a view accompanying Alexander Taylor's map of County Kildare, 1783

FIGURE 1b
John Rocque's map of Maynooth, 1757 (Cambridge University Ms Plans x.4).

That some sort of master scheme for a new Maynooth was envisaged sometime in the late 1740s or 1750s is evident from a projected street layout shown on an undated plan accompanying Rocque's 1757 map (see Fig. 2). This plan shows some features already created by the mid-1750s, including part of the long tree-lined avenue that still exists and which gives physical expression to the link between Carton and Maynooth. North of the avenue is the new Protestant charter school founded in 1749 (this site was later occupied by the Presentation convent and is now shared between apartments and a primary school). The avenue leads directly to a wide, straight, main street off which are side and back lanes. According to leasing records, a row of seven two-storey, slated

Chapter 10 Thomas Roberts (1747–77)

TOP *The Bridge in the Park with Workmen Landing Logs from a Boat.*

ABOVE *A View in the Park at Carton with the Ivory Bridge in the Foreground.*

Private collection.

Chapter 10 Thomas Roberts (1747–77)
TOP *A View in the Park at Carton with Haymakers,* 1776.
ABOVE *The Sheet of Water at Carton, with the Duke and Duchess of Leinster about to Board a Rowing Boat. Private collection.*

Chapter 10 William Ashford (1726–1824)

TOP *A View of the Park of Carton, County Kildare, with an Angler and a Gamekeeper*, 1779.

ABOVE *A View of the Park of Carton, County Kildare, with the Duke and Duchess of Leinster Riding in a Carriage*, 1779. *Private collection.*

Chapter 11 William Robert FitzGerald (1749–1804),
2nd Duke of Leinster. *Courtesy of Mallaghan family.*

Chapter 11 Lord Edward FitzGerald (1763–98).

Chapter 14 G. Thompson, *Augustus Frederick FitzGerald, 3rd Duke of Leinster c.*1840.
Courtesy of Mallaghan family.

Chapter 13 Carton Avenue, Maynooth 2013.
Courtesy of Arnold Horner.

Chapter 13 Leinster Cottages, Maynooth 2013.
Courtesy of Arnold Horner.

ABOVE
Chapter 17 Lord Frederick FitzGerald
(1857–1924).

ABOVE RIGHT
Chapter 18 Edward FitzGerald
(1892–1976), 7th Duke of Leinster.

RIGHT
Chapter 18 Henry Mallaby-Deeley
(1863–1937).

Chapter 19 Carton House. *Courtesy of Mallaghan family.*

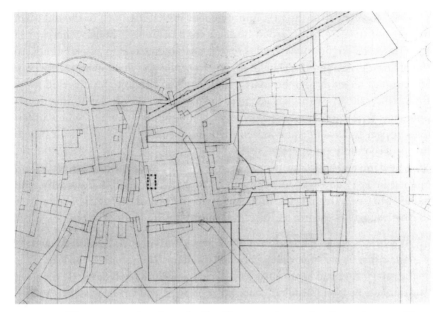

FIGURE 2 *The 1750s master scheme for the village superimposed on Rocque's survey (Cambridge University Ms Plans x.4)*

houses had been commenced sometime after 1754 along the north side of this new street. The avenue, the charter school and these houses – now over 250 years old – mark the first stage in the redevelopment process.

As foreseen in the initial plan of the 1750s, the wide main street was to lead to a large open space within which a single building, presumably the market house, would be set. That scheme was only partially implemented. Progress to 1773, the year in which James, now the 1st duke of Leinster, died, is recorded on a map by Bernard Scalé. Showing almost 50 new houses in total, this map also identifies a new location for the 'Roman chaple'[4] and shows a new market house and pump recessed on an open area on the south side of the new main street. By then, the Protestant church had also been refurbished, and three rows of single-storey, slate-roofed cottages had been built behind the street on its north side, in all 28 dwellings which served as residences for many of the labourers who worked on the Carton estate.[5] Along the main street itself, 21 two-storey houses had been completed. Progress had thus been significant but also slow, perhaps for various reasons such as a lack of demand to live in Maynooth, and because the improvement of the village was driven with much less urgency and fewer resources than the improvement of Carton. The FitzGeralds appear to have been rarely directly involved, with many of the building leases passing through the hands of an agent, Peter Bere, and with redevelopment usually only occurring as earlier leases expired.

Over 30 years after the first improvement initiatives, 'part of the old town not yet out of lease' is recorded beside a map made by Thomas Sherrard in 1781. It took a further two decades for the new main street to extend almost to the old castle. Around the time of the death of the 2nd duke in 1804, the construction of a new bridge beside the mill enabled traffic to be diverted away from the castle. The bridge was one of the last major physical planning developments of the improvement period. By the late eighteenth century, new initiatives appear to have become increasingly more concerned with the vitality of the local economy and society.

A new inn and ballroom, occupying a large site beside the market-place, had opened in 1777 and was initially run by Richard Vousden, followed by men named Maxwell, Grehan and McDonnell. As the text of this newspaper advertisement suggests, the inn had a central role in the life of the village:

> NEW INN, Maynooth. Richard VOUSDEN, begs leave to acquaint his Friends and the Public that he has removed from his old dwelling in Maynooth to the Sign of the Leinster Arms, and is provided with Accommodations of all Sorts. He has good Four Post Beds and Bedding, constantly well aired, and large convenient Stables. He begs Leave to assure the generous Public, that he will spare neither Care nor Expence to render his Entertainment as complete as possible. He is now supplied with the best Wines, and will endeavour to procure the best Meats the Market can afford. From the great Success he has met with since his commencement in Business, particularly in his Post Chaises and Horses, that for the more easy Mode of travelling he has got Stables at the new Inn, where he means constantly to keep Chaises and Horses, which will enable him to drive that long Stage between Maynooth and Kinnegad with more Expedition, without advancing the Expence to the Travellers. He hopes the impartial Public will consider he was the first that set up Chaises on that Road. Post Chaises, as usual, in Maynooth, and also at the New Inn, which is Mid-way between Maynooth and Kinnegad. Post Chaise and Pair at Thirteen Pence a Mile, four Horses at Nineteen Pence Halfpenny. Gentlemen may be accommodated with Horses to their own Carriages at the above Price.[6]

With stabling for 100 horses, the inn was an attractive first stop on the route west from Dublin. As various other newspaper entries attest, the inn, with its ballroom, could also be a focus for the local society with gatherings of over 200 people being noted. The 'Friendly Brothers of the County Kildare Knot' organised an annual dinner, usually in Maynooth, while balls appear to have been held regularly during the 1780s.[7] Other celebrations were also reported, for example, in 1779:

> a Number of Gentlemen from Dublin, and from the Neighbourhood of Maynooth, celebrated the Birth-day of that truly patriotic and amicable Nobleman, his Grace the Duke of Leinster, at Maynooth, where they dined, had Bonfires and illuminations, and spent the Evening in the greatest Harmony and Festivity.[8]

Little more than six weeks after the storming of the Bastille had ignited the French Revolution, the socially superior late-night clubbing of 1789 Maynooth was described in some detail in the *Dublin Evening Post* of 3 September:

MAYNOOTH BALL

The Friendly Brothers Ball, given at Maxwell's, at Maynooth, last Monday night, was in a stile of splendour, and conducted with a regularity redounding very highly to the honour of the stewards.

The company, among whom their Graces of Leinster – the Earl and Countess of Arran, and several personages of the first distinction, were assembled by eleven – and danced till one – when they retired to the supper rooms, which were laid out in very admirable stile of plenty, decoration and excellence.

About three the company disappeared, expressing the highest satisfaction at the elegant entertainment of the night.

The wines were claret, Vin de Grave, Lunelle, Madeira, and Sherry, and were excellent in their kinds – and there was a very excellent and complete desert [*sic*] of the best fruits. Among other dishes which seemed to have occupied the peculiar fancy and art of the cook, was a dish of brown, in which his Worship the SHAM made his appearance in effigy, mounted on a boar.[9]

A generation later, the coming-of-age of the 3rd duke was the occasion for great celebration in August 1812. As Napoleon advanced toward Moscow, the *Dublin Evening Post* was concerned to report events in Maynooth as follows:

The Dinner at Maynooth, by which the numerous Tenantry of his Grace celebrated his Birth-day, exceeded in number and splendour the festivities which took place at Athy and its neighbourhood. Several hundred persons, consisting of the respectable Tenantry on his Grace's estate, and also of some Gentlemen who were invited from Dublin, dined at the Inn. The lower orders of the inhabitants were plentifully regaled in the demesne of Carton, and the evening concluded with a brilliant Illumination of the Town and College of Maynooth.

Among the several Gentlemen who, in honor of their characters, had been separately invited, were Henry Hamilton, James Hamilton, Robt. Morgan, and William Murphy, of Smithfield, Esqrs.; the Protestant and Roman Catholic Clergymen of the Parish; the Superiors of both Colleges at Maynooth, and the Officers of the Regiment quartered in the Town and Neighbourhood.[10]

In 1815 the annual ploughing match of the Kildare Farming Society was followed by dinner at the inn.[11] Ten years later, in August 1825, a ball and supper was held at 'McDonnells Great Rooms' under the patronage of the duke and duchess of Leinster on the occasion of the Kilcock races. It was promised that a military band would attend.[12]

Initiatives in economic activity also helped promote late eighteenth- and early nineteenth-century Maynooth. One such was the 'Factory' which is shown located on the main street on Sherrard's map of 1781 (Fig. 3). This was probably a small-scale and quite genteel enterprise. A newspaper notice of 1785 gives some amplification, indicating that there were:

> two factories at present in Maynooth, under the immediate patronage of the Duke of Leinster, which are arriving to a very great degree of extensiveness and perfection. Tapes, threads, and garters are manufactured at the one, and stockings at the other.[13]

The garter manufactory is recorded as still being in operation in 1797. However, by 1804, the factory was being considered as a temporary barracks for troops.[14]

The Royal Canal and the new Roman Catholic college were two developments of the mid-1790s. The line of the canal had apparently been influenced by the duke of Leinster. Constructed at great expense and over a protracted period, the canal featured a harbour at Maynooth, as well as a private quayside near the Dublin road entrance to Carton. But traffic always seems to have been light, and the greatest long-term benefit of the canal was arguably that in the 1840s it defined the route taken by the Midland and Great Western Railway.

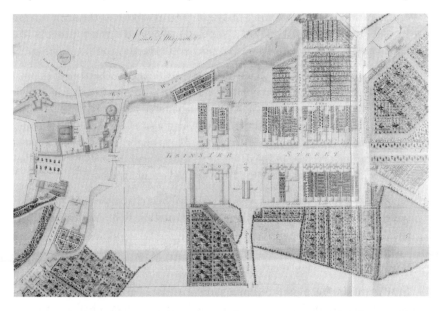

FIGURE 3 *Maynooth in 1781. By this time much of the east-end planning had been completed, whereas the west end remained largely untouched. The blank area represents sites awaiting redevelopment on the expiration of leases (Cambridge University Ms Plans x.4).*

The college site, made available through the duke, was located close to the old castle on a 58-acre property formerly part of the old 'Council House' and recently held by John Stoyte. In contrast to the canal, the college had an immediate and enduring impact. Established as a seminary for the training of Roman Catholic priests, it rapidly grew to have around 600 students by the early decades of the nineteenth century. As such it had a significant economic impact on the local area, contributing to the sustenance of shops and providing significant direct employment.

Throughout the nineteenth century the influence of the FitzGeralds remained strong in Maynooth. Located at opposite ends of the town, Carton and the college were the chief sources of local employment. Compared to the second half of the eighteenth century, however, the FitzGeralds made fewer interventions affecting the physical fabric. The more significant included the redevelopment (around 1820) of the square to incorporate a court-house to the rear of the market house building and, in the 1840s, perhaps in anticipation of the visit of Queen Victoria to Carton, an extensive tidying and railing-in of the old castle area. In the 1880s the court-house was modified to serve as a new town hall. Perhaps significantly, this key central feature remained in the ownership of the duke. Other developments directly involving the FitzGeralds included a redesign of the Protestant church and the construction of a small one-room Protestant school house, both about 1860.

Across much of Maynooth, the long leases that had been issued, particularly from the 1780s onward, ensured that most property-holders had considerable independence. The situation was described by James Montgomery when he made a valuation of the town in 1850.[15] Building works linked to the college and the new railway meant that the town was full of labourers and tradesmen. Describing the town as clean, with the houses generally of good order and built of substantial materials, he contrasted the properties of the duke of Leinster and those of other landlords. The 30 small houses (the cottages shown on the 1773 map) and half a dozen large ones held from the duke were linked to rents below the rateable valuation. In contrast, the remainder of the town belonged to middle landlords 'most of whom are of the avaricious class', who had taken advantage of the building boom to charge high rents – Montgomery repeatedly used the term 'rack rent'.

Throughout the century, the link between the FitzGeralds and Maynooth involved elements of both harmony and tension. Parts of County Kildare close to Maynooth had been the scene of intense turmoil during 1798, and some expressions of unrest were recorded involving townspeople during the risings of 1803 and 1867. But the 2nd duke opposed the Union, and his brother, Lord Edward FitzGerald, had sided with the United Irishmen. Tensions sometimes surfaced, for example in the 1870s over leases for farms. Yet for most of the nineteenth century the FitzGeralds were almost always resident at Carton, and appear to have enjoyed a reputation for being well-disposed patriots and fair in their local dealings. Although not intensely involved in the daily life of Maynooth, they offered benevolent support to local community activities, for example in the early nineteenth century supporting schools and maintaining the local dispensary. A particular example was in August 1813 when the *Dublin Evening Post* advertised a charity sermon to be held in the College chapel in aid of the Maynooth poor schools and supported by both Catholic and Protestant clergy:

ROYAL CHAPEL OF MAYNOOTH

On Sunday, the 8th of August, a SERMON will be preached in the ROYAL COLLEGE CHAPEL of MAYNOOTH, at Two o'Clock, by the REV. A.LUBE, in aid of the POOR SCHOOLS of that Town and District, wherein upwards of One Hundred Children, of both sexes, are educated – Forty of whom will be clothed, and all, during the severe seasons of the year, provided with breakfast.

These Schools have, since their establishment, during a period of six years, been supported by private contributions; during the last hard Summer they had been involved in considerable debt notwithstanding. This debt his Grace the Duke of Leinster, by a most generous donation, has discharged. His Grace also has, with kind condescension, promised to collect at the Sermon – to receive subscriptions; and has directed that his beautiful Demesne shall be opened for the accommodation of passage to those whose charity will conduct them to Maynooth on that day.[16]

During the 1880s and 1890s, newspapers based in Naas sometimes included reports on events in Maynooth. In the early 1890s there is news of parties for local children organised by the duchess of Leinster, and of the town hall being made available for concerts and similar entertainments. An emotional and crowded meeting assembled in December 1893 to express the sympathies of the townspeople following the untimely death of the 4th duke. Chaired by the parish priest, the meeting heard the observations of the Protestant rector:

I can confidently say that there is scarcely a family in the town of Maynooth that has not directly or indirectly experienced the advantages of having a residential duke at Carton ... The Duke and Duchess of Leinster were seldom absent from Carton. They lived in the midst of their people. They were anxious about their welfare. They knew their wants and relieved them. It is only a few days since that I received a letter from the Duchess enclosing a list of the poor widows who, as usual, were to receive blankets, &c, at Christmas, and asking me to revise the list for the coming Christmas, and apologising for the Duke not writing, he being very ill, and promising to receive the applications from the poor as usual, thus evincing the greatest anxiety for the poor people of Maynooth.[17]

Newspapers of around 1900 portray a small town of mixed and changing fortunes. Within the college the great centenary spire, over 260 feet in height, was a new physical assertion of Maynooth being at the core of a strong Irish

Catholic Church.[18] In contrast, other descriptions draw attention to the fact that, particularly away from the main street, the town suffered from noxious odours and problems of sewage disposal. Cholera outbreaks in 1832 and 1849 had left over 80 dead within the town. Yet over 50 years later, in 1901, the recently established and nationalist-dominated Kildare County Council was still drawing attention to unsanitary conditions in its annual report.[19] Such conditions are a reminder that daily life in the town could be a world away from that enjoyed by the FitzGeralds.

But during this period there are also signs of other changes. Extensive reports on the Maynooth football tournament in 1888 herald the rise of the Gaelic Athletic Association.[20] Lord Frederick FitzGerald, guardian of the young 6th duke, gifted a football park to the people of Maynooth about 1900. However, when he stood for election to the new county council in 1899 he was represented as being the unionist candidate and struggled against a nationalist strong farmer. The Kildare Hunt continued to meet, and on occasion, parade down the main street. But in the early 1900s there were also meetings of an active Gaelic League, with an 'aeridheacht' in September 1903 drawing a crowd of 1,500.[21] The shifting, and sometimes competing, loyalties increasingly confronting the people of Maynooth were evident in several other events of 1903. When King Edward VII visited the college in July, the town was decorated, large crowds turned out and the king was 'cordially cheered'.[22] Two months later another large gathering witnessed the 'imposing spectacle' of the funeral procession of the Gaelic scholar, Father O'Growney, as his body was brought from the station to the college.[23] Another happening of autumn 1903 was, however, of the greatest, most enduring significance. In late September, following the new land act, the trustees of the Leinster estate reached agreement for the transfer of the estate to the tenants[24] – a final, decisive act in curtailing the landed wealth that had sustained the FitzGeralds over many centuries.

Notwithstanding the far-reaching nature of these changes, the coming-of-age of the 6th duke was celebrated in traditional fashion in 1908. An address of welcome 'illuminated with Celtic ornamentation' was prepared, with the support of over 140 subscribers, including such leading nationalists as Domhnall ua Buachalla (later the last governor-general of the Free State).[25] Replying to the address, the duke observed that he intended 'following in the footsteps of his ancestors in looking after the welfare of the people of Maynooth, and in identifying himself with their interests'. The *Kildare Observer* could report that the duke received 'an enthusiastic reception' from the townspeople and that: 'The town was brilliantly illuminated, and flags hung from the houses. Opposite the Town Hall there was an immense bonfire, and there was a magnificent display of fireworks.'[26]

Within 15 years, Maynooth and Carton was changed forever. During the revolutionary period 1920–3, the police barracks was burnt down and the town hall bombed. There were ambushes, killing, arrests and reprisals, and, in parallel almost, the Carton FitzGeralds self-destructed. As the young duke entered Maynooth in 1908, few could have anticipated just how quickly the old order would change.

NOTES

1   The main sources used in this chapter are cited in detail in Arnold Horner, *Maynooth, Irish Historic Towns Atlas No. 7* (Dublin, 1995).

2   Thomas Monk, 'A descriptive account of the County of Kildare in 1682', in *Journal of the County Kildare Archaeological Society* (hereafter *JCKAS*), vi (1909–11), pp 339–46.

3   National Library of Ireland reports on private collections, 493 (Report on the O'Hara Papers), p. 46.

4   At a building still standing on Pound Street/Back Lane, later in use as a boys' school and as a band hall.

5   Although considerably refurbished and modified, these cottages still stand along parts of Double Lane, Convent Lane, and Cross Lane.

6   *Dublin Journal*, 15–18 Nov. 1777.

7   For the context of the Friendly Brothers, see Patrick Guinness, 'The meeting book of the County of Kildare knot of the Friendly Brothers of St. Patrick, 1758–1791', in *JCKAS*, xix:1 (2000–1), pp 116–60.

8   *Dublin Journal*, 18–20 Mar. 1779.

9   *Dublin Evening Post* (hereafter *DEP*), 3 Sept. 1789.

10   *DEP*, 13 and 25 Aug. 1812.

11   *DEP*, 25 Feb. 1815.

12   *DEP*, 2 Aug. 1825.

13   *DEP*, 17 Mar. 1785.

14   Arnold Horner, 'A note on the fate of the "factory" at Maynooth', in *JCKAS*, xix:3 (2005), pp 562–5.

15   Town of Maynooth, Valuation Office house book 5.2857 available at the National Archives of Ireland (reprinted in Horner, *Maynooth*, p. 11).

16   *DEP*, 3 Aug. 1813.

17   *Kildare Observer* (hereafter *KO*), 9 Dec. 1893.

18   *Leinster Leader*, 2 Nov. 1895; *KO*, 7 Oct. 1899.

19   *KO*, 26 Oct. 1901.

20   *KO*, 1 Sept. 1888.

21   *KO*, 26 Sept. 1903.

22   *KO*, 1 Aug. 1903.

23   *KO*, 3 Oct. 1903.

24   *KO*, 26 Sept., 10 Oct. 1903; see also chapter 16.

25   *KO*, 7 Mar. 1908.

26   *KO*, 18 Apr. 1908.

CHAPTER 14

Whig Politics and the 3rd Duke of Leinster (1791–1874)

Elizabeth Heggs

Recognised as the 'premier' Irish peer from 1804 until 1874, Augustus Frederick FitzGerald (1791–1874), the 3rd Duke of Leinster, played a significant role in nineteenth-century politics, his life straddling a most significant and formative period in modern Irish history. When he was born in 1791, Ireland was in the midst of a glorious era of Protestant patriot activity. However, Augustus was to witness the transformation of Protestant Ireland from this period of confident enthusiasm to the altogether less secure unionism of the nineteenth century. He observed first-hand the rise of Daniel O'Connell and the Catholic Association in the 1820s, and the campaign for a repeal of the union in the 1830s and 1840s. These developments, along with the continued evolution of modern Irish nationalism in the 1850s and 1860s, heralding as it did the eclipse of Protestant political influence and control, fundamentally affected how the duke thought about his country and the role he played in its politics.

Despite the centrality of the 3rd duke to Irish politics and the wider social arena over such an extended and important period in Irish history, no full biography has been written about him, and research into his life is so limited that he was not even included in the *Oxford Dictionary of National Biography*. He has been the subject of only three, short, biographical articles which have been produced at remote intervals. The first, an extremely deferential piece, complete with autograph, appeared in the *Dublin University Magazine* just before the duke's death in 1874. A second interpretation by Brian FitzGerald in *The Dublin Magazine* in 1949 is admittedly dated, but arguably presents a more balanced analysis. The only modern, if succinct, analysis written by Bridget Hourican appeared in the *Dictionary of Irish Biography* in 2009.[1] This relative lack of interest is all the more astonishing considering the sheer volume of extant material available to historians and researchers. The restricted nature of previous research means, therefore, that modern understandings of Augustus's politics have been markedly two-dimensional, as his career has often been scrutinised tangentially through his reactions to national and parliamentary politics. This approach has resulted in a rather distorted view of how Augustus himself approached politics and government. The aim of this chapter is both to provide an overview of his political career, and to suggest the need for a much more thorough investigation of his life.

Augustus was born at Carton House, Maynooth, in August 1791 to William Robert FitzGerald, the 2nd Duke of Leinster and his wife, Emilia St George.[2] By then the story of the 10th Earl of Kildare, executed as a traitor in 1537 and known to posterity as Silken Thomas, had become the stuff of legend. More recently, the FitzGerald family had been forced to come to terms with the death of the 3rd duke's revolutionary uncle, Lord Edward FitzGerald, who died in 1798 from wounds received while resisting arrest on charge of treason. This inheritance was viewed with fascination by some members of the family, as shown by Augustus's son and heir, Charles William, in his *The Earls of Kildare and their Ancestors* published by popular demand in 1858. The 3rd duke shouldered this inheritance, and it had a significant impact on how he approached politics, government and his own identity.

Augustus was one of the largest landowners in the country, owning approximately 73,000 acres in Meath and Kildare – albeit an indebted estate, his debts totalling more than £87,000 in 1821.[3] During his lifetime, Augustus was deputy lieutenant for County Kildare, a peer in the House of Lords, and grand master of the Irish Freemasons. When he died in 1874 he was laid to rest in the family mausoleum he had built at St Mary's Church in Maynooth. But what were the political ideals of the 3rd duke of Leinster? It is safe to say that throughout his life, he upheld with valour, if not always with complete conviction, the Whig politics of the FitzGerald family. This is hardly surprising since contemporaries considered him to be the hereditary leader of the Irish Whigs in the House of Lords.[4]

In 1813, Augustus certainly emerged as the most significant Irish peer to favour Catholic emancipation, speaking in the House of Lords on the necessity of 'admitting our Catholic fellow subjects to all the benefits of the British constitution'.[5] While he made no effort to speak again in parliament on the subject, he did make significant efforts to orchestrate Protestant activity in Ireland in support of Catholic relief. In 1819 he signed a requisition for a Protestant meeting in favour of emancipation, and was chosen to forward the resulting Protestant petition to the House of Lords. In October 1828 he prepared a 'Protestant declaration' in favour of emancipation which was signed by a significant number of Irish liberal Protestants, and which was undoubtedly of huge influence in 'preparing the public mind' for emancipation. He voted in favour of all Catholic relief bills in the Lords – those of 1825 and 1828, as well as the successful bill of 1829.[6] Even after emancipation Augustus remained favourable to religious toleration in principle, as evidenced by his ongoing defence of the parliamentary grant to St Patrick's College, built on his lands in Maynooth.[7]

However, in 1830 when Daniel O'Connell launched the Repeal movement,

Augustus, along with most of the other Irish Whigs, reacted strongly. The Act of Union which came into effect on 1 January 1801 had abolished the Irish parliament and placed responsibility for governing Ireland with the imperial parliament at Westminster. O'Connell's intermittent campaign for its repeal in the 1830s and 1840s, while purposely ambiguous in its focus, aimed at the re-establishment of a domestic parliament. Augustus spearheaded a unionist campaign and organised the famous 'Leinster declaration' against repeal; recently, this has been interpreted as part of a more widespread effort on the part of the Irish administration to cultivate unionist public opinion in Ireland. Immensely successful as it was in attracting unionist support, Douglas Kanter has argued that the declaration represented 'a propaganda coup for the government'.[8] Stating that repeal would 'be productive of consequences prejudicial in the highest degree to the interests of Ireland, and the empire of which she forms a part',[9] the declaration was adopted at a Dublin unionist meeting on 29 October 1830. If nothing else, the declaration was highly suggestive of Augustus's own perception of Ireland as an integral part of the British empire, and provides a strong hint of his ambiguous attitude towards British and Irish identity. An earlier draft of the declaration – available among the Leinster Papers and written in more dramatic language than that eventually adopted – spoke of his fear of 'encountering a civil war' if the repeal campaign was further pursued.[10]

In this context Augustus seems to have been a model 'liberal Protestant' in these years, supporting religious toleration and a degree of reform, but shying away from any perceived hostility or disloyalty to the government and Irish administration. Nevertheless, unlike other Irish liberal Protestants, the duke's approach to politics was in many ways bound by an inherent detachment. In this way, while he was content to chair meetings that adopted declarations in favour of emancipation or the union, and even to write these declarations himself, he rarely spoke in public or in parliament on these matters. Similarly, as a commissioner of education he was happy to act as a figurehead and let others deal with the daily issues. He was more comfortable when simply lending his influence to political questions.

The duke's relationship with Daniel O'Connell is also revealing. Throughout the 1820s O'Connell recognised the importance of maintaining the support of the Irish Whigs for emancipation, and in 1820 he called Augustus 'the excellent duke', telling Valentine Lawless, Lord Cloncurry, that: 'I recognise in this country no political party but that of which the duke of Leinster is the head'.[11] But as the campaign for emancipation gathered momentum in the late 1820s, O'Connell became increasingly frustrated by the duke's apparent inactivity, calling on him to join the Catholic Association and denouncing the Leinster declaration as 'paltry' and 'just enough to serve as an excuse for doing nothing'. Thus, O'Connell continued his complaint to Lord Cloncurry: 'There is, indeed, a duke who you say ... means well, but allow me mournfully to ask you of what value are his intentions? What a glorious opportunity is he not letting slip to serve Ireland and exalt himself?'[12] By the 1830s, after he had launched the repeal campaign, O'Connell was so impatient with the duke that he called him 'the most miserable of dukes' in 1832 and 'the first of his race who was un-Irish and he is un-Irish to the backbone'.[13] The cooling of relations between the two men was reflective of a much wider rift between O'Connell and the Irish Whigs in the aftermath of the granting of emancipation in 1829.

Likewise, it is clear from Augustus's conduct that he wanted as little as possible to do with a man he increasingly considered a demagogue. For example, in 1828 O'Connell attacked what he called the duke's 'tyrannical' actions towards his tenants – a blatant effort to gain the support of the latter, as well as to provoke Augustus into making a widely expected speech in the House of Lords in favour of emancipation. Augustus responded with a circular, in which he contended that O'Connell's denunciations would never influence his conduct:

> Be assured of it, I shall never allow them [the O'Connellites] to become the managers of my estate ... Whatever may be their views of policy, expediency and justice, I shall claim and exercise a right to act upon my own.[14]

Despite this, O'Connell never lost hope (at least in public) of convincing Irish Protestants to support repeal. Indeed, by 1834, O'Connell was optimistic that Augustus would aid him in establishing an anti-Tory alliance of Whigs and Repealers, the purpose of which was to campaign for the return of anti-Tory candidates at the 1835 general election. But relations between them continued to worsen and, by 1844, O'Connell was denouncing Augustus once more, contending savagely that 'his name operates like a vomit'.[15]

In the 1830s one of Augustus's main political interests was the improvement of Irish agricultural conditions, and it is testament to his Whig views that he maintained this belief in 'progress' throughout his life. However, it is here that the evidence of the duke's behaviour and his reputation in popular memory are increasingly at odds. Historians have sometimes pointed to his inactivity during the Famine years as proof of his aloofness and even alienation from Irish life.[16] Indeed, Hourican suggests that the duke oversaw evictions at Athy during the Famine.[17] The nineteenth-century inheritance was keenly felt in the twentieth, explaining why Augustus might have come in for steady criticism – essentially because of his position as the premier Irish Protestant landlord in a period of social catastrophe, when the entire system which supported his class was coming under increasing attack. However, evidence of other actions has led to alternative interpretations. During the debate on poor relief legislation in the 1830s, Augustus looked to public works as a means of alleviating Irish poverty.[18] In 1846, when the potato blight was causing much suffering, he voted in favour of a bill to import corn into Ireland to feed the poor. After the Great Famine he was active in promoting the establishment of an emigration centre in Ireland, in the shape of a harbour from which Irish emigrants could sail directly to America.[19]

While Augustus was highly criticised by many contemporaries (and later by historians) for lethargy during the Famine and his attitude to tenant rights after it, it was actions such as these just described that also led him to be hailed by some contemporaries as 'the good old duke of Leinster, the most liberal and generous of landlords', and by at least one modern historian as 'that rare phenomenon in Ireland, a conscientious landlord'.[20] He genuinely sought to take a leading role in agricultural improvement, investing over £17,500 on improving the buildings on his estate and over £14,000 on drainage schemes between 1860 and 1870.[21] For many years Augustus was the president of the Royal Agricultural Improvement Society, and was a constant promoter of the development of Irish agriculture through the introduction of new ideas such as crop rotation, crop diversity, and improved animal husbandry. It is probably fair to conclude that he was very much an aristocrat of his time; if he was genuinely conscientious about agricultural improvement on his estates, the ideas and plans he conceived were promoted very much on his own terms.

Moreover, Augustus remained innately suspicious of what he viewed as the 'politicisation' of relief societies. In September 1846 he was asked by Edward Buller to lend his support to a campaign for applying the funds of the Agricultural Society meant for famine relief to a new scheme of 'developing the land'. Seeing this as an attempt to transform the society into an O'Connellite body that would divert relief funds for essentially political purposes, Leinster responded with hostility, and promptly handed in his resignation (although he did eventually return). He may have been misguided and his response on this occasion has, therefore, often been interpreted as an attempt to thwart popular famine relief policies, and to a certain extent there is some truth in this. But again, it could equally be interpreted as the response of a man who was very much a product of his environment, at a time when his class and position in Irish life were coming under increasing attack from Catholic agitators; he may even have perceived it as his duty as leader of the Irish Protestant community to take control of the situation on his own terms. Such an interpretation might also go some way to explaining Augustus's previous anathema to O'Connell's Registry Association in 1839, which he thought would be used as an instrument for repeal agitation.[22]

Augustus's reputation suffered greatly after the passing of the 1870 Land Act and his introduction of the infamous 'Leinster lease' (see chapter 16), in which he effectively attempted to have his leaseholders contract themselves out of compensation for improvements legislated for under that act. While there is evidence to suggest that the main opposition to the lease came not from his tenants but from tenant rights agitators, the controversy severely strained landlord-tenant relations on the estate. In 1872 a Tenants Defence Association was established in Athy, and by 1881 the Leinster lease had become such a national symbol of oppression and tyranny that it was burned by a leading Land

League agitator, Michael Boyton, at a mass meeting in Athy.[23] This irrevocably tainted the social memory of the 3rd duke. Yet, while there is little doubt that the lease was rigorous, tough and threatening to tenants who did not obey its terms, it was not especially 'tyrannical' in the context of the period. Indeed, the Leinster lease is most interesting for its extraordinary detail, particularly in relation to the duke's perceptions of how his tenants should work their holdings. It stipulated in elaborate terms everything from the kinds of crops the tenants were to sow, to the punishment to be meted out if thistles and other weeds went to seed on the land. Significantly, the controversy led to no major outbreak of agitation on the estate, but it did portend events to come in the following 30 years or so.[24]

Augustus's interest in preserving the stability of the Established Church presents another intriguing insight into his attitude toward Irish life and politics. In 1828 he 'completely repaired and improved' St Mary's church in Maynooth, turning the fifteenth-century tower into a family mausoleum. In 1859 he ordered another 'complete restoration', this time extending the main building so that it incorporated the tower, slating part of the roof, and plastering the interior. He seems to have been, what might be termed, a 'low churchman' and had very little patience for what he considered to be the extravagance of the Church hierarchy. In 1833 he attracted the wrath of Richard Whately, the Archbishop of Dublin, for comments he made concerning the 'overgrown church' in Ireland.[25] Another letter written by the duke in 1841 is particularly revealing in this regard: 'I am not a high churchman. I have a respect for the religious opinions of all classes, but as a member of the Church of England, I feel deeply how essential it is for our clergy now to attend their flock'.[26]

Augustus also opposed the growing trend in the nineteenth century, begun by the Oxford Movement in the 1840s, for strengthening elements of liturgy and ritual in Anglican Church practice. In 1866 he told J. H. Monahan, the rector of Maynooth, that his parish music society should steer clear of what he called 'new ritualism'.[27] Similarly, in 1869 Augustus told the Anglican archbishop of Dublin that he hoped 'that the innovations now spreading in England will be kept out, which lead so many to … the Church of Rome'.[28] Yet despite this inherent suspicion of Catholicism, Augustus remained a friend and patron of the temperance campaigner, Fr Theobald Mathew (1790–1856). Of course, this may very well have been driven by the duke's own aversion to alcohol, and his abhorrence of what he termed 'debauchery and sloth', as well as the fact that Fr Mathew's teachings mirrored the duke's own conviction that the Irish people should act with 'steady, orderly, and peaceful habits'.[29]

In 1869 Augustus voted in favour of disestablishment, despite the real and symbolic blow it dealt to the Protestant interest in Ireland. As a 'low churchman' and a long time friend of civil and religious liberty, this stance was in some respects more than a simple towing of the British Liberal party line. It is further revealing of the duke's perception of his dual role as both a British and Irish peer. Yet he remained optimistic about the future of the Protestant faith in Ireland, telling several correspondents in September 1869 that he 'had no fear' but that the church would 'flourish'.[30] He led the subscription fund to aid the Anglican clergy while the Representative Church Body was being established, and supported the laity's right to choose their lay representatives. Despite his low-church leanings, Augustus became a model Anglican in post-disestablishment Ireland.

Augustus was also keenly interested in education. He acted as patron and member of the board of the Kildare Place Society from 1815, although he avoided playing a leading role, lending the society the influence of his name rather than his active involvement. In 1819 when O'Connell denounced the Kildare Place Society as a proselytising body and resigned, he hoped that the duke would follow suit. However, Augustus refused to publicly condemn the society,[31] and it was some years before he eventually resigned. In the meantime he played a significant role as mediator during the government's deliberations to establish the Board of National Education, a groundbreaking decision that was ultimately publicised in a letter Lord Stanley addressed to the duke. In 1831 Augustus was appointed chairman of the new board. While the duke's involvement in education has been more thoroughly scrutinised than any other aspect of his career,[32] questions remain as to why he was content to pass on the duty of Education Commissioner to the marquis of Kildare in 1840.

From this brief examination of Augustus's politics, it is possible to draw several conclusions. Clearly he took his role in Irish society as the country's most important nobleman very seriously. He tried assiduously to uphold the Whig traditions of his family. Yet, despite his support for emancipation and for social improvement, he was always conscious of his role as a Protestant figurehead. He was never a political animal in the way that O'Connell was. It is possibly indicative of his hierarchical views and his perception of the traditional role of the Irish aristocracy that Augustus was happy to lend his name, but often not his heart, to political issues. There is little doubt but that he occupied an oftimes influential intermediate role between the Irish liberals on the one hand, and the government and wider British opinion on the other. His relations with the Crown similarly resonate with his ability to be diplomatic; his relations with King George IV had been strained in 1820–21 by his leadership of the defence, in the House of Lords, of Queen Caroline against the king's accusation of adultery.[33] Yet his relations with Queen Victoria were much more positive, with the young queen calling him 'the kindest and best of men' after her visit to Carton in 1849. Her attitude in 1869 was equally positive, when she told him that Carton was 'a place now associated in my mind with pleasant memories of the past'.[34]

The most obvious conclusion one can draw from this overview is that Augustus's varied involvement in Irish life and politics warrants a comprehensive biography to rightly appraise his situation and role and, indeed, to illuminate further his own ambivalent attitude in terms of his national identity. In forwarding an explanation as to why this has not happened, it is perhaps fair to say that not enough attention has been paid to the relatively comprehensive collection of his personal papers in the surviving Leinster archive (which is lacking in so many other respects). It is perhaps also fair to say that the 3rd duke, as a leading Protestant peer, has to a certain extent been a victim of historical trends. The portrait of the duke painted in 1874 for the *Dublin University Magazine* envisioned him as the single most important Irish nobleman of the century. But by the mid-twentieth century, historians such as Brian FitzGerald viewed Augustus as a single member of that doomed class of Irish Protestant landlords, describing him as 'one of the last, perhaps the very last, of his kind to regard Irish events from a consciously Irish viewpoint'.[35] The very fact that Augustus has been largely ignored is indicative of the often limited consideration afforded to nineteenth-century Protestant politics by orthodox nationalist interpretations of Irish history in the post-independence era. It is an unfortunate effect of the eclipse of Protestant political supremacy in the nineteenth century that it has been understudied in the twentieth. It is now time for Augustus Frederick FitzGerald, 3rd Duke of Leinster, to be recognised in his true context, at the very heart of nineteenth-century Irish liberal politics.

NOTES

1   'Our portrait gallery, second series – no. 6: Augustus Frederick, Duke of Leinster', *Dublin University Magazine: A Literary and Political Journal*, lxxxiv (July–Dec. 1874), pp 42–56; Brian FitzGerald, 'After the Union', *Dublin Magazine*, xxiv (1949), pp 13–19; Bridget Hourican, 'Augustus Frederick FitzGerald, 3rd Duke of Leinster', in McGuire and Quinn (eds), *Dictionary of Irish Biography* (hereafter *DIB*), vol. iii, pp 818–19.

2   Lord William's first born son and heir, George, had died in 1784; see *Burke's Peerage and Baronetage* (London, 1853 edn.), p. 818.

3   W. E. Vaughan, *Landlords and Tenants in Ireland, 1848–1904* (Dublin, 1984), p. 5; E. Tickell to Leinster, 18 Oct. 1821, Public Records of Northern Ireland (PRONI), Leinster Papers, D3078/3/13/10.

4   Frederick Ponsonby to the duke of Leinster, 8 Jan. 1836, PRONI, Leinster Papers, D3078/3/26/3.

5   *Hansard's Parliamentary Debates*, 1st series, xxiv, col. 498 (12 Feb. 1813).

6   Ibid., 2nd series, xviii, col. 766 (17 May 1825); xix, col. 1294 (10 June 1828); xxi, col. 694 (10 Apr. 1829).

7   Ibid., 3rd series, xxx, col. 126 (30 July 1833), lxxxi, col. 270 (10 June 1845); cxxv, col. 1328 (18 Apr. 1853); clx, col. 266 (27 July 1860); *Dublin University Magazine*, p. 51.

8   Douglas Kanter, *The Making of British Unionism, 1740–1848: Politics, Government and the Anglo-Irish Constitutional Relationship* (Dublin, 2009), p. 176.

9   'Leinster Declaration', Oct. 1830, PRONI, Leinster Papers, D3078/3/21/12.

10   A printed version of the 'Leinster Declaration', Oct. 1830, PRONI, Leinster Papers, D3078/3/21/12.

11   Daniel O'Connell to Lord Cloncurry, 14 May 1820 and Daniel O'Connell to Henry Brougham, 14 Dec. 1820, in Maurice O'Connell (ed.), *The Correspondence of Daniel O'Connell* (8 vols, Dublin, 1972), vol. ii, p. 841

12   Daniel O'Connell to Lord Cloncurry, 4 Sept, 1828 in ibid., vol. ii, p. 1483.

13   Daniel O'Connell to P. V. Fitzpatrick, 22 Sept. 1832, in ibid., vol. ii, p. 1921

14   The duke's address to his 'Friends and Tenants', [?] Feb. 1828, PRONI, Leinster Papers, D3078/3/19/3.

15   Daniel O'Connell to Mary O'Connell, 26 Nov. 1834; Daniel O'Connell to Richard Lalor Sheil, 16 June 1844, in O'Connell (ed.), *Correspondence of Daniel O'Connell*, vol. v, letter 2142, vol. vii, letter 3073.

16   For example, Brian FitzGerald, 'After the Union'; Bridget Hourican, 'Augustus Frederick FitzGerald, 3rd Duke of Leinster'.

17   Hourican, 'Augustus Frederick FitzGerald'.

18   *Hansard's Parliamentary Debates*, 3rd series, xxxiii, 898–99 (13 May 1836).

19   Ibid., 2nd series, lxxxvi, col. 1405 (28 May 1846); Sir George Grey to the Duke of Leinster, 3 June 1850, PRONI, Leinster Papers, D3078/3/37/9.

20   James Macaulay, *Ireland in 1872: A Tour of Observation with Remarks on Irish Public Questions* (London, 1873), p. 279; D. H. Akenson, *The Irish Education Experiment: The National System of Education in the Nineteenth Century* (London, 1970), p. 128.

21   'Our portrait gallery, second series – no. 6: Augustus Frederick, Duke of Leinster', p. 49.

22   Edward Buller to Leinster, several letters Sept.–Nov. 1846; Lord Ebrington to Leinster, 12 Sept. 1839, PRONI, Leinster Papers, MSS D3078/3/33/12–15; 21–2; D3078/3/30/3.

23   *Dublin University Magazine*, p. 50; Macaulay, *Ireland in 1872*, p. 279; T. W. Moody and F. X. Martin, *The Course of Irish History* (Cork, 1994, 3rd edn), p. 290.

24   See chapters 15 and 17 of this volume.

25   Chief Secretary P. J. Littleton to Leinster, 12 Nov. 1833, PRONI, Leinster Papers, D3078/3/23/11; Richard Whately to Leinster, 20 Nov. 1833, PRONI, Leinster Papers, D3078/3/23/12.

26   Leinster to unknown recipient, Apr. 1841, PRONI, Leinster Papers, D3078/3/31/4.

27   Revd J. H. Monahan to Leinster, 9 Nov. 1866, and the duke's reply, 10 Nov. 1866, PRONI, Leinster Papers, D3078/3/46/13–14.

28   Leinster to R. C. Trench, Archbishop of Dublin, 16 Sep. 1869, PRONI, Leinster Papers, D3078/3/50/15.

29   Address of the Duke of Leinster to his 'Friends and Tenants', Feb. 1828, PRONI, Leinster Papers, D30783/19/3.

30   Duke of Leinster to J. Bonham, 12 Sept. 1869; Duke of Leinster to R. C. Trench, Archbishop of Dublin, 16 Sept. 1869. PRONI, Leinster Papers, D3078/3/50/9, 15.

31   Mary O'Connell to Daniel O'Connell, 7 March 1820, in O'Connell, *Correspondence of Daniel O'Connell*, vol. ii, letter 814; Joseph D. Jackson to Leinster, 30 June 1823, PRONI, Leinster Papers, D3078/3/15/3.

32   'Our portrait gallery, second series – no. 6: Augustus Frederick, Duke of Leinster', pp 42–56; Brian FitzGerald, 'After the Union'; Bridget Hourican, 'Augustus Frederick FitzGerald, 3rd Duke of Leinster'.

33   *Hansard's Parliamentary Debates*, 2nd series, ii, col. 612 (17 Aug. 1820); iv (25 Jan. 1821).

34   *Dublin University Magazine*, p. 52; Col. Elphinstone to Leinster, 18 Apr. 1869, PRONI, Leinster Papers, D3078/3/50/2.

35   Brian FitzGerald, 'After the Union'.

CHAPTER 15

A Middleman in the 1840s
Charles Carey and the Leinster Estate

Ciarán Reilly

On the eve of the Great Famine (1845–51), the ubiquitous middlemen were perceived to be the cause of many of the social evils which existed in rural Ireland, particularly in relation to the system of land tenure and the general condition of the people.[1] While many middlemen were large farmers, prosperous and Protestant, some were also members of the Catholic 'demi-gentry' that had emerged in the eighteenth century.[2] These men had been granted extended leases, in some cases as long as 500 or 1,000 years.[3] Initially the system was attractive to landlords because it facilitated the easy collection of rents and meant that land agents did not have to deal with the lower orders. However, by the early 1840s middlemen were being increasingly blamed for the subdivision of land into tiny uneconomic holdings, which had led to overcrowding and inevitable agrarian disputes. They were accused of greedily squeezing extortionate rents from their subtenants. At the same time it became increasingly frustrating for landowners, whose ancestors had granted extended leases, who were now unable to raise their rents to exploit market forces during periods of economic growth.

Thus, by the 1840s land agents such as Arthur Fitzmaurice, who managed estates in Carlow, Kildare and King's County, were convinced that the middleman system was 'ruinous'. In his evidence to the Devon Commission in 1845, Fitzmaurice pointed out that that the number of middlemen was declining because landlords were refusing to renew their leases as they began to fall in. This he considered to be a good thing as 'they [middlemen] take no interest to encourage improvements. They take all they can of the land knowing that they will have done with it shortly'.[4] The generality of his claim may be questionable, but it did suggest that in the future middlemen would come under increased scrutiny and pressure from agents and landlords alike.[5] The Leinster estate was probably no different to most at this time; unfortunately the dearth of estate rentals and accounts for the period makes it impossible to determine with certainty. However, what does exist in the National Library of Ireland is a very

important and rather rare document – the unpublished journal and correspondence of Charles Carey, a middleman on the Athy estate of the 3rd duke of
Leinster – which reveals much about the changing relationship between landlord and tenant during the Famine.[6]

Let us first consider what is known about the Leinster estate and the landlord during that time. Augustus Frederick FitzGerald (1791–1874), 3rd Duke
of Leinster, lived through an extraordinary period in Irish history – from the
success of O'Connell's Catholic Emancipation movement (which he supported) through the Repeal movement (which he opposed), the Great Famine, the
later emergence of the Home Rule movement and the simultaneous coming to
prominence of the land question. The period of the Great Famine looms large
in Augustus's life. The traditional perception has been that he came out of it
with his reputation largely unscathed, as noted by Bridget Hourican in her
brief survey of his life.[7] He was one of the few landlords that Cecil Woodham
Smith commended in her pioneering study of the Famine.[8] In a broader context, James Macaulay described him as 'the good, old duke of Leinster, the most
liberal and generous of landlords'.[9]

In the pre-Famine period, the Leinster estate was undoubtedly one of the
best situated in Ireland.[10] Holdings were generally let in parcels of ten to 50 acres
but there were, it seems, quite a large number of farms of over 100 acres.[11] Augustus avoided issuing leases to smallholders, who in most cases could not support
themselves: 'I never made a 40s. freeholder and when a lease fell out with small
tenants on it, I bought them up and improved long before it became general', noted the duke.[12] In an effort to generally improve husbandry on the estate, several
agricultural instructors were brought over from Scotland. Consolidation of
holdings had taken place in the pre-Famine period possibly in response to the
passing of the Poor Law Act of 1838. There is evidence that Augustus removed
tenants from the estate during this period and emigrated them to America. Robert Rawson, a large-holder near Athy, noted in evidence to the Devon Commission that 'farms have been consolidated in a few instances and the duke of
Leinster gives to the ejected tenant, money to bring them to America'.[13] This
period also coincided with the extension of the railway system linking Maynooth
to Dublin and beyond. Thus, to facilitate it coming through his estate, Augustus
paid a tenant named Boylan from Athy, £27 to quit his holding.[14]

However, as is the case with many landlords praised for their benevolence
during the Famine, his generosity in modern terms would seem negligible. His
charitable donations and investment in relief measures may have been generous in comparison to many of his peers, but given his wealth it could arguably
have been much greater. But it must be remembered that he worked within the
prevailing *laissez faire* ideologies of the time. This was possibly most evident in
his public criticism of the efforts of the Royal Agricultural Society in establishing relief employment schemes for the labouring classes, stating that it was not

the role of the society to do so. His stance resulted in him resigning his position as president in 1846. In the early stages of the Famine he denied that there existed the need for local relief committees in Kildare so delaying their establishment.[15] R. V. Comerford has argued that the duke's tenants at Maynooth should have been better circumstanced owing to the building of the Midland Great Western Railway which was completed in 1847, the enlargement of Maynooth College following the 'infamous' grant of 1845 and the lavish refurbishments of Carton and Kilkea Castle in 1849.[16] However, despite the existence of such works, the population of Maynooth declined by about 20 per cent during the Famine.

Charles Carey, as noted above, lived on the Athy estate which was described in 1840 as the 'neglected step child' about whom nobody cared.[17] Besides a substantial farm, Carey leased a considerable number of houses and other properties in the town at Emily Square, Offaly Street, Leinster Street, Market Square and Meeting Lane. The accumulation of urban property had been begun by Carey's father, Michael, towards the end of the eighteenth century when he was described as being, amongst other things, a shoemaker, a chandler, a cordwainer and a publican. By 1833 Charles Carey had succeeded to his father's properties and quickly added to his portfolio by leasing premises on Meeting Lane. He was openly pro-Union and anti-Catholic. He was extreme in his religious views: in his journal he venomously attacked 'spalpeen priests' and their 'lousy crew' and even went as far as to suggest that 'St Patrick salted the fish with plenty of salt and pepper to give them [the Catholics] a thirst for fish'. In the early 1840s, he actively opposed the Repeal party in Athy town, pouring scorn on the 'arch agitator', Daniel O'Connell, declaring that 'no country can thrive where popery is predominant'. While Carey's landlord did not support Repeal, he had been an ardent emancipationist. The 3rd duke was also an ardent supporter of Fr Theobald Mathew but Carey condemned the work of the temperance reformer believing that he was planning to arm his converts: 'I am certain the Protestants of this country if tomorrow the papist war whoop was sounded would beat them into the sea; and I am thinking that it must come to a battle in the end.'[18]

These sentiments were at some variance with Carey's attitude towards the Catholic poor. His journal suggests a deepening of poverty in the Athy area in the early 1840s; he lamented that it was 'a pity to have the country convulsed by a set of broken down paupers'.[19] By February 1842 he admitted that it was the first time in 20 years that he was not himself able to pay his rent. Although obviously struggling to meet his obligations, he insisted that he would not 'give up the fight' and looked forward to the coming mowing season. In contrast to the stereotypical image of middlemen grinding tenants for rent, Carey remarked that he was reluctant to push his subtenants: 'I will never turn out my own while I have potatoes and milk to give them'.[20] Thus, on the eve of the Great

Famine he appears to have been constantly borrowing and struggling to get by – this while beset by his own family strife.[21]

The 3rd duke of Leinster was absent from the country when the potato blight first appeared in September 1845. Upon his return to Carton he was informed about conditions in a report by his agriculturalist, Mr McLennan, and was said to have been distressed to learn that at least one-third of the potato crop would be lost.[22] (It was to prove even worse than anticipated as another half of those potatoes orginally thought to be free from disease were also lost.) In October, Carey's journal reveals that the potato blight had also reached Athy: 'There is a curse on Paddy's Land. The people here are finding out to their sorrow the failure of the potato crop ... I hope the calamity will not be found to be so great as is represented.'[23] By September 1846 his tenants were in dire circumstance: 'I am really frightened when I look around and see the awful situation of the country. The people are pulling the weeds out of their land, for the potatoes have all gone regularly died away and gone to nothing'. The following month he lamented: 'we teem here with the dread word, "Famine". The frost can't hurt them now, for those that went out to dig had none'. Carey's journal also graphically depicts the suffering of the duke of Leinster's tenants, which peaked in the early months of 1847; he could remember nothing comparable since the town was plagued by cholera in 1834:

> The post teems with deaths, and our poor house is daily sending out its dead, and the poor in the country are bringing their deal coffins through the streets on their little ass's cars. It is equal to the time of the cholera, when the deep wailings of the living for the dead woke us from our midnight slumbers. How awful are these wailings now! I wish I was out of reach of the mournful sounds. I am in good health, but these miserable scenes sicken me.[24]

Carey feared that 'the country will be thinned of one half of its inhabitants and that contagion will spread, and sketch its devastating hand among the lords of the land'.[25] At first he tried to be proactive, pleading with his subtenants to re-sow the land with crops. As the Famine progressed he became disillusioned with the local landlords, asking: 'What happens if the land is left unsown? Then the lordly landlords may look for their rent on the barren waste, while their slaves who used to labour with light hearts are near their last homes, leaving a blank behind'. In February 1847 he was critical of the fact that 20 out of every 100 persons were to be taken off the public works schemes, leaving only 'the shivering child and the poor naked mother'. He was vocal about the nature of the schemes in County Kildare, believing that the labour would have been better put to use in agriculture than building roads to nowhere. He vowed never to 'prosecute the thief for he will only do what I would do myself if I was hungry', philosophising that 'The want of potatoes and living on bread has changed our nature, but when we look around and see the starving multitude, where hunger is depicted on every face, we must drop our gourmandising and be thankful'.[26]

But hunger often led to crime. The Leinster estate experienced a significant breakdown in law and order, particularly at Athy and Castledermot where it was claimed that people were committing crime in an effort to be sent to gaol or transported away from the harsh realities. According to Carey: 'famine is making sad savages here ... it matters little what king reigns, for the king of terrors stalks through the land'. And as crime levels rose, he reappraised his opinions: 'the peasantry have become a complete set of blackguards and until there is a great reformation and the people brought round to put their shoulders to the wheel, we must remain a poor, degraded, pauperised community and I think the landlords must set the wheel going'. In July 1847 Carey decided to withhold his rents from Leinster writing: 'it is better disappoint the duke than distress poor honest men that always paid me and will pay me when the harvest comes in'.[28] He was dismayed by relief efforts; although the charitable efforts of Quaker communities have long been acknowledged, those in the immediate vicinity of Athy do not appear to have contributed to Famine relief. Consequently, in 1847, the workhouse in Athy, originally built to house 600 people, housed over 1,500 inmates. A further 1,102 people were receiving outdoor relief and additional accommodation was provided at Barrack Street and Canal Side. By August 1848 the total number of people receiving outdoor and indoor relief had risen to over 2,800.[29]

While these were not all tenants of the duke of Leinster, given the extent of his lands in the area, it is reasonable to assume that many of them were. In October 1848 a cholera outbreak added to the woes of the inhabitants of Athy and, to counteract the influx of strangers into the town, the magistrates decided that only locals would be entitled to relief. By now the duke had decided to initiate 'a programme of emigration', believing this to be a prerequisite to the agricultural improvement of Ireland. In April 1849 his tenants were amongst those who departed from Athy for Quebec on board the *Hannah*. The following month there were further reports that 'the *Princess Alicia* brought a large number from the counties of Wicklow and Kildare. From the latter county there were many of the duke of Leinster's tenantry'.[30] The duke then proceeded to consolidate the vacated lands and advertised large tracts of land in the Athy area; however, he specifically looked for Scottish tenants, offering them 'substantial farms with new dwelling houses in south Kildare'.[31]

Seventeen Presbyterian families arrived from Perthshire in Scotland and settled in Athy in the early 1850s, building a church in the town in 1856.[32] The duke evidently felt that they would bring much-needed agricultural expertise but, undoubtedly, he also had an eye on improving the rental capacity of the estate. In 1868, the lawyer, economist and government policy adviser, Nassau William Senior (1790–1864), commented on the management of the Leinster estate under Francis Trench, and the policy of taking in the Scottish tenants:

He [the duke] cleared the land by an extensive emigration [scheme] and advertised widely in the Scotch papers for tenants. In time, the estate was re-let, the rental, which had be £35,000 a year, was, by improved management, and by the falling in of very old leases, raised to £45,000; and the tenants (especially the Scotch) are doing well.[33]

By the end of 1848, it seems that Carey's own inability to collect rents from an impoverished tenantry meant that he could no longer afford to pay his own rent and so he was served with notice to quit; he expressed his anger at the 'over-fed lords of the soil'.[34] He wrote to the law agent, William Crosby, stating that he had held the land for 53 years, had made several improvements to his holdings and had plans for the establishment of an agricultural school. Although he was not initially evicted, he continued to be critical of the duke of Leinster and his fellow grandees; in December 1850, he wrote to his nephew, Michael, of his distaste for 'haughty usurpers of the soil', claiming that 'nothing but the pound of flesh will suffice on the Leinster estate'.[35] Unfortunately he provided no evidence of how much he was in arrears, or why he was not actually evicted. Perhaps some indication of his own growing indebtedness can be gleaned from his having to borrow £1 from Michael Lawler's wife in 1851; and his comments in the same year regarding an offer by agents of the duke to allow a £2 abatement if he paid up all of his arrears: 'Good News!! A grand specimen of the great duke, and shows the really good times coming!'[36] By 1853, however, Carey was so indebted that agents and bailiffs of the duke of Leinster 'took the land without any remuneration ... The bloody Trench – the curse of Ireland'.[37]

Carey's attitude towards the duke of Leinster had changed radically over the course of a decade. In December 1841 he had widely praised him and his representatives for acting kindly to the poor of Athy, giving them land, cabins and abatements of rent. He encouraged his nephew to publish evidence of the fact in the *Leinster Express* as an example to other landlords: 'he has made glad the hearts of many who bless him from delivering them from the grinding middleman'.[38] The beginning of the Famine coincided with the change in Carey's attitude, although, in November 1846, he instructed his nephew to burn a letter he had written to him describing the duke as a harsh landlord. In 1847 he grudgingly credited Leinster with helping the poor tenants to till and sow their lands – but hastened to add that it was necessary to do so for 'if his land lies idle he loses cat and game'.[39]

Carey's personal circumstances had undoubtedly changed by the 1850s; writing in the last days of his life (around 1859), he told his nephew in a letter recorded in the journal that 'the duke never did anything for me or mine'.[40] While Carey does not appear to have suffered destitution he does seem to have lost a good deal of his property, and consequently a loss of social status. When he died in 1859 his nephew, Michael, sold the possessions he had left: a pot, basin, bedsteads, ladders, a heap of straw, three jaunting carts, two tables and a winnowing machine. Michael was further obliged to pay off £22 in debts and to surrender part of Carey's remaining holdings in Emily Square to James Freeman, the estate bailiff, as his uncle had been over £30 in rent arrears.[41]

There were others who had suffered a similar fate and who also decried the 3rd duke of Leinster as a 'grasping landlord' with an 'unprincipled agent'.[42] Unfortunately for Carey and other middlemen, the Famine provided the pretext and opportunity for landlords like the duke to wrestle back their lands from the men who had been profiting from them by virtue of holding long-term leases. The Famine brought the middleman system to an end; as James Donnelly Jnr has concluded, middlemen 'were ground into dust between the upper and nether millstones'.[43] Their demise was inevitable both because of the socio-economic impact of the Famine, and the deliberate policy of some landlords to end what came to be perceived as a pernicious system. As Margaret Power noted: 'it took patience, vigilance, careful management and the catastrophe of the Famine to effectively get rid of the system of middlemen'.[44]

As for the 3rd duke of Leinster, the point has already been made that he rode out the Famine according to the prevailing philosophies of the day. He considered that he had done his duty towards his tenantry, claiming many years later that he had acted fairly; he had 'built houses and offices, sunk rivers and improved long before it became general. I gave leases for 21 years or a life, which I was induced to do as without a life, no matter how large the farm, the tenant has no status in the county'.[45] However, no expense was spared for the visit of Queen Victoria to Carton in August 1849, which came at a time when 141 cases of cholera and typhoid were reported in Maynooth, many resulted in death. Cholera was also rampant in Athy 'adding fear to the distress and hunger of the local people'.[46] Moreover, as well as the refurbishment of Carton around this time, improvements were carried out at Kilkea Castle in 1849; and town houses were maintained in grandeur at 13 Dominick Street, Dublin and 6 Carlton House Terrace, London. There was also significant outlay for the marriage celebrations of the duke's son, the marquis of Kildare, to Lady Caroline Sutherland-Leveson-Gower in October 1847. The following month the marquis's parents gave a 'hospitable entertainment to their tenants and neighbours' at Carton. The *Freeman's Journal* described the scene: 'As early as one o'clock, large crowds were observed in all directions bending their way towards Carton, the tenantry of his grace's estate having being invited to dine at the mansion.'[47] The guests were undoubtedly prominent townsmen as well as members of the class of large farmers that the duke of Leinster had been so careful to create.

In the years following the Famine, the Leinster estate settled into a period of relative stability and prosperity which was not broken until the introduction of the so-called 'Leinster lease' in the 1870s. This, and the extended Land War from that period, focused negative attention on virtually all landlords in Ireland

– with many subject to allegations regarding alleged deeds (or misdeeds) which had occurred during the Famine period. Thus, in 1872 a large farmer from Athy, whose rights, as he perceived them, were to be compromised by the Leinster lease, claimed that the 3rd duke had carried out 'sundry evictions in the Famine years' and thus did not deserve the reputation of an improving landlord.[48] The duke's land agent, Charles Hamilton, advised the tenantry not to believe falsehoods which had been uttered and urged them to remember that their landlord had looked after them very well, particularly during the Famine.[49] There were, in retrospect, elements of truth in both claims.

NOTES

1   For studies of nineteenth-century middlemen, see, for example, F. S. L. Lyons, 'Vicissitudes of a middleman in County Leitrim, 1810–27', in *Irish Historical Studies*, 9 (1955), pp 300–18; David Dickson, 'Middlemen', in Thomas Bartlett and D. W. Hayton (eds.), *Penal Era and Golden Age, Essays in Irish History, 1690–180*0 (Belfast, 1979), pp 162–85 and Kevin Whelan, 'An underground gentry? Catholic middlemen in eighteenth-century Ireland', in James S. Donnelly and Kerby Miller (eds.) *Irish Popular Culture 1650–1850* (Dublin, 1998), pp 118–72.

2   Arthur Young, *A Tour in Ireland 1776–1779*, ed. A. W. Hutton (Shannon, 1970), p. 26.

3   Examples can be found in the Dowdall Papers, National Library of Ireland (NLI), John Ainsworth, *Report on Private Collections*, no. 99; see also Lloyd Papers, NLI, MS 44,810 (5).

4   *Report from Her Majesty's Commissioners of Enquiry into the State of the Law and Practice in Respect of the Occupation of Land in Ireland, with Minutes of Evidence, Supplements, Appendices and Index* (Devon Commission) (hereafter cited as Devon Commission), HC 1845, [605] [606] xix.1, 57, p. 573.

5   It should however be noted that not every landlord or agent advocated the ending of the system of middlemen: some preferred to retain middlemen believing that there was a better chance of collecting rents from such persons than from impoverished tenant farmers.

6   'Journal of Michael Carey, Athy, Co. Kildare, including (indexed) copies of leases etc. but largely consisting of copies of letters to him from Charles Carey, 1840–1859', NLI, MS 25,299. (Hereafter cited as 'Carey journal').

7   Bridget Hourican, 'FitzGerald, Augustus Frederick, 3rd Duke of Leinster', *Dictionary of National Biography*, online edn (http://dib.cambridge.org/viewReadPage.do?articleId=a3133) (accessed 29 Nov. 2011).

8   Cecil Woodham-Smith, *The Great Hunger* (London, 1962), p. 18, 295.

9   James Macaulay, *Ireland in 1872: A Tour of Observation (London, 1873), p. 279.*

10   Hourican, 'FitzGerald, Augustus Frederick'.

11   Evidence of Patrick Dunne, Devon Commission, [605], xix. l, p. 579.

12   Brian FitzGerald, 'After the Union', in *The Dublin Magazine*, xxiv (Apr.–June, 1949), p. 14.

13   Devon Commission, p. 577.

14   Ibid.

15   Duke of Leinster to Relief Commissioners, 22 Mar. 1846, National Archives of Ireland (NAI), Relief Commission Papers, RLFC 3/8/881.

16   R. V. Comerford, 'County Kildare and the famine', in Kildare County Council, *Lest We Forget: Kildare and the Great Famine* (Kildare, 1995), p. 13.

17   *Leinster Express*, 27 June 1840.

18   'Carey journal', 9 Sept. 1840.

19   Ibid., 11 July 1843.

20   Ibid., 27 Oct. 1846.

21   Frank Taaffe has highlighted the number of items pawned by the inhabitants of Athy on the eve of the Famine as being an indicator of their declining fortunes, see 'Athy and the Great Famine', in Kildare County Council, *Lest We Forget*, p. 58; 'Carey Journal', 22 Oct. 1846.

22   Duke of Leinster to Relief Commissioners, Dublin Castle, 7 Dec. 1845, NAI, Relief Commission Papers, 2/Z17412.

23   'Carey journal', 29 Oct. 1845; in the same month another commentator claimed that Athy had been largely unaffected and that the blight had only affected potatoes sown in drills, see Taaffe, 'Athy and the Great Famine', p. 58.

24   'Carey journal', 20 Jan. 1847.

25   Ibid., 20. Jan. 1847.

26   Ibid., 21 Mar. 1847.

27   Taaffe, 'Athy and the Great Famine', p. 61.

28   'Carey journal', 14 July 1847.

29   Taaffe, 'Athy and the Great Famine', p. 66.

30   *Leinster Express*, 14 Apr., 12, 19 May 1849.

31   Taaffe, 'Athy and the Great Famine', p. 65.

32   See: www.athyheritagecentre–museum.ie/religiousdiversity (accessed 24 Mar. 2011).

33   N. W. Senior, *Journals, Conversations and Essays Relating to Ireland* (London, 1868), p. 85.

34   'Carey journal', 31 Oct. 1848.

35   Ibid., Dec. 1850.

36   Ibid., 12 June 1851.

37   Ibid., n.d. (1853).

38   Ibid., 21 Mar. 1847.

39   Ibid., 19 Feb. 1847.

40   Ibid., 10 Feb 1859.

41   See for example a variety of correspondence in the Carey journal.

42   H. Norwood Tyre, *Tyre v. Leinster: or, An Englishman's Experience of the Working of the Landlord and Tenant (Ireland) Act, 1870* (Dublin, 1874), p. 12.

43   James S. Donnelly Jnr, *The Great Irish Potato Famine* (Stroud, 2001), p. 134.

44   Margaret M. C. Power, 'Sir Richard Bourke and his tenants 1815–55', in *North Munster Antiquarian Journal*, xli (2001), p. 76.

45   FitzGerald, 'After the Union', p. 14.

46   Taaffe, 'Athy and the Great Famine', p. 70.

47   *Freeman's Journal*, 2 Nov. 1847.

48   Ibid., 10 Dec. 1872.

49   Norwood Tyre, *Tyre v. Leinster*, p. 59.

CHAPTER 16

'Sacrificed for Ready Money'
The Leinster Estate and the Irish Land Question, 1870–1908

Patrick Cosgrove

From the 1870s until the coming-of-age of the 6th Duke of Leinster, Maurice FitzGerald (1887–1922) in 1908, the Irish land question increasingly impacted on the FitzGerald family and the Leinster estate. During these years the policy of making Irish tenant farmers the owners of their holdings assumed increased significance for successive British governments and, like all members of the Irish landed gentry, the FitzGeralds were not immune from the repercussions of land legislation enacted during this period. According to an 1876 government return of landowners in Ireland, the Leinster estate consisted of just over 68,000 acres yet within a few decades almost all of the FitzGerald's ancestral lands had passed into the hands of tenant-purchasers.[1] This essay traces the effects of the various legislative attempts made to resolve the Irish land question during this period and how they impacted on the FitzGerald family and the Leinster estate.

The 3rd Duke of Leinster, Augustus Frederick FitzGerald (1791–1874), was widely admired as a resident and patriarchal landlord who took a great personal interest in the management of his estate. However, the introduction of the 1870 Land Act led to growing tensions between the tenants and his successor, Charles William FitzGerald (1819–87). In this period, tenant organisations were firmly focused on securing what became known as the '3 Fs': freedom to sell their interest in their holding, fair rent and fixity of tenure. The 1870 legislation stipulated that any tenant who was evicted from his holding for any reason, other than the non-payment of rent, was entitled to compensation from his landlord. However, the 3rd duke attempted to get around this requirement by drawing up a document which became known as the 'Leinster lease'. This document, issued by both the 3rd and 4th dukes to tenants throughout the Leinster estate, contained a clause absolving the dukes from their responsibility to pay compensation in such cases. The issue of the lease quickly assumed a political tenor after it was publicly opposed by the Athy Poor Law Guardians and many tenants, including the trustees of Maynooth College, refused to sign it. Consequently, in 1877, the college trustees were evicted from a farm they rented from the 4th duke at Laraghbryan.[2] William J. Walsh, the president of the college, was fully aware of the implications for both landlords and tenants throughout the country, stating that:

> ... the great reason why our trustees were so unwilling to sign the lease, was that being all Roman Catholic bishops, they felt that they would place themselves in a false position before the country ... Of course the fact of their signing it would be quoted all over the country as an argument for calling on other people to do so.[3]

One of the most evocative images of the Land War in County Kildare is the burning in 1881 of the 'Leinster lease' on a 1798 pike in Kildare town by Michael J. Boyton, a member of the Irish National Land League. Established in 1879 by Michael Davitt and with Charles Stewart Parnell as its chairman, the Land League was a reaction to the agricultural depression of 1877–9 which had led to considerable unrest amongst Irish tenant farmers. In response to calls for reductions in rents and a growing social unrest, the Liberal prime minister, William Gladstone, introduced the 1881 Land Act. This legislation granted the '3 Fs' to tenants, established the Land Commission and set up land courts to decide on fair rents. There was also a provision to enable tenants to purchase their holdings from their landlords, but the terms were not attractive and very few tenants actually purchased under the Act. Like many landlords throughout the country the 4th duke of Leinster faced increased demands for rent reductions from his tenants. Having agreed to reductions of 20 to 25 per cent in 1880, he was forced to grant further reductions by the land courts established after the introduction of the 1881 Land Act.[4] In the land courts, rents were fixed by a judicial tribunal for a period of 15 years, after which they could be re-assessed. Tenants on the Leinster estate, like Robert Mooney who rented 262 acres at Smithstown and Rooske in Maynooth, were quick to take advantage of the new legislation. Mooney got his rent reduced from £210 to £197 while John Bailey, another substantial farmer who rented 500 acres at Laraghbryan and elsewhere on the estate, got his rent reduced from £771 to £600.[5]

With the rental income on the Leinster estate considerably diminished, debts steadily rose. When Finlay Dun visited the estate in the early 1880s he calculated that the 4th duke was spending 20 per cent of the gross annual income (£12,000) from the estate on improvements such as arterial drainage and buildings.[6] When the 5th duke, Gerald FitzGerald (1851–93), succeeded in 1887, the encumbrances on the estate amounted to £290,000 – almost half of which related to family charges.[7] As a result, Gerald was forced to sell 19,200 acres, primarily in the manors of Kildare, Rathangan and Maynooth, under the 1885 (Ashbourne) Land Act; virtually all of the £246,400 he received went towards paying off debts.[8] Tenants who purchased holdings on the Leinster estate, such as Mathew Moran in Rathangan and Patrick Moore in Clonmoyle, repaid their loans over a 49 year period.[9]

Although £5 million had been set aside by the Conservative government for land purchase, the Ashbourne Land Act did not resolve the land question in County Kildare or elsewhere. Economic difficulties and an agricultural depression from 1884 to 1887 added to further unrest in the Irish countryside. This phase of the land question was dominated by the 'Plan of Campaign', where tenants on numerous estates throughout the country, entered into combinations and refused, with the support of the National League, to pay their rents until the landlord granted rent reductions. Large numbers of tenants were evicted on several estates, and many never returned to their former holdings. The plight of these 'wounded soldiers of the Land War', as nationalists referred to them, became a highly emotive issue and a major obstacle in any attempt to settle the land question in Ireland. In 1888 Pope Leo XIII condemned the Plan of Campaign and the agrarian agitation associated with it and, by the early 1890s, the plan had collapsed on most estates. Significantly, the tenants on the Leinster estate did not join the Plan of Campaign and avoided the worst of the Land War. The rent reductions granted by the 4th duke and the commencement of labour intensive drainage schemes on the estate during the period may well have prevented any agitation gaining a foothold.[10] In 1895, following the deaths of the 5th duke and his wife Hermione (1864–95), the Leinster estate passed into the hands of two trustees as the 6th Duke, Maurice, was still a minor. The two trustees who now controlled the destiny of the estate were Maurice's uncle, Lord Frederick FitzGerald (1857–1924), and a Scottish relation, Arthur FitzGerald (1847–1923), the 11th Lord Kinnaird of Inchture and 3rd Baron Kinnaird of Rossie.

Lord Frederick FitzGerald held the rank of lieutenant-colonel in the army and served in Afghanistan, Egypt and South Africa. He was also a member of Kildare County Council and was a national commissioner for education in Ireland (see chapter 17). Arthur FitzGerald was related to the FitzGeralds through his grandfather Charles FitzGerald, 8th Lord Kinnaird of Inchture (who had married Olivia Letitia Catherine FitzGerald (1787–1858), the youngest daughter of the 2nd duke of Leinster). Arthur was a prominent figure in the development of soccer in Britain. He was an accomplished footballer, winning five Football Association (FA) Cup medals with Old Etonians and Wanderers in addition to representing Scotland. His record of 11 FA Cup final appearances is still unequalled. He was an enthusiastic advocate of 'hacking' which, as the name suggests, involved trying to kick an opponent in the shins, believing that it was vitally important to assure the 'manliness' of soccer. His notoriety as one of the toughest tacklers in the game led his mother to express the fear that he would one day break a leg. Hearing her comment, a friend, who knew Kinnaird, is said to have responded: 'If he does, it won't be his own.'[11] In 1890, he became president of the FA. Outside of football, he had a successful career in banking becoming a director of Barclay's Bank Ltd in 1896.

The 1903 Land Act was intended to solve the Irish land question. Its principal objectives were land purchase, the relief of congestion, particularly in the west of Ireland, and the resolution of the evicted tenants' question. For the Irish Parliamentary Party, led by John Redmond (1856–1918), the two latter objectives carried as much if not more weight than the policy of land purchase.[12] The act quickly became known as the Wyndham Land Act after George Wyndham (1863–1913), the Conservative chief secretary from 1900 to 1905. (Interestingly, Wyndham was related to the FitzGeralds being the grandson of Pamela, the daughter of Edward who took part in the 1798 rebellion.) Although sales under the act were voluntary, in that there was no compulsion on landlords to sell their estates, there were a number of inducements which greatly encouraged sales. The purchase money was paid in cash, unlike earlier acts where landlords had been paid in government stock; and, most importantly, all vendors received a 12 per cent cash bonus from the government based on the purchase money of the estate sold. Tenants were provided with loans from the government to purchase their holdings which they repaid with interest in the form of annuities over sixty-eight and a half years. Trustees of estates were given powers to sell land on behalf of a minor and so it was that the trustees of the Leinster estate decided to sell on behalf of the 16-year old duke of Leinster. Thus, the estate was one of the earliest and largest estates to be sold under the 1903 Act. According to Horace Plunkett, the trustees 'took advantage of the government's desire to make a big show for their act at an early date.'[13]

The Leinster estate comprised approximately 45,000 acres in 1903 and was mainly situated in County Kildare around Maynooth, Athy, Kilkea and Castledermot with a few hundred acres in County Meath.[14] After the trustees informed the tenants that they were willing to sell, a committee from Athy/ Kilkea quickly began purchase negotiations with the estate agent, Charles R. Hamilton, in Dublin on 17 September 1903. Stephen J. Browne, a solicitor and chairman of Kildare County Council, attended on behalf of the Maynooth tenantry. The agent informed the committee that the trustees had decided not to sell for less than 26 years' purchase.[15] One year's purchase was the equivalent of one year's rent, therefore, an annual rent of £10 at 26 years' purchase was equal to £260. (This method of calculating the purchase price based on tenants' rent had become standard practice under the various land acts passed by the British government since 1881.) However, many felt that it was unjust to expect all the tenants on any estate to pay the same standard price for their holdings and that their varying positions and circumstances had to be taken into account.

There was a general perception on many estates that the larger farmers would dictate the pace and terms of purchase negotiations. Almost immediately divisions began to emerge on the Leinster estate between tenants with large, economically viable farms and those with poorer smaller holdings. The *Freeman's Journal* commented that the sale of the Leinster estate was being 'run by the big men and Scotchmen' and that these were wealthy men who had 'heaps of money'.[16] (The mention of Scotchmen referred to the introduction of a number of Scottish tenants to the estate by the 3rd duke after the Great Famine.) The Maynooth portion of the estate was described, for instance, as being 'mostly made up of grazing lands, held by some of the leading graziers of Kildare and Meath.' There were, however, some portions of these lands 'under tillage, and this, needless to say, is of the poorer quality, and is let in comparatively small farms.'[17] The first meeting of the Maynooth tenantry was held on 21 September in Maynooth town, with approximately 50 tenants present. The *Leinster Leader* reported that Stephen J. Browne, chairman of Kildare County Council, had informed the gathering that the trustees had reconsidered their original offer to the tenants and had intimated a willingness to sell at 25 years' purchase.[18] However, this price still did not reflect the variations in the quality of lands in different parts of the estate. It did, however, bolster claims that the larger tenants were setting the purchase price. In fact, the *Leinster Leader* observed that 'the grazier element predominated and took charge of the meeting'.[19] Most of the Maynooth meeting was concerned with the appointment of a deputation which would attend a further meeting in Athy on the following day.

On 22 September 1903, a general meeting of the Leinster estate tenants was held in Athy to consider the report of the Athy/Kilkea committee which had opened negotiations with the agent, Charles R. Hamilton, only a few days earlier. However, the meeting was not entirely representative of the Leinster tenantry as tenants from the Castledermot section of the estate were not present. This was called to the attention of the meeting by Edward Heydon, Kildare county councillor; as the *Leinster Leader* reported: 'it was a serious thing to come to an arrangement and only one tenth of the tenants [on the Leinster estate] present.'[20] The concerns of the smaller tenants were also articulated, particularly in relation to the number of years' purchase that had to be paid, and Heydon made the point that '25 years' purchase is frightening everybody'.[21] The outcome of the tenants' meeting on 22 September was the appointment of a deputation, with the power to make terms for the purchase of their holdings, to meet with the trustees.

Thus, on 24 September a 'joint deputation representing the tenantry of Maynooth and of the Manor of Athy [and Kilkea]' met with Lord Frederick FitzGerald in Dublin.[22] The *Irish Times* reported that the meeting was brief, lasting between 30 minutes and an hour, with the press being informed that the tenants had agreed to pay 25 years' purchase for their farms.[23] Although it was a deputation representing Maynooth and Athy/Kilkea only, the *Leinster Leader* considered 'the terms of sale as accepted by practically the whole of the Leinster tenantry'.[24] This was in spite of the fact that the Castledermot tenants had not had an opportunity to meet and to select representatives to negòtiate on their behalf. The Castledermot tenants only met for the first time on 27 September. The purpose of their first meeting was not to discuss the terms of purchase of their holdings, but to decide whether or not to accept the terms agreed on 24 September by the Maynooth and Athy/Kilkea deputation. The newspaper accounts of the meeting indicate that much of the Castledermot tenantry were anxious about agreeing to 25 years' purchase because they considered their land to be inferior to the rest of the estate. One Castledermot tenant, John Keogh, commented that: 'It's all very well for the big bugs about Athy to give twenty-five years' purchase, but it's different with us.'[25] Eventually, however, the Castledermot tenantry decided to accept the terms already agreed by the Athy/Kilkea and Maynooth deputations.

In analysing the sale of the Leinster estate, it is instructive to consider the composition of the 18-man deputation from Maynooth and Athy/Kilkea who negotiated the purchase terms with the trustees. The Maynooth deputation consisted largely of strong farmers and graziers, many holding well over 100 acres. Richard McKenna, Laurence Ball and Stephen Browne were all Justices of the Peace (JPs). McKenna was also a county councillor while Browne was chairman of Kildare County Council. Thus, the members of the Maynooth deputation were no ordinary tenants. In fact, they would be considered the elite of the tenantry, owing to the significant tracts of land they rented and the prominent positions held by some in local government. Similarly, the majority of the members of the Athy/Kilkea deputation held well over 150 acres each. Edward Heydon, as mentioned, was a county councillor while Matthew Minch, Thomas Anderson, Richard Wright and John Gannon were all JPs. Minch was also a former Irish Parliamentary Party MP and a wealthy malt and corn merchant.

While such men might be expected to be prominent in negotiations for any sale, the lack of small tenant farmer representation surely influenced the outcome of the negotiations. Between them, the combined 18-man deputation rented approximately 3,580 acres and, even with the best of intentions, it is questionable as to whether or not these large farmers actually appreciated or understood the needs and concerns of the smaller tenants.[26] According to nationalists, the weakness of the principal nationalist organisation, the United Irish League, in the region and its absence from the sale negotiations undoubtedly contributed to the prices paid by the Leinster tenants. At a league meeting held in Redwood, County Wicklow, D. J. Cogan, MP for East Wicklow, warned of the dangers of hasty negotiations and the absence of tenant organisation. He believed that on the Leinster estate: 'the wealthier and stronger tenants rushed the sale to the disadvantage of their poorer neighbours, and the sale was anything but a businesslike one, and he did think that it was one that won't prove advantageous either to the tenants themselves or to their posterity.'[27] It is also significant to note that the nationalist MP for North Kildare, Edmund Leamy, played no role in the sale negotiations (although this may have been due to his ill-health as he died in the south of France late in 1904). Similarly, Denis Kilbride, the nationalist MP for South Kildare, took little part although he later gave an instructive speech on the new land act in Athy on 17 October 1903.[28]

The sale of the Leinster estate received considerable attention both locally and nationally. Much of this attention was, however, negative. The sale was regarded by many as a prime example of how the Wyndham Act could be exploited by those in least need of assistance to purchase their holdings. The tenants came in for severe criticism over the price they had paid for their holdings. Even the typically pro-landlord *Irish Times* was taken aback at the financial scale of the sale and sounded a note of caution: 'Businesslike and agreeable as is such an agreement as the Leinster tenants have made, we should prefer to see the smaller landlords and poorer tenants coming in for the fruits of this piece of beneficent legislation.'[29] The grievances of many tenants on the Leinster estate concerning the manner in which the sale had been negotiated were given voice by Stephen Heydon, another Kildare county councillor. The *Nationalist and Leinster Times* reported:

> In south Kildare at the present time the headline has been set but he was afraid it was the wrong headline for south Kildare. It was set generally by those north Kildare men, graziers, who are living within easy access of Dublin, and having prime grassland. Those are the men who proposed 25 years' purchase, which he considered was not fair for this part of the country at all.[30]

The principal nationalist newspaper, the *Freeman's Journal*, hoped that the 'wild first plunge of the Leinster sheep' would not be imitated by other tenant-purchasers.[31] William O'Brien, the nationalist MP for Cork and one of the most prominent advocates of the Wyndham Act, condemned what he considered as the selfishness of the Leinster estate tenants and asserted that the sale inflated the prices paid by tenant-purchasers in the province of Leinster: 'The [nationalist] panic-mongers were aided by the selfishness of the wealthy tenantry of the duke of Leinster, who had always held aloof from the national organisation [United Irish League] and were the first to rush into a precipitate bargain on extravagant terms'.[32]

The fact that virtually the entire Leinster estate was sold while the 6th duke was still a minor led to criticism in some quarters. The 4th Baron Muskerry severely censured the actions of the trustees in this regard, declaring in the House of Lords: 'one great estate, which used to support the highest dignity in the Irish peerage, has been sacrificed for ready money by the guardians of a minor, with little respect for the future of a title divorced from property and residence.'[33] Vernon Cochrane, another contemporary, was scathing of the trustees's treatment of the property of the young duke, accusing the chief secretary, George Wyndham, of using 'his influence to secure part of the bonus to sell the

Leinster estate, which, whatever is its legal aspect, is a crime to the minor.'[34]

The total purchase money from the sale of the Leinster estate amounted to £766,647, a sum which included the 12 per cent cash bonus of £80,108.[35] In today's terms (2013), this would have amounted to approximately £44 million.[36] According to a statement made in December 1905, on the legal and beneficial ownership of the purchase monies of the Leinster estate, approximately £272,076 of the purchase money was tied up in family charges. All of the surviving children of the 4th duke of Leinster, aunts and uncles of the 6th duke, received a portion of the purchase money. The bulk of the purchase money, £603,000, was invested in mortgages to other members of the landed gentry, mainly in Britain, while £61,706 was invested in stocks.[37] The agent for the estate, Charles R. Hamilton, received the considerable sum of £15,000 for his services during the sale, a sum which would equate to over £860,250 in 2013.[38]

When new land legislation was required in 1908–09, owing to the financial difficulties encountered by the Wyndham Act, the sale of the Leinster estate came under increased scrutiny. The Liberal attorney-general, Richard R. Cherry, stressed in the House of Commons in 1908 that 'those large tenants of the duke of Leinster's estate were certainly not the class of people intended to be benefited by the land purchase acts.'[39] Indeed, many well-circumstanced tenants on the estate did receive substantial loans under the act to purchase their holdings. On the Maynooth portion of the estate, for example, Philip Brady received £7,000 to purchase 270 acres in Moneycooley while John Maxwell Shaw received £6,332 to purchase 261 acres in Griffinrath.[40]

By 1909 the total money available for land purchase under the Wyndham Act was exhausted by the early sale of large properties such as the Leinster estate. These estates, mainly in the east of the country, contained large economic holdings whose tenants were in less need of assistance than those on uneconomic holdings in the west of Ireland. The sale of the Leinster estate had also used up a significant portion of the bonus fund available to other landlords who wished to sell their estates. The Liberal chief secretary, Augustine Birrell, noted that the bonus had not been introduced to allow well-circumstanced landowners to make a financial killing but to provide the poor and encumbered landlords, especially in the west, with the opportunity to sell: '...nobody will say that for a well-managed estate like that of the duke of Leinster's the duke should get £80,000 [bonus] into his breeches pocket for selling at market value an excellent estate upon which there has never been any particular amount of trouble.'[41] In fact, Birrell was certain that the purchase money of the Leinster sale, when invested, brought in a much greater annual income than the estate rental ever had.[42]

Maurice FitzGerald, the 6th Duke of Leinster, did not reach his majority until 1 March 1908, almost five years after the trustees had decided to sell the Leinster estate.[43] While he was now the first subject in Ireland and premier duke, the connection with those lands which had been for so long associated with his family had been severed. Although Carton House still remained in the family's possession this was only to be temporary. Within 14 years Maurice and his brother Desmond would both be dead, and ownership of Carton would soon pass from the FitzGerald family.

NOTES

1   *Landowners in Ireland. Return of Owners of Land of One Acre and Upwards in the Several Counties...*31 and 69 [C.1492] H.C. 1876, lxxx, 61.

2   Patrick J. Corish, *Maynooth College, 1795–1995* (Dublin, 1995), pp 185–6.

3   *Report of Her Majesty's Commissioners of Inquiry into the Working of the Landlord and Tenant (Ireland) Act, 1870, and the Acts Amending the Same* (Bessborough Commission), 1111, [C.2779] [C.2779–I] [C.2779–II] [C.2779–III] H.C. 1881, xviii.1, 73, xix.1, 825. See also William Nolan and Thomas McGrath (eds), *Kildare: History and Society* (Dublin, 2006), pp 549–85.

4   Terence Dooley and Conor Mallaghan, *Carton House: An Illustrated History* (Celbridge, 2006), p. 72.

5   *Return of Judicial Rents Fixed by Sub Commissions and Civil Bill Courts, Notified to Irish Land Commission, Apr.–May 1882*, 58–59, [C.3260] H.C. 1882, lvi, 303.

6   Finlay Dun, *Landlords and Tenants in Ireland* (London, 1880), pp 24–5.

7   Dooley and Mallaghan, *Carton House*, p. 72; Terence Dooley, 'The decline of Carton House and estate, 1870–1950', in *Journal of County Kildare Archaelogical Society* (hereafter *JCKAS*), xviii:2 (1994–5), pp 215–16.

8   Terence Dooley, *The Decline of the Big House in Ireland* (Dublin, 2001), p. 105. The 1885 Act was better known as the Ashbourne Land Act, after the Lord Chancellor of Ireland, Edward Gibson (1837–1913) first Baron Ashbourne.

9   'Irish Land Commission. Purchase of Land (Ireland) Act, 1885', Public Records of Northern Ireland (PRONI), Leinster Papers, D3078/2/11/3.

10   Tom Nelson, *The Land War in County Kildare* (Maynooth, 1985), pp 16–17.

11   Nicholas Fishwick, 'Kinnaird, Arthur FitzGerald, eleventh Lord Kinnaird of Inchture and third Baron Kinnaird of Rossie (1847–1923)', in H. C. G. Matthew and Brian Harrison (eds), *Oxford Dictionary of National Biography* (hereafter *ODNB*), xxxi (Oxford, 2004), pp 732–4.

12   See Patrick John Cosgrove, 'The Wyndham Land Act, 1903: The final solution to the Irish Land Question?' (Unpublished PhD thesis, National University of Ireland, Maynooth, 2008).

13   Quoted in Chas. P. Johnson to Frederick FitzGerald, 31 Jan. 1905, PRONI, Leinster Papers, D3078/2/15/15/9.

14   *Return of Advances Made Under the Irish Land Act, 1903 during the period from 1st Nov., 1903 to 31st Dec., 1905*, vol. I parts i, ii, and iii [Cd.3447, Cd.3560, Cd.3547] H.C. 1907, lxx, 1.

15   *The Times*, 19 Sept. 1903; *Nationalist and Leinster Times*, 19 Sept. 1903.

16   Quoted in *Nationalist and Leinster Times*, 19 Sept. 1903.

17   *Nationalist and Leinster Times*, 20 Sept. 1903.

18   *Leinster Leader*, 26 Sept. 1903

19   Ibid.

20   Ibid.

21   Ibid.

22   *Irish Times*, 25 Sept. 1903.

23   Ibid.

24   *Leinster Leader*, 26 Sept. 1903.

25   Ibid.

26   Patrick Cosgrove, 'The sale of the Leinster Estate under the Wyndham Land Act, 1903', in *JCKAS*, xx:1, (2008–9), pp 20–1.

27   *Irish Independent*, 6 Oct. 1903.

28   *Nationalist and Leinster Times*, 17 Oct. 1903.

29   *Irish Times*, 25 Sept. 1903.

30   *Nationalist and Leinster Times*, 17 Oct. 1903.

31   Cited in *Times*, 29 Oct. 1903.

32   William O'Brien, *An Olive Branch in Ireland* (London, 1910), p. 301, 274.

33   *Hansard 4*, xxx, 521 (22 Feb. 1904).

34   *Irish Times*, 14 Dec. 1903.

35   'Statement of applications of sums received on the sale of the Leinster Estates in Ireland', PRONI, Leinster Papers, D3078/2/15/5.

36   Based on the currency converter for the year 1905, available on the website of the National Archives (UK) (http://www.nationalarchives.gov.uk/currency) (10 Sept. 2013) .

37   Statement of applications of sums received on the sale of the Leinster Estates in Ireland, PRONI, Leinster Papers, D3078/2/15/5.

38   'Leinster Estate Sale' (PRONI, Leinster Papers, D3078/2/15/16/3). Based on the currency converter on the National Archives (UK) website for the year 1905 (http://www.nationalarchives.gov.uk/currency) (10 Sept. 2013).

39   *Hansard 4*, cxcviii, 243 (8 Dec. 1908).

40   *Return of Advances Made Under the Irish Land Act, 1903 During the Period from 1st Nov., 1903 to 31st Dec., 1905*, vol. I parts i, ii, and iii [Cd.3447, Cd.3560, Cd.3547] H.C. 1907, lxx, 1.

41   *Hansard 5 (Commons)*, iii, 194–5 (30 Mar. 1909).

42   Augustine Birrell, 'Proposed [Irish] Land Bill' 13 Nov. 1908, The National Archives (UK), CAB 37/96/151, p. 7.

43   *Irish Independent*, 29 Feb. 1908.

CHAPTER 17

Lord Frederick FitzGerald (1857–1924) and Local Politics in County Kildare

Thomas Nelson

The intriguing figure of Lord Frederick FitzGerald (1857–1924) features prominently in the break-up of the Leinster estate in the early 1900s. However, Frederick's prominence at Carton actually began much earlier in 1891 when his elder brother, Gerald, 5th Duke of Leinster, died prematurely, followed by his wife, Hermione, less than two years later. The three surviving children were all minors; the eldest, Maurice, was not due to come of age until 1908. Thus, the management of the estate passed into the hands of trustees under Frederick (see chapter 16). Arguably, from the early 1890s until his death in 1924, he was the duke of Leinster in all but name (as Maurice would be institutionalised as 'insane' shortly after coming-of-age). Yet, despite the fact that he oversaw the sale of Ireland's most prestigious estate in 1903, virtually nothing is known about him. The main reason for this is that he left few papers and certainly none of a personal nature which might inform on so many aspects of life at Carton during this dramatic period in its history. However, an examination of local newspapers, supplemented by local government records and other sources, allows at least an insight into the political role he assumed, one which traditionally had been expected of the head of the household at Carton. It is this aspect of his life which forms the basis of this essay.

Frederick was born on 18 January 1857 to Charles William FitzGerald (1819–87) and his wife, Caroline Leveson-Gower (1827–87). He was one of 15 children, the eighth child and the third son. Three of his siblings died in infancy and the eldest, a daughter, Geraldine, died aged 19.[1] His parents had married in 1847 shortly before the Leinster family was fully rehabilitated among the royal establishment by the visit of the young Queen Victoria to Carton in August 1849.[2] The visit was public proof that the quiet and diligent loyalty of Frederick's grandfather, the 3rd duke, and of his father, had dissipated any lingering doubts about the allegiance of the FitzGeralds, particularly in the wake of the very public rebellion of Lord Edward FitzGerald in 1798. Throughout Frederick's life the FitzGerald family benefitted from their privileged access to the very highest levels of elite social and political life in the British empire; whereas in Ireland, they benefitted from the residual gratitude of Irish nationalists for the contribution of Lord Edward to the reality and the mythology of rebellion against the Crown. The FitzGeralds, and Frederick in particular, were not slow to exploit these seemingly contradictory advantages when the need arose.

Frederick, like most of the male members of his family, attended Eton and from there went to Sandhurst and thence to the King's Royal Rifle Corps to begin an army career in the expanding British empire. He was listed as a sub-lieutenant in the corps in 1875 and as a lieutenant in 1876.[3] His rapid promotions were probably in large part due to his prominent aristocratic background; at the time, it seems that the only other officer from a higher social background listed for the regiment was its colonel-in-chief, the duke of Cambridge.[4] In 1879 Frederick was ordered to do duty with the Royal Scots Fusiliers as they embarked for India to join the British Expeditionary Force in Afghanistan.[5] The British had always been worried about the Russians' expanding empire encroaching onto their north-west Indian border, which had resulted in the earlier Anglo-Afghan War (1839–1842). From then on, British policy was to support a friendly regime in Afghanistan, to act as a buffer zone, while keeping the trade routes between Russia and British-India open. This worked until 1878 when the Amir, Sher Ali Khan, hesitated to accept British influence, while admitting the Russians to Kabul. At the same time, a British envoy, General Sir Neville Chamberlain, was refused entry to the country at the Khyber Pass and so the British invaded.[6]

On 27 July 1880, British troops under General Burrows were completely defeated by Ayub Khan at Maiwand in the biggest British disaster – and the greatest Afghan victory – of the conflict. Ayub then besieged the remainder of the garrison at Kandahar. General Roberts, commander of the Kabul and Kandahar field force, set out with his army of 10,000 from Kabul on 8 August to relieve Kandahar, which lay over 300 miles away. Frederick FitzGerald was decorated with a medal and two clasps for his role in this conflict, and he may well have been on the famous march from Kabul to Kandahar in 1880 that brought the British victory. Almost immediately, Frederick's regiment was shipped to South Africa to deal with the aftermath of the Zulu uprising there.[7] By now he had been away from Ireland continuously for over five years. In early 1882, now with the rank of captain, Frederick paid a brief visit home to Carton. The *Kildare Observer* claimed that the locals surrounded him and 'peered closely into his face to see what changes an Indian sun had wrought upon his face'.[8] He was still in Maynooth in April 1882, when his sister, Alice, was married in the local church.[9] Reports on both the wedding and Frederick's earlier return from abroad clearly suggest great warmth and regard for the FitzGeralds among the local people around Maynooth.

The idyllic picture of a peasantry and aristocracy displaying harmony and mutually-supportive regard may well be close to the reality of that specific time and place, but it is instructive to note that these glowing reports were published at the height of the Land War. A note announcing that C. S. Parnell's period of detention in Kilmainham Jail was to be extended for a further three months appeared in the same newspaper that reported Frederick's triumphant return.[10] (The wedding of Lady Alice FitzGerald occurred with great glamour and style, on the very same day that Parnell was finally released from prison.[11]) Some of those engaged in the campaign for a better deal for tenants actively challenged the legitimacy of landlordism and almost all involved resented and opposed the type of privilege that the FitzGeralds and other landlords enjoyed.[12] Rent strikes, mass meetings, boycotting and even criminal damage to property were common throughout the country. In Kildare the Land League was well organised and vocal in its agitation.[13] The Carton estate did not escape this agitation. In the 1870s, the 4th duke of Leinster insisted that its tenants agree to the so-called 'Leinster lease' introduced by his father which effectively evaded the provision of the 1870 Land Act that provided for compensation to tenants for improvements they made to their holdings. Resented by hundreds of tenants, the lease became the focus of protracted disaffection and was publicly burned at a Land League meeting in Kildare town in 1881. Indeed, one of the speakers at the meeting promised that the ashes of the lease would be posted the following day to the duke himself.[14] There is no record of it having been received.

One commentator has attributed the beginning of the 'downward spiral' of the dukes of Leinster to the turmoil of the Land War.[15] However, it is difficult to reconcile the alleged breakdown in landlord-tenant relations with the rapturous reception Frederick received in Maynooth in January 1882, or with the tremendous celebrations enjoyed by locals when his sister married a few months later.[16] Indeed, much of the virulence of the Land War that was evident in many parts of the country was, in fact, avoided in County Kildare because of a deal struck between the 4th duke of Leinster and his tenants. Initially, the former offered reductions in rent on the understanding that he would have to lay off many of the labourers directly employed by him. He wanted an agreement that the larger tenants would now employ these men themselves. This was debated throughout the county and some groups of tenants agreed to it. However, in the end the duke offered a reduction without the threat of letting the labourers go. This, being generally acceptable to his tenants, kept the Leinster estate relatively peaceful – at least until the advent of the 1881 Land Act.[17]

Frederick was away from Maynooth for most of the next decade: he left Ireland in 1882 and returned to his regiment which was soon asserting the empire's interests in another theatre of war, this time Egypt, where the ultimate objective was the safety of British ships using the Suez Canal, now government-owned.[18] He was not the only son of a Kildare landlord in Egypt at this time. Richard and George Wolfe, officers in the Royal Irish Fusiliers, were sons of the owner of over 4,000 acres in Kildare and Wicklow.[19] Their regiment was involved in the famous battle of Tel El Kebir in 1882; George Wolfe received the Khedive's Star medal for his efforts that day.[20] Frederick's Royal Rifles arrived in Egypt after this battle but he too was decorated for his exploits later in the campaign. Richard Wolfe, the heir to his family's estate at Forenaughts near Naas, was killed in the battle of Abu Klea in 1885. He was part of a small detachment sent overland to try to relieve General Gordon at Khartoum while the main force travelled by boat. In a 15-minute battle the British force inflicted over 1,000 casualties while losing only 74 of their own men, one of whom was the Kildare man.[21] George Wolfe inherited the estate in his brother's place.[22] Frederick and George Wolfe would later be colleagues on the Kildare County Council for over 20 years.

Frederick was back at Carton in 1887 for the funeral of his father, the 4th duke of Leinster.[23] The duke was buried in the private cemetery in Carton which he had established only a few years earlier for the re-interment of his four children who had pre-deceased him.[24] Frederick's elder brother, Gerald, became the 5th duke of Leinster but he did not live long to enjoy the title, dying of typhoid fever in 1893. As executor of Gerald's will, and chief trustee, Frederick was placed at the centre of the administration of the Leinster estate – along with the estate's land agent, Charles Hamilton. Frederick was also named, along with the duke's widow, Hermione, as legal guardian of the young 6th duke and his two brothers.[25] (He was not living at Carton at the time, his address being given as the Isle of Wight.) Two years later, Hermione died and the guardianship of the three sons of the late duke, namely, Maurice, Desmond and Edward, was now shared between Frederick and Hermione's sister, Lady Cynthia Graham.

From this time on, Frederick lived at Carton with his sister, Mabel, and various combinations of the three young boys, who tended to spend most of their time in England, either with their maternal grandparents, Lord and Lady Feversham, or at school at Eton. According to returns for the 1901 census, Frederick was head of household at Carton and was attended by eight live-in servants (the total number employed is likely to have been higher).[26] Interestingly, none of the servants named in the 1901 census were returned in 1911. Similarly, of the 15 demesne houses occupied by servants in 1901 and the 17 occupied in 1911, only two were in the same family name. Local folk memory describes Frederick as being amorously predatory on the female servants and, if there is an element of truth in this piece of local lore, it may explain the rate of turnover among servants!

The FitzGeralds of Maynooth had a long legacy of active participation in the administration of Kildare, dating back to the Middle Ages, and this would continue for as long as Carton remained in their hands.[27] After settling at Carton, Frederick gradually established himself in the usual areas of interest among the landlords of the county. Ironically, he was first selected for the Kildare County Grand Jury in 1898 just as the legislation, the Local Government (Ireland) Bill, was published by the government to effectively remove all local administrative duties from the grand juries and vest them in democratically elected county councils. Frederick was unfazed by this and threw himself enthusiastically into the task of getting elected to the new bodies. Reform of local government had been on the agenda of liberal European thought and politics for most of the nineteenth century, and it had been attempted in half-hearted ways in Ireland on various occasions. In England, elected county councils replaced the grand juries in 1888 but this was not extended to Ireland until ten years later. It is worth noting that in England the reform resulted in the electorate returning as county councillors the same landowners – more or less – who had controlled the grand juries.[28]

When the bill to introduce the new representative system of local government into Ireland was proposed in 1898 it was met with a strange variety of responses. Unionists were suspicious that it might be the first step on the way to full Home Rule in Ireland; while nationalists thought it might be given as a sop to quell demands for a Home Rule parliament. Others saw the proposals as a 'revolution' that would usher in a new era of democratic control of Irish affairs. Some nationalists were also determined to use the new councils as a training ground for Home Rule governance. Many saw it as a chance to show the world, and the British administration in particular, that the Irish were capable of administering their own affairs.[29] A few voices cautioned about expecting too much from an act that was concerned primarily with collecting rates and repairing the roads. Given the widely-held belief that landlords would lose the control of local government which they had enjoyed for centuries, one assize court judge in Kildare described it as 'an act for the abolition of gentlemen.'[30]

Given the recent history of landlord-tenant relationships in Ireland (outside of Ulster) the election results were inevitable. From a position where they had been completely dominant on the grand juries, unionist landlords were almost completely excluded from membership of the new county councils; the new membership was almost entirely nationalist, with tenant farmers, shopkeepers and publicans predominating. In fact, those elected throughout the country tended to be men who had been actively involved in the land agitation of the 1880s and the rhetoric of the election campaign replayed and recalled that earlier struggle.[31] The county council election in Kildare followed this pattern, but the outcome was somewhat more subtle than the national results would indicate – a reminder that any overall picture of history consists of many nuanced shades and tones.

Among those elected was Frederick FitzGerald. In Kildare there were 21 electoral divisions, with contests in 15 of these. Of the uncontested seats, five were, as one would expect, taken by nationalist candidates, but the sixth, Celbridge, went to a Catholic unionist, Gerald Dease. Dease had been lord chamberlain to several lords lieutenant in Dublin Castle but obviously this did not diminish his reputation amongst the electors in Celbridge, the majority of whom were Catholic nationalists.[32] Another Catholic unionist, Ambrose More O'Ferrall, was elected in Carbury, winning a seat against two nationalist opponents and outpolling their combined vote. He showed some fancy political footwork in dealing with the issue of his unionism, in the following ambiguous manner:

> The county councils were not political organisations ... and politics were foreign to their constitution. For that reason he did not think it necessary in his address to deal with that question (cheers). But, if elected, he would, when burning questions of the day came before them, know how to treat them and without telling the mode, he would do so in a manner that he did not think his unionist friends would be disgusted with (more cheers).[33]

In spite of his unionism, More O' Ferrall was not above using his 'green' ancestry to good electoral effect; he did not demur when one of those who spoke in his favour at his selection as candidate said of him: 'he was thoroughly conversant with county business, one who was in sympathy with the people, a descendant of Rory O'More and one whose forefathers stood up against Cromwell in defence of his country (cheers)'.[34]

 Frederick FitzGerald played a similar card in Maynooth, drawing on the residual memory of the exploits of his ancestor, Lord Edward, during the 1798 rebellion. The previous year's centenary celebrations had brought the FitzGerald family connection back to public memory and on his election posters Frederick's supporters were urged to 'remember the spirit of Lord Edward and 1798'. Not everybody bought this line. A supporter of FitzGerald's electoral opponent, William Rutherford, declared: 'Lord Frederick was a bitter unionist who believed that the Irish people were not fit to be trusted with self government'[35] An editorial in the *Freeman's Journal* urged the electorate to reject all such landlord candidates, describing Frederick as the representative of a family that had oppressed the people of Kildare for centuries in a similar manner to a Russian oligarch.[36] The editorial was very much reflective of the direction which nationalist rhetoric had taken since the beginning of the Land War when all landlords were associated with oppression and decadence, and their homes portrayed as symbols of colonial oppression.

 But Frederick's election, and that of another Kildare landlord, George Wolfe, to the county council serves to illustrate that broad generalisations often hide significant anomalies at local level. Wolfe, too, was a Protestant landlord, owner of some 1,300 acres in the east of the county near Ballymore Eustace and of 2,764 adjoining acres in Wicklow. As noted above, he had served in the British army in Egypt and had inherited his estate on the death of his older brother, Richard, in the same campaign. He stood in his area as a nationalist, advocating that the county councils should be used as the first step in a campaign for Home Rule: 'One hundred and seventeen years ago Grattan used his volunteers to force from the government of that time what is now known as Grattan's parliament. In this year, 1899, they should use this local government act to force Home Rule.'[37] His identification with Grattan's volunteers is noteworthy, particularly in light of his own involvement in the National Volunteers in Kildare in 1914. Wolfe later won a seat for Kildare in Dáil Éireann as a pro-treaty candidate in 1923 and a Cumann na nGaedheal candidate in 1927.[38]

In the country as a whole, the county council elections of 1899 resulted in a complete rout of unionist landlords from local government: 558 nationalists won seats as against 119 unionists. Outside of Ulster the ratio was even starker: unionists winning only 39 of a possible 495 seats.[39] In Kildare, 18 nationalists and only three unionists were returned. The old landlord influence on local government was ended. Fourteen of the nationalists elected had been active participants in the Land War of the 1880s, thus signalling the pivotal role this event had played in the county in terms of having formed political networks and built local political profiles.[40] Yet Frederick FitzGerald's victory was welcomed locally amongst unionists and nationalists alike, and further afield within traditional establishment circles. *The Times* reported that on his arrival back at Maynooth railway station after his election, Frederick was met by his supporters who unhitched the horses from his carriage and pulled him home to Carton themselves.[41] It was nothing more than might have been expected of a class of people who were aware of the importance of the FitzGerald dynasty to the local economy. Frederick was duke in all but name, and the pulling of the cart was a ritual symbolic of loyalty and deference traditionally associated with celebratory events such as this.

At the first meeting of Kildare County Council, Frederick was left in no doubt about the aspirations of the majority when his nationalist colleague proposed a vote in support of Home Rule: 'That we affirm the right of the Irish nation to a full measure of self-government. We accept the Local Government Act as the first installment of the same and call on the imperial parliament to proceed with the further restitution of our rights.'[42] The council further called for an Irish board of agriculture and industries, a Catholic university and for a commission to enquire into the excessive rates charged by the Irish railway companies. The three unionists – Gerald Dease, Ambrose More O'Ferrall and Frederick – abstained from voting on these requests after they were merged in a composite motion calling for Home Rule.

Despite his unionism and prominent membership of the Irish Unionist Alliance, Frederick went on to have a long and distinguished career on the council. His attendance at meetings was highly impressive. In its first year, from April 1899 to April 1900, he attended 11 out of 13 meetings; in 1912–13 he was at all of the meetings, and in his last year on the council, 1919–20, he was at six out of eight, and that at a time when the Irish War of Independence made travel within the county dangerous. He never attended less than half of the meetings in any year.[43] He would also have had to come to accept that, far from being the radical boards of feckless nationalists expected by the unionist press, the council was characterised by conservatism and caution, anxious as they were to disprove those who doubted their ability to administer local affairs and to prove themselves worthy of further responsibility under Home Rule. As property owners themselves, the majority of councillors were also, of course, eager to avoid any increase in the payment of rates which would have appealed equally to Frederick, probably one of the largest ratepayers in the county. The council tended to strike and collect the annual rates in a very diligent and competent fashion. Indeed, for almost all of the time Frederick was a councillor, the rates charged in Kildare remained at or near the level they had been under the grand jury in the 1890s (see Fig.1).

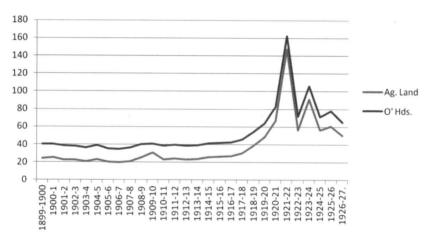

FIGURE 1 *Rates in Kildare, 1899–1927*[44]

The noticeable increase in the years 1907–10 is directly attributable to Frederick's own role in the sale of the Leinster estate to the tenants under the 1903 Wyndham Land Act (see chapter 16). Under this Act almost 45,000 acres of the Leinster estate were purchased by the tenants throughout Kildare. Notably, some of the larger purchasers were themselves county councillors and at all of the land purchase meetings in 1903 councillors were prominent. Both sides seemed happy with the deal, the tenants being advanced the funds to buy the land and the Leinster estate getting not only the generous 25 years' purchase price but also a 12 per cent sale bonus. However, in the spring of 1907, Kildare County Council was informed that, under an obscure subsection of the 1903 Act, over £8,000 of its agricultural grant (the subsidy from central funds to make up for the half-rating of farmland) would be withheld, on account, it was said, of arrears in tenants's repayments of annuities for the loans advanced to buy the farms.

It turned out that arrears were an insignificant part of the problem and the real issue was that the cash was raised by the British government to advance to the tenants from the issue of guaranteed stock. The section of the Act that caused the trouble made the agricultural grant for Ireland liable for any short-fall in the yearly value of the stock. In 1906–7 the value of the stock tumbled and the county councils in Ireland had their agricultural grants cut in propor-tion to the amount of funds advanced to tenants in the respective counties. Since the Leinster estate had received the lion's share of the funds, Kildare County Council's deduction was proportionately far in excess of that in any other county.⁴⁵ The immediate result was a threat by the council to double the rates in County Kildare. There was no particular animosity towards Frederick FitzGerald on the council, which was hardly surprising given that, as noted above, some of the councillors had been tenant purchasers themselves and the chairman, Naas solicitor, Stephen J. Browne, had represented many of them in the negotiations. The chickens had effectively come home to roost and all were complicit. While Frederick attended all of the meetings which considered this crisis, there is no evidence of any of councillors apportioning blame to him. In the end it was decided not to double the rates but to try to make good the short-fall in funding by a combination of a small increase, severe cutbacks to services and deferred payments to suppliers and contractors. It was also decided to take legal action in the form of a 'petition of right' to force the restoration of the withheld funds.⁴⁶ The issue was raised in parliament by the Irish Party leader, John Redmond, and the controversial section of the Act was eventually repealed,⁴⁷ but not before the rate payers of Kildare had to suffer slightly higher rates for a few years until the impact of the deduction passed.

Frederick FitzGerald continued as a county councillor for 21 years but nev-er had to fight an election after 1899. A provision existed under the Local Gov-ernment (Ireland) Act 1898, for elections and new councils every three years, but a significant feature of local government in County Kildare was how very few council seats were, in fact, contested after the first set of elections in 1899. In 1902 for instance, only four out of 22 seats were contested; in 1905, there were three contests and one in 1908. In 1911, there were two elections but in 1914 there was, again, only one. Seats were filled by nominees, usually the incumbent. The local elections due in 1917 were postponed, initially on account of World War One (1914–18) and then because of the deteriorating political and military situation in Ireland.

The result of this lack of political contest was that, by 1920, the same group of councillors had been, more or less, in control of local government since 1899. Furthermore, as noted earlier, given that the majority of nationalist representatives had come together initially as a coherent political group during the Land War of the early 1880s, this local political elite had been able to consolidate its position over a 40-year period before having to give way to a much younger and more radical group of Sinn Féin and Labour candidates in 1920.[48]

Until then, the more moderate nationalists of Kildare County Council were very much at ease with the monarchy and its attendant aristocracy. Thus, in 1903, when King Edward VII (1841–1910) visited Ireland, the chairman of the county council, Stephen Browne, wrote an address of welcome and presented it on behalf of Naas Town Commission. Two other nationalist members of the county council, Matthew Minch and George Wolfe, were formally presented to the king at Dublin Castle; Frederick was also in attendance at this event.[49] The members of Kildare County Council were also among those who formally congratulated the 6th duke of Leinster on his coming-of-age in 1908: 'They might couple with their congratulations the wish that the duke might soon be able to reside amongst them in Kildare and that he might be long spared to carry on the great tradition of his family'. Frederick, as the duke's uncle, thanked the council stating: 'Some day when he is on the county council, I hope he will meet with the same attention and kindness I have always had'.[50] In 1911, when King George V (1865–1936) visited Maynooth College, a committee of welcome asked Stephen Browne to help them draw up their address of welcome. The king was not only visiting the national seminary, thereby paying respect to the Catholic Church, he was also visiting Ireland's only ducal village. The locals were keen to show their support and so when his car arrived at the local Royal Irish Constabulary barracks 'the village folk' greeted him enthusiastically and the town band escorted him to the College where the flower-beds had been laid out, arranged in royal colours.[51]

Three years later when John Redmond called on nationalists to support the British war effort, county councillors were prominent at recruitment meetings throughout Kildare and George Wolfe was the provincial organiser. Councillor Matthew Minch's two sons enlisted, as did the nephew of John Healy.[52] When Frederick's nephew, Desmond, younger brother of the 6th duke, was accidentally killed at the front in May 1916, the council's reaction to his death came at the same meeting as their official response to the Easter Rising and is revealing of the attitude of conservative nationalist Ireland at this crucial point in Irish history. The following was proposed and seconded by nationalists:

> That we, the members of the Kildare County Council, hereby express our sympathy with our colleague, Lord Frederick FitzGerald, and the other members of the Leinster family in their sad bereavement through the death, while on active service in France, of Lord Desmond FitzGerald, and we are confident that the sympathetic knowledge which is shared by an appreciative and grateful people, that he gave his life for his country after a brief but glorious period of service will tend

to mitigate in some degree the great sorrow which they feel for the early ending of a promising and brilliant career.[53]

The sentiment was unequivocal: Desmond FitzGerald's death in the Great War had been in the service of his country, Ireland, and all nationalists were reportedly grateful. Within a few minutes the council then unanimously passed the following motion condemning the recent rebellion (Easter Rising) in Dublin:

> That we, the members of the Kildare County Council, strongly deprecate the recent deplorable action of a section of our countrymen in resorting to force of arms. At the same time we strongly appeal in what we consider the best interests of this country, and the empire as a whole, to the government to extend the greatest possible clemency to the rank and file, who we believe were deceived into taking part in the rising. That we take this opportunity of again recording our unabated confidence in Mr. J. E. Redmond and the Irish parliamentary party, and we thoroughly endorse the attitude they adopted during the crisis we are passing through.[54]

The interests of 'this country' (Ireland) were also those of 'the empire'. However, the events of the following years meant that this type of middle-ground, constitutional nationalism was sidelined. This was first evident at the 1918 general election and emphasised when the much-delayed county council elections were finally held in 1920: very few of the outgoing councillors even stood for election, realising the futility of doing so (most were quite elderly anyway). The only unambiguous old Home Ruler to get re-elected was Michael Fitzpatrick; otherwise all the seats went to Sinn Féin and Labour representatives and the story of Kildare County Council for the next few years centred on the struggle for dominance between Labour and farmers.

Frederick FitzGerald did not stand for election in 1920 and was replaced by Maynooth shopkeeper, Daniel Buckley (1866-1963), now known as Domhnall Ua Buachalla, representing Sinn Féin.[55] Buckley had made a name for himself as a veteran of the 1916 Rising and the attitude towards such men had changed dramatically from the night that the county council decried what they had done in the name of the Irish people. When Frederick died four years later in 1924, he was no more than a glorified caretaker at Carton, the property having been lost to the FitzGerald family in 1922 by his nephew, Edward, the 7th Duke of Leinster.

Frederick straddled that period in Irish history which proved a major watershed for the aristocracy and, in particular, his own family who had played such an important part in the life of Maynooth and County Kildare since the twelfth century. He oversaw the transfer of the most significant estate in Ireland at a remarkable (and highly controversial) price under the 1903 Land Act, as well as the subsequent investment of the funds. He remained at the helm at Carton after the 6th duke was institutionalised and it must have come as a severe blow to him when the eventual heir's reckless behaviour resulted in the transfer of the life interest of the estate to Henry Mallaby-Deeley (1863–1937), the so-called 'forty-shilling tailor'. Unfortunately, as aforementioned, Frederick seems to have left no accessible papers, perhaps as much by design as accident. If any were to surface in the future they would undoubtedly shed light on an intriguing character who lived very much as his ancestors had (and possibly even better-off given the proceeds from the sale of the estate to which he had significant access), and who continued to enjoy a degree of local political power and prestige when most of his peers were denied any form of access to the corridors of political power, even at local level.

NOTES

1   Charles Mosley (ed.), *Burke's Peerage, Baronetage & Knightage*, (3 vols, Wilmington, Delaware, U.S.A., 2003, 107th edn), vol. ii, p. 2299.

2   *Illustrated London News*, 18 Aug. 1849.

3   Nesbit Willoughby Wallace, *A Regimental Chronicle and List of Officers of the 60th, or the King's Royal Rifle Corps, Formerly the 62nd, or the Royal American Regiment of Foot* (London, 1879), p. 282, 284.

4   Ibid., p. 283.

5   *Irish Times*, 3 Feb. 1879.

6   Bryan Robson, *The Road to Kabul* (London, 2007), p. 3; see also, R. K. Webb, *Modern England: From the Eighteenth Century to the Present* (London, 1969), p. 350.

7   Edward T.H. Hutton, *A Brief History of the King's Royal Rifle Corps, 1755–1915* (London, 1917, 2nd edn), pp 23–5.

8   *Kildare Observer* (hereafter *KO*), 21 Jan. 1882.

9   *KO*, 6 May 1882.

10   *KO*, 21 Jan. 1882.

11   *KO*, 6 May 1882.

12   R. V. Comerford, 'Land War' in S. J. Connolly (ed.), *The Oxford Companion to Irish History* (Oxford, 1998), pp 300–1.

13   See Thomas Nelson, *The Land War in Co. Kildare* (Maynooth, 1985).

14   *Illustrated London News*, 8 Jan. 1881.

15   William Nolan, 'The land of Kildare: valuation, ownership and occupation, 1850–1906', in William Nolan and Thomas McGrath (eds), *Kildare: History and Society* (Dublin, 2006), p. 579.

16   *KO*, 21 Jan. 1882; *KO*, 6 May 1882.

17   *KO*, 8 Jan. 1881.

18   Webb, *Modern England*, pp 356–8.

19   *Return for 1870 of the Number of Landed Proprietors...*(167), H.C. 1872 xlv11; *Summary of the Return of Owners of Land in Ireland...*(422), H.C. 1876, lxxx.

20   *Leinster Leader*, 13 Dec. 1941

21   *Encyclopaedia Britannica* (Cambridge,11th edn, 1911), ix, p. 124.

22   *KO*, 28 Mar. 1885.

23   *KO*, 19 Feb. 1887.

24   *KO*, 23 Mar. 1895.

25   *Irish Times*, 5 Feb. 1894.

26   http://www.census.nationalarchives.ie/pages/1901/Kildare/Maynooth/Carton_Demesne/1437790/ (accessed 19 July 2011).

27   Thomas Nelson, 'Kildare County Council, 1899–1926' (Unpublished Ph.D. thesis, NUI Maynooth, 2007), pp 30–9.

28   B. Keith-Lucas, *English Local Government in the Nineteenth and Twentieth Centuries* (London, 1977).

29   *Leinster Leader*, 12 Mar. 1898.

30   *KO*, 26 Feb. 1898.

31   Nelson, 'Kildare County Council', p. 74.

32   Ibid., p. 61.

33   *KO*, 18 Mar. 1899.

34   Ibid. Rory O'More (*c.*1600–55) was a Gaelic chieftain from Laois who played a major role in the 1641 rebellion and was eventually forced into exile. *Freeman's Journal*, 20 Mar. 1899.

35   *Leinster Leader*, 18 Mar. 1899.

36   *Freeman's Journal*, 20 Mar. 1899.

37   *KO*, 18 Mar. 1899.

38   Brian Walker, *Parliamentary Election Results in Ireland, 1918–1992* (Dublin, 1992), p. 112, 121.

39   Virginia Crossman, *Local Government in Nineteenth-Century Ireland* (Belfast, 1994), pp 95–6.

40   Nelson, 'Kildare County Council', pp 71–80.

41   *The Times*, 25 Apr. 1899.

42   Kildare County Council (KCC) minutes, 22 Apr. 1899.

43   Figures from KCC minutes held in Kildare county library local studies department, Newbridge.

44   Nelson, 'Kildare County Council', pp 137–51. 'O'Hd' means 'Other Hereditaments', i.e. all property except farmland.

45   Ibid., p. 140.

46   *KO*, 24 Aug. 1907.

47   *KO*, 19 Dec. 1908.

48   Nelson, 'Kildare County Council', p. 298.

49   *Irish Times*, 25 July, 1903.

50   KCC minutes, 7 Mar. 1908.

51   *KO*, 15 July 1911.

52   Nelson, 'Kildare County Council', p. 204.

53   KCC minutes, 29 May 1916.

54   Ibid.

55   Nelson, 'Kildare County Council', p. 297.

CHAPTER 18

'The Fairy Godfather as Regards the Estate'
Henry Mallaby-Deeley and Carton
1922–37

Terence Dooley

The transfer of the Leinster estate from landlord to tenant proprietors illustrated that the FitzGeralds, like many of the great landowners of Ireland at the time, were effectively bailed out by the British government under the terms of the 1903 Land Act. Undoubtedly the political and social connections cultivated by the family over successive generations, and recent connections with George Wyndham, chief secretary for Ireland (1900–05), and Arthur Balfour, British prime minister (1902–05), ensured that the Leinster estate had qualified as a priority. Given that, after the sale of the estate, the estimated income from investments was around £50,000 per annum and that estate charges that had previously diminished annual rental income were now minimised, the FitzGeralds might very well have survived at Carton much longer into the twentieth century were it not for a convergence of other factors. In 1903, as they rushed to sell their estates, few of the Irish gentry and aristocracy could have foreseen the devastation that would be wrought by the Great War; the decimation of their investment portfolios by the economic depression that followed; the impact of the Irish revolution (1916 to 1923); or the radical terms of post-independence land legislation under which the Irish Land Commission stripped quite a few surviving 'big houses' of their remaining estates.[1]

While these national and international developments were largely outside the control of the FitzGerald family, there were other personal and tragic developments much closer to home that acted as catalysts in their decline; these were the type of personal and family crises which are all too often ignored in any analysis of the fall of the Irish aristocracy.[2] To understand these we have to look at certain aspects of the FitzGerald family history from the 1890s. In 1893, the 5th Duke of Leinster, Gerald FitzGerald (1851–93), died from typhus at the age of 42. His wife, Hermione Duncombe (1864–95), often described as one of the most beautiful women of her generation, died from consumption less than two years later, at the age of 31. The care of the three young boys who survived them, ranging in age from one to six years, was left in the hands of Gerald's brother, Frederick, and Hermione's sister, Lady Cynthia Graham. The eldest of these, Maurice, born in 1887, began life as a bright, healthy young boy but within a few years his mother began to have maternal anxieties about his health and future. She wrote to a trusted friend: 'Kildare, too, is a happy [?] sensitive child & likely to suffer <u>torture</u> with anyone incapable of understanding him – this gives me a great sense of responsibility about the child & a great wish to spare him all the suffering I can.'[3] She did not live to see her fears eventually realised; shortly after coming-of-age in 1908, Maurice was diagnosed with epilepsy and, largely because of medical ignorance of the condition at that time, was confined to an asylum in Edinburgh where he would spend the rest of his life.

In contrast, his younger brother, Desmond, always looked, according to his mother, to be 'bursting with health.'[4] Given that it was believed at the time that those who suffered from epilepsy would die young, Desmond was probably groomed by his uncle, Frederick, who continued to reside at Carton, to eventually succeed to the estate and title. After he completed his education at Eton, Desmond went to the Royal Military College at Sandhurst. During World War One he rose to the rank of major in the 1st Regiment of the Irish Guards. Revealingly, while he was at the Front, close family friends worried about the fate of the family and Carton; when he was wounded early in the war, Dr Donald Pollock, Maurice's personal physician, wrote: 'I am glad that Desmond's wound is no worse. Personally I feel thankful that he is not in the middle of it and may be kept out of it for good. With Ed. as successor things would be too dreadful.'[5] ('Ed' was the youngest of the boys who, even then, was showing signs of profligacy.) Pollock's letter is interesting: it suggests that attempts may have been made to keep Desmond out of the thick of battle. But he was having none of it and, as was the nature of the war in which junior officers were expected to lead their men over the top, Desmond could not be kept out of danger.

Indeed, from an early stage Desmond foresaw a certain patriotic heroism that would come with death, not dissimilar to that shared by other Irishmen of a different political persuasion in 1916, although their sense of 'country' was very different. On 17 November 1914, shortly after reaching the Front, he wrote:

> This is just to say that except for the sorrow it may cause to my dear relations, I have no reason to fear death and I hope this will be a comfort to anybody who sorrows over it. I am most anxious that on no account should there be a memorial service for me and as far as possible that nobody should mourn. I should however like a small tablet put up for me in the Guards Chapel and at Eton where I spent the happiest days of my life. Silence alone can express my love for and gratitude to my relations for all they have done for me. To a great extent I am a futurist but if I am granted to die for my country, it is the one death above all others that I should wish for and gladly accept.[6]

This was a letter composed in the aftermath of a period of slaughter at the Front when the Irish Guards had suffered terrible losses. The day before he had written to his Aunt Dolly, the wife of Henry FitzGerald (1863–1955), that 'the casualties have been so awful that I shall not find more than 2 officers out of the 30 that started with me and not so many as 100 men out of the original lot'.[7] Six months later, his battalion suffered further decimation at the Battle of Festubert (15–27 May 1915) but he showed the type of leadership qualities that his uncle Frederick hoped he would someday bring to the management of Carton. The battalion doctor, W. H. L. McCarthy, later wrote:

> I will never forget his cheery optimism during and after those days in May when the battalion had such heavy casualties at Festubert. I myself felt then that the spirit of the battalion was broken forever, our losses in officers and men were so serious. But Desmond, with wonderful confidence and capacity, devoted himself at once to the task of building up the unit afresh, and before many weeks had passed the old spirit and tradition had returned.[8]

Desmond was awarded the Military Cross and mentioned twice in dispatches. But it seems that Festubert had left a deep psychological mark on him; thereafter, like many of his fellow aristocratic officers he felt a sense of inevitability about his death. He was killed on 3 March 1916. In the end, it was more of an accident: it seems that the chaplain whom he was accompanying picked up a live hand grenade that exploded wounding him but killing Desmond instantly. Immediately upon hearing the news Edward, Prince of Wales (1894–1972), wrote to Desmond's aunt, Cynthia Graham:

> Please forgive my troubling you with a letter at such a time as this, but I must ask you to accept my very sincere sympathy on the great loss you have sustained. I got a wire this evening to say that dear Desmond had been accidentally killed in a bombing accident at Calais. It is one of the greatest blows or shocks I have ever had for in Desmond's death I have lost my greatest friend. I can't yet realise what has happened or bring myself to think I shall never see him again ... It is too terribly tragic for me to be able to express myself better ... Please do not bother to answer this; but I can't help writing to you who I know was ever first in Desmond's thoughts! He was my greatest friend and that is really why I write.[9]

While obviously extremely poignant, this letter also highlighted the extent to which the FitzGeralds's social standing had continued to allow them access to the highest echelons of British society.

All this while, Edward, the youngest of the three boys, (who, it should be noted, had a decent wartime record until wounded) had lived something of a reckless and carefree youth. In 1913, at the age of 21, he married May Etheridge, the so-called 'pink-pyjama girl' of Shaftesbury Theatre, London; it was a marriage scorned in aristocratic circles and was to be short-lived, not because of the disdain heaped upon him but because of his own lifestyle. He spent lavishly and when he could not get access to family allowances simply turned to moneylenders, one of the earliest of whom, William Cooper Hobbs, charged him extortionate interest rates of 400 per cent. But easy access to money, facilitated by the mere fact that he was a duke's brother, allowed him to luxuriate in extravagance and thus he recalled many years later: 'The world was as rosy as the pink champagne I drank at the Cavendish Hotel'.[10]

In 1914, a year after his marriage, he was declared bankrupt for the first time, at the age of 27. It was then that he first met Henry Mallaby-Deeley (1863–1937). Edward would later claim that they were introduced by a man named Fraser, the son of a Scottish gillie: 'a strange individual who delighted in meeting young men in trouble ... whose business was to introduce them to money-lenders and then collect a nice commission.'[11] But despite Edward's mythologizing to that effect, Henry Mallaby-Deeley was no ordinary money-lender. Henry (also known as Harry) was born in 1863, the son of William Deeley, a prosperous oil merchant who lived at Curzon Park in Chester. He was educated at Shrewsbury School and later graduated as a barrister from Trinity College, Cambridge, but, it seems, he never actually practiced. Instead he entered the world of financial investment and property speculation, becoming possibly the most daring and successful real estate dealer of the early twentieth century. He first rose to public prominence in 1913 when it was reported that he had purchased the duke of Bedford's Covent Garden property in London, the *New York Times* estimating its worth at $50 million. By 1918, he had become Conservative MP for Willesden East and was created a baronet in 1922. He was also a leading golfer who played off scratch at the Prince's Golf Club at Mitcham Commons, Croydon, a course which he re-designed himself in the 1890s. In fact, he was described in 1914 by Josiah Newman, editor of the American magazine *Golf*, as 'the finest amateur golf architect in the world.'[12]

As a result of Mallaby-Deeley's intervention, Edward's 1914 bankruptcy was annulled on 9 July 1918.[13] Under the terms of a legally binding agreement, Mallaby-Deeley agreed to pay off Edward's debts of over £67,000 – estimated at around £16.4 million in today's terms [14] – and to pay him £1,000 per annum (tax free) as an allowance. The pay off was that if Edward inherited the title of duke of Leinster, Mallaby-Deeley would become the owner of Carton and all the income from the estate entailed with the dukedom. Edward's naivety and his desperation for money was a dangerous combination in face of Mallaby-Deeley's financial astuteness. It was said of the latter that:

> ... when the idea of acquiring any particular property had occurred to him he would follow it up with an interview with the owner, and usually, if the latter had the least intention of disposing of his interest, Mallaby-Deeley would come from the meeting place with a half sheet of notepaper recording the proposed contract.[15]

Mallaby-Deeley very quickly insured Edward's life for £300,000 because, as he put it, of 'his mode of life & family history.'[16] The mention of 'family history' probably refers to Maurice's state of mind, which Mallaby-Deeley may have feared was genetic, but he was more concerned with Edward's 'mode of life'. Two examples will suffice to show grounds for Mallaby-Deeley's fears: in July 1922, five months after inheriting the title of 7th duke of Leinster, Edward placed a huge bet of £3,000 that he would drive from London to Aberdeen in less than 15 hours. Driving a Rolls Royce, he made the journey of just over 400 miles (or 650 kilometres) with some time to spare. He then tried to accept another bet to cross the Atlantic in a 36-foot ketch (a two-masted sailing boat), but Mallaby-Deeley forbade this endeavour claiming that it might threaten his life; Edward lost the £1,000 deposit he had paid on the ketch.

Mallaby-Deeley became the legal owner of Carton in 1922 but never considered a move to Carton; if he had, how might he have been received? Lore has it 'that he would have been shot if he set foot there.' While that was hardly likely, there certainly was an outpouring of popular support and sympathy for the FitzGeralds and a latent disdain directed at the largely anonymous 'usurper'. Shortly after news of the transfer of Carton broke in June 1922, the local nationalist newspaper extolled the role of the FitzGeralds as patriots and rebels, from Garret Oge (Gearóid Óg) in the fifteenth century through to his rebellious grandson, Silken Thomas, and on to the iconic Edward of the 1798 United Irishmen rebellion:

They [the FitzGeralds] were not many generations in the country until having made common cause with the people they became more Irish than the Irish themselves. For centuries the Geraldines held a foremost place in the Irish national struggle. The names of Garret Oge, Silken Thomas and Lord Edward are as imperishable as Irish history itself.[17]

However, underpinning any local apprehensions was the more immediate fear of economic loss to the area, fuelled by rumours that the staff numbers on the estate were to be reduced. The estate agent, Charles Hamilton, felt it necessary to point out to Mallaby-Deeley that 'Carton has been run in the past with the view of giving as much employment as possible to the people in Maynooth.'[18] In the early years Mallaby-Deeley accepted this advice and interfered minimally; in fact, he raised the farm labourers' wages to 34s. per week, four shillings above the county average. Moreover, Frederick FitzGerald, who was still resident in the house, was allowed to retain a large indoor staff.[19] Frederick was certainly not shy about writing to Henry, regularly requesting substantial sums of money (usually around £2,000) for expenses in running Carton, which, it should be added, Mallaby-Deeley was not legally obliged to provide.

The first two account books sent by the trustees to Mallaby-Deeley showed that prior to his agreement with Edward, now 7th Duke of Leinster, the Leinster estate had been running at a loss of over £8,000 per annum, which had to be covered by the dividends from English investments. It was 'admitted that the rate of expenditure in the [6th] duke's lifetime had been lavish'. While a portion of this pertained to the 6th duke's medical expenses at Craighouse in Edinburgh, much of the rest could be put down to the ducal lifestyle being enjoyed by Frederick FitzGerald. Mallaby-Deeley was not prepared to support this level of expenditure and he wrote to Frederick inviting him to prepare a statement 'for certain economies in administration'. This Frederick did, but 'it showed an estimated expenditure not much less than that which was made during the duke's lifetime.'[20] It is probably safe to conclude that a certain amount of peevishness on Frederick's behalf led him to test Henry's resolve. In 1923 around £9,000 was again diverted from the trust investments to cover 'estate expenses'.[21] In this way the invested capital was dwindling slowly but surely, much to Mallaby-Deeley's annoyance. In May 1923, one of Frederick's legal advisors, Henry Nix, calculated that income from the Leinster investments had now diminished to around £23,500 per annum, less than half of what it had been a decade earlier.[22]

Consequently, Mallaby-Deeley announced he would sell the reversionary rights to Carton to some member of the family or to the trustees – 'but to no other person' – for £180,000, with £5,000 to be paid on deposit.[23] The eminent London lawyer, Charles Ashworth James, advised the trustees that 'if something is not done, there is a danger and even a probability that Carton will be lost to the family forever'.[24] The trustees, however, did not make a move. His offer refused, Mallaby-Deeley now demanded quarterly estimates of expenditure from Frederick FitzGerald and Charles Hamilton, the least he could expect, he contended, given 'the position he [was] entitled to occupy'.[25] When the first quarterly report arrived on 1 December 1924, Mallaby-Deeley was annoyed that proposed expenditure had not been reduced and so he insisted again that costs 'be further materially decreased, consistently with the due preservation of the property in proper repair.'[26] Of note here, is the fact that he constantly insisted that Carton was to be maintained to high standards.

Frederick FitzGerald died in March 1924 and, in the weeks that followed, the cook and a number of servants were made redundant at Carton. While Mallaby-Deeley was concerned about 'the very heavy and unnecessary cost' of the house, he was careful to balance any redundancies against 'causing friction and hardship' or 'any ill feeling'; he accepted Hamilton's advice to reduce indoor staff and estate workers 'in a gradual way' and to pay those made redundant a gratuity of £1–2 per annum.[27] Meanwhile, the demesne continued to be farmed as Hamilton, the agent, later told Mallaby-Deeley: 'we are more or less bound to do a certain amount of tillage to prevent the government from interfering with the demesne.' This was one way to circumvent the compulsory acquisition terms of the 1923 Land Act which gave the state powers to compul-sorily acquire lands deemed necessary for the relief of local congestion. How-ever, in May 1924, as the economic and agricultural crises worsened, 16 labourers at Carton were let go.[28] Two months later Hamilton was happy to report to his employer that the redundancies were likely to save the estate around £3,000 annually but warned that any more lay-offs would 'cause a lot of hardship and lead to trouble and distress in Maynooth which I think right to be avoided.' A year later farm wages on the estate[27] were reduced and the so-called harvest bonus abolished.[29] It led to a brief standoff with the Irish Transport and General Workers' Union.[30] To allay Mallaby-Deeley's concerns, Hamilton assured him: 'I expect to keep Carton up just as well if not better with the reduced number of men.'[31]

For a few months after Frederick's death, Carton remained empty except for a handful of servants. In July 1924, Mallaby-Deeley's private secretary wrote to Hamilton: 'Please let Sir Harry know what can be done, as he cannot go on bearing this enormous expense for the benefit apparently of nobody at all, and so far as he knows none of the family seem to evince any interest in the matter.'[32] Hamilton suggested allowing Edward's spinster aunts, to live there. Given his close relationship with the family, the content of his letter and the tone were hardly remarkable: 'They are most anxious', he wrote to Henry,

> ... for Carton to be preserved as the home of the Leinster family and are most grateful to you for what you have done ... I have always heard all the members of the family I have met say how well you have acted about Carton in the last two years and how much they hoped that the place would be kept up and come back to the family eventually.[33]

Nesta subsequently moved in and Henry allowed her to retain a skeleton staff – for which he bore full financial liability.

By the late 1920s, even the shrewdest and most successful of businessmen found it difficult to maintain previous lifestyles and Mallaby-Deeley was no exception. On 23 October 1929, just a week before the New York Stock Exchange crashed on Black Tuesday, he sent a cheque for £1,000 to Hamilton, regretting that it could not be the £2,000 he requested; he informed his agent he would not have it until his dividend in the London and North Eastern Railway Com-pany was paid.[34] Over the next few years, Henry's financial difficulties wors-ened as evidenced in a letter of Hamilton's in 1932: 'I fully realise the difficulties Sir Harry has owing to increase of taxation both income tax and super tax in England and also the war loan conversion I know have hit him very hard.'[35] Hamilton was referring to fact that the standard rate of income tax had increased from 5.8 per cent in 1914–15 to 30 per cent in 1920–21 and did not fall below 20 per cent in the late 1920s. Mallaby-Deeley had also been one of the largest single contributors to the war loan; in 1932 the British government took the decision to convert 5 per cent war loan bonds (the largest single block of the national debt) to new 3.5 per cent bonds, greatly diminishing his investment.[36]

That same year in Ireland, the beginning of the so-called Economic War with Britain had a devastating impact on the Irish agricultural economy. At a local level, Hamilton pointed out that the letting (or conacre) value of lands plummeted, while the value of fattening cattle showed a heavy loss. Great houses such as Carton were now, more than ever, proverbial white elephants on the landscape. Rather than pay the hefty rates imposed by the new Fianna Fáil government, hundreds of owners simply abandoned them and had their roofs removed. At Carton, economic exigencies demanded that labourers' wages be reduced again, this time to 25s a week – a dramatic cut from the 34s paid a decade earlier. Charles Hamilton pointed out other areas where cutbacks could be made, for example, having Nesta FitzGerald live at Kilkea Castle instead of Carton would save the wages of the butler (£100), the cook/housekeeper (£52), and the coachman (£90 without board wages). But Henry was reluctant to disturb Nesta and the elderly butler who had been employed by the 5th duchess of Leinster in the 1890s.[37] At any rate, he could see no alternative; in the existing economic climate it was unlikely that another tenant would be secured. In December 1932 Hamilton reported that the Shannon Electrical Scheme had got as far as the town of Maynooth but the £1,500 required to install the electric light at Carton was prohibitive: 'Wiring costs a good deal,' he informed Henry, 'and nobody but a rich American would take it [Carton].'

In 1937, a year after Edward had been declared bankrupt for the third time with debts of £140,000, Henry Mallaby-Deeley died. Years later, Edward recalled their first meeting and remembered Henry as a 'well-dressed, shrewd and charming' man.[38] The latter two adjectives hint that he may have wanted the readership of the tabloid to which he sold his life-story to feel that he had been somehow duped, but ultimately it was that meeting that probably saved Carton. Given Edward's track record, it would be difficult to imagine that the house would have survived in a better state into the late 1940s (when it was sold by Mallaby-Deeley's family) if he had inherited. It would most likely have been abandoned just as hundreds of other big houses had been – in a short radius of Maynooth alone, Donadea, Hortland and Rathcoffey were amongst the houses abandoned to decay.

Edward's own family later recognised the contribution and generosity of Mallaby-Deeley. Gerald FitzGerald (1914–2004), the 8th Duke of Leinster, claimed that his father had simply made a bad deal and Henry a good one. Edward's granddaughter, Rosemary FitzGerald (b. 1939), claimed that Henry and his son, Meyrick, behaved 'most honourably throughout the entire history' of their dealings with her family.[39] A good illustration of Henry's consideration towards the family is evident in a decision taken by him in September 1926 when approached by Hamilton, the agent, for money for a new boiler at Carton.

Henry replied to the request: 'I think one ought to be installed, it is not fit for Lady Nesta to be there in the winter without one.'[40] Under the terms of the original agreement, Mallaby-Deeley was under no obligation to spend any of his personal income on boilers or any other form of maintenance at Carton, but he did, and this was not just out of consideration to the elderly tenants; he was at all times adamant that Carton should not fall into dilapidation. He was equally considerate (as much as he could be in the economic circumstances of the time) of the repercussions that the decline of the estate as a key local employer might have on the local community.

Henry Mallaby-Deeley evidently took a certain pride in preserving Carton. In 1930 he wrote to Hamilton: 'Lord Frederick wrote me not long before he died that I had been the fairy godfather as regards the estate, which, without me, would long ago have been in the hands of the d[uke]'s Jew moneylenders,' the reference here being to Frederick Seymour Salaman whose proceedings against Edward as a result of his second bankruptcy resulted in a major sale of Carton contents in the 1920s.[41] That Edward was declared bankrupt twice more before World War Two (1939–45) is probably evidence enough of Mallaby-Deeley's assertion.

NOTES

1   For the wider context of decline, see Terence Dooley, *The Decline of the Big House in Ireland: A Study of Irish Landed Families 1860–1960* (Dublin, 2001).

2   This will be developed in a forthcoming book by this author, *The Decline and Fall of the Dukes of Leinster: Love, War, Debt and Madness* (Dublin, 2014).

3   Hermione Leinster to Evelyn de Vesci, n.d., Somerset Records Office, DD/DRU/90. Unless otherwise stated, the manuscripts cited below are in private possession.

4   Ibid.

5   Quoted in Michael Estorick, *Heirs and Graces: The Claims to the Dukedom of Leinster* (London, 1981), p. 151.

6   Note written by Desmond FitzGerald, 17 Nov. 1914.

7   Desmond FitzGerald to Aunt Dolly, 16 Nov. 1916.

8   Copy W. H. L. McCarthy to Lord de Vesci, 2 Apr. 1916.

9   Edward, Prince of Wales, to Lady Cynthia Graham, 3 Mar. 1916.

10   Quoted in Marcus Scriven, *Splendour and Squalor: The Decline and Fall of Three Aristocratic Dynasties* (London, 2009), p. 35.

11   Quoted in ibid.

12   See http://www.mitchamcommon.org/golfclub.htm (accessed 17 Nov. 2009).

13   'Official Receiver's report to the court heard on 25 June 1953', The National Archives (UK), PRO, B 9/953.

14   Scriven, *Splendour & Squalor*, p. 36.

15   See: http://www.mitchamcommon.org/golfclub.html (accessed 17 Nov. 2009).

16   Henry Mallaby-Deeley to Charles Hamilton, 16 Aug. 1924.

17   *Leinster Leader*, 17 June 1922.

18   Charles Hamilton to Henry Mallaby-Deeley, 8 Apr. 1924.

19   Ibid., 3 Apr. 1924.

20   Freshfields Leese and Munns to Johnson Raymond-Barker & Co., 18 Jan. 1923.

21   Cecil Raymond-Barker to Frederick FitzGerald, 26 Nov. 1923.

22   Henry Nix to Frederick FitzGerald, 30 May 1923.

23   Duke of Leinster's estate: opinion of C. Ashworth James, 29 May 1923.

24   Ibid.

25   Freshfields Leese and Munns to Johnson Raymond-Barker & Co., 18 Jan. 1923.

26   Freshfields, Leese, Munns to Charles Hamilton, 1 Dec. 1924.

27   Henry Mallaby-Deeley to Charles Hamilton, 12 Apr. 1924, 16 Aug. 1924.

28   Ibid., 10 May 1924; Charles Hamilton to Henry Mallaby-Deeley, 24 May 1924; Charles Hamilton to Henry Mallaby-Deeley, 5 Dec. 1932.

29   Charles Hamilton to Henry Mallaby-Deeley, 8 Apr. 1924, 24 July 1924.

30   Thomas Kennedy to Charles Hamilton, 29 May 1925.

31   Charles Hamilton to Henry Mallaby-Deeley, 12 May 1924.

32   Ibid., 24 July 1924.

33   Ibid., 21 July 1924, 24 July 1924.

34   Henry Mallaby-Deeley to Charles Hamilton, 23 Oct. 1929.

35   Charles Hamilton to Mr Arnott, 14 Aug. 1932.

36   *The Times*, 15 Aug. 1932.

37   Charles Hamilton to Mr Arnott, 14 Aug. 1932; Charles Hamilton to Henry Mallaby-Deeley, 5 Dec. 1932.

38   Estorick, *Heirs and Graces*, p. 12.

39   Quoted in Scriven, *Splendour and Squalor*, p. 37.

40   Henry Mallaby-Deeley to Charles Hamilton, 29 Sept. 1926.

41   Ibid., 1 Apr. 1930.

CHAPTER 19

The FitzGerald Legacy

Christopher Ridgway

The vicissitudes of the FitzGerald family and their estate at Carton might easily prompt one to reach for Edward Gibbon's seminal text, *The History of the Decline and Fall of the Roman Empire*, for here is a grand tale of decline and fall. Unsurprisingly, however, the narrative that encompasses their great Palladian mansion is more nuanced and more continuous than might appear at first sight. For Gibbon (1737–94) the fall of the Roman empire resulted, ultimately, in a series of spectacular ruins and monuments and a corpus of writing that was transformed into one of the founding narratives for Western civilisation. The traces of the past at Carton have not vanished so comprehensively, and significantly this is a narrative that continues today albeit without the FitzGeralds.

The fate of Carton exemplifies perfectly the question raised by the English author Simon Jenkins: 'which lasts longer, a house or a family?' Jenkins concedes that usually the house outlasts the family, and at Carton this has been true since the FitzGeralds' departure in 1949.[1] The story of Carton and the FitzGeralds is one that is characterised by triumphs and reversals. Among the great accomplishments was the consolidation of their lands (eventually totalling almost 70,000 acres); the building of the mansion by Richard Castle in 1739 and its remodelling less than a century later by Richard Morrison; the elevation of the family first as earls of Kildare and then as dukes of Leinster, thereby becoming the premier titled family in Ireland; their distinguished artistic patronage with the Lafranchini brothers' decoration of the Gold Saloon; the creation of the Chinese Room by Emily, countess of Kildare; the building of the Shell Cottage; the fashioning of the 1,100-acre demesne, circumscribed by its five-mile perimeter wall; and the commissioning of a set of topographical views by William Ashford.

Beyond this corner of Kildare the FitzGeralds signalled their importance nationally with the building of Leinster House in Dublin, their grant of land to St Patrick's College, Maynooth, and a life of political activity across successive generations. As befitted a family with such wealth and pedigree the FitzGeralds were made to strut the grandest stage possible. Indeed it is hard to think of any other family or estate in Ireland that could command such levels of social, political and cultural influence for so many centuries. Indeed, one would be hard pressed to find many equivalent families in England: obvious counterparts might be the ducal families of the Churchills and the Cavendishes with their spectacular creations at Blenheim and Chatsworth; and perhaps the Cecils of Hatfield House, a political dynasty that included both Robert Cecil (1563–1612) and the 3rd Marquis of Salisbury (1830–1903). Such parallels could be debated endlessly but whether Churchills, Cavendishes, Cecils, or even other great families like the Howards, Percys, or Russells, such English examples are all marked by one enormous difference. These families are still attached to their estates, even if they have largely stepped down from national political life.

The FitzGeralds' triumphs are, of course, offset by calamities: the rebellion of Silken Thomas; the death of Lord Edward FitzGerald in 1798; fire at Carton in 1855; indebtedness and profligacy of staggering proportions; the enigmatic machinations of Harry Mallaby-Deeley; untimely death, bankruptcy, and finally the relinquishing of Carton. While they are not the only landed family to have experienced such an implosion of fortune, their later decline must be understood in the context of Irish political upheaval, as land war yielded to land acts and the massive disposal of estate holdings, followed by disastrous reinvestment. The FitzGerald family and their estates dwindled in scale, wealth, and influence, and they showed a marked inability to hold on to what remained, let alone manage any diminished estates prudently.

But as with Gibbon, in surveying this majestic sweep of accomplishment and deliquescence, one is profoundly aware of a narrative that has etched itself upon Irish history. This very volume, offering the fruits of research that were first aired at a conference in 2010, offers an assessment of the multiple strands of life and activity on the part of the FitzGeralds and their seat in Kildare. Carton House and its history are a major focus of this work, much of which, admittedly, is refracted through the FitzGerald family. Because, in Simon Jenkins's words, the house endures, the watershed of 1949 does not signal the end of this narrative: indeed it could be argued that more has happened at Carton in recent decades than in the previous 100 years.

1949 is exactly 40 years before the, briefly fashionable, concept of 'the end of history' was first articulated; and many would concur with this assessment in relation to Carton after 1949. The departure of the family marked a definitive hiatus in the story of the house and family as an integrated ensemble. Many would claim that to take away the family is to diminish the house and estate; cut adrift from its founding inhabitants and their successors the house and its history comes to a halt. This is a challenge that has been faced by countless houses and estates in the twentieth century: ownership surrendered in the face of intractable pressures (money, death, sustainability, or, in more extreme circumstances, political hostility and violence). The retreat of the family often entailed the disposal of land, farms and properties, as well as collections and archives (in the case of Carton this meant crateloads of treasures sold to the American newspaper magnate Randolph Hearst). What is left is merely a shell for the new occupier.

The new occupant may or may not revere all that has gone before, and even if they do choose to respect and preserve the past, it is of course not their own past. Fresh ownership of a house might mark an entirely new departure, but it can also occasion a subtle and respectful engagement with history. Such crisis points of transition abound across Europe as numerous houses and their owners gave way to new forms of occupation. Buildings were institutionalised, turned into schools, state enterprises, museums, corporate headquarters, or hotels. For many of these new owners the imperative of historical continuity did not fall within their remit; a charitable institution, or commercial organisation, must look to answer to its own directives before engaging extensively in the business of conservation and interpretation. It can be difficult to justify expenditure outside of the core mission. Beyond making the structure sound and secure, money for further conservation, in both a physical and intellectual sense, is generally not available. While new owners in old buildings will often throw up conflicting priorities, there are also examples of where the two do combine successfully. The union can be harmonious and fruitful.

To this must be added the idea of public access. Even the grandest houses were open in the past to visitors, whether these were the handfuls of individuals furnished with the correct social credentials, or, later in the railway age, early mass-excursionists admitted by ticketed entrance. There are many instances of houses that once granted access but whose subsequent owners retreated behind locked gates; at Carton the 5th duke chose to open the grounds to the public – only for Frederick to close the gates in the 1890s. More positively, since the end of the Second World War, there have been a multitude of examples of houses throwing open their doors as owners take advantage of the boom in heritage tourism. In many cases this has been achieved through the transfer of the property to guardian bodies such as the Office of Public Works, or the National Trust, and English Heritage in Britain, all of whom manage a growing portfolio of the built heritage that is recognised as part of the national patrimony in their respective jurisdictions. Under suitable management policies, physical access and intellectual access combine to offer a visitor attraction of considerable calibre. As is well-recognised, these actions not only safeguard the past, but also ensure that the house, the estate, the collections, and even the families in question, have a future that is both sustainable, and which is also predicated upon the public value of this endeavour.

As the fortunes of the FitzGeralds contracted in the late nineteenth and early twentieth centuries, so too did any sense of this noble seat and noble family playing a significant role in national affairs. Beleagured by financial and political adversity, the best Carton could hope for was merely to hold on. Aside from its manifest decline, Carton was also representative of a governing elite that embodied a style of ruling by the 'haves' over the 'have-nots'. Those who were hostile to the 'Big House' would have considered that such families deserved the ruin brought upon themselves by a combination of their own imprudence or the rise of a new social and political order. The reputation of Carton was decidedly mixed, however, and the FitzGerald family were able to invoke nationalist sympathies through the figures of Silken Thomas and Lord Edward FitzGerald; the latter's martyrology is even said to have helped spare Carton from the incendiary fate suffered by so many big houses during the Irish war of independence and the civil war.

This ineluctable financial and social dismemberment was accompanied by a sense of the past that became increasingly mute as the FitzGeralds literally turned in upon themselves. It is no coincidence that this climacteric is matched by a paucity of understanding – much about these terminal years remains obscure. A great deal still requires more investigation: Terence Dooley has only just begun to unlock the actions and motivations of Mallaby-Deeley and the family settlements of this time; little is known about the requisition of the house from 1939 to 1945; and even less is understood of the final sale to, and ownership by, the Brocket family after 1949.

The estate was sold for an estimated £80,000. It continued to be farmed with some success, and the house was partially mothballed. Even when occupied, only a fraction of the interiors would be utilised and there were no longer cadres of servants to run a full and permanent household on the scale of old. Had Carton been an English home it is very possible that a way would have been found to transfer house and estate in some form to the National Trust (or perhaps a local authority). It would not be hard to imagine a figure such as James Lees-Milne visiting the house in the 1940s and entering into discussions with the family.[2] But this was not an option available in Ireland.

An auspicious moment arose in the 1950s when Desmond and Mariga Guinness leased Carton, and in 1958, wholly appropriately, the couple (re) founded the Irish Georgian Society at Carton. Here was a union between occupant and building that was apt and productive. Carton, the grandest Palladian house in Ireland, cherished and inhabited by the doyen of one of the country's foremost preservation and lobbying bodies for the built heritage. The limelight continued to flicker glamorously in the 1960s with well-publicised visits by international celebrities including Prince Rainier and Princess Grace of Monaco, Mick Jagger, Marianne Faithful, Peter Sellars and Julie Andrews. But for all the dedication of Desmond Guinness and his Georgian colleagues there was a limit to what could be achieved during their period of tenancy. There was no foundation from which to create a secure future. The FitzGerald universe had atomised, with much of the collections dispersed to the Hearst residence at

San Simeon in California or on the art market; the fragmented archives deposited in the Public Record Office in Northern Ireland; and the family relocated to more modest dwellings in Oxfordshire. Crucially, however, the house and demesne remained intact, although it was no longer possible to speak of Carton and the FitzGeralds in the same – singular – way.

Yet the grandeur of the house was at odds with the realities of the estate, which struggled as a going concern. In 1977 Carton was sold once more, for £1.5 million, to Powerscreen International Ltd, an engineering company based in County Tyrone, which was looking to relocate to the Republic in the face of the upsurge of violence north of the border. In 1988 one of the directors, Lee Mallaghan, assumed control of Carton at which point the remarkable story of Carton's renaissance really begins.[3]

Years of decline throughout the twentieth century meant that the house, park, and outbuildings were in poor repair. The estate was not economically sustainable despite a 600-acre farm operation, and although dairy farming continued, with successful breeding trials resulting in very high-yield cattle, these herds were twice decimated in the 1990s. While still functioning as a company headquarters, Carton was presented with the challenge faced by countless similar properties of how to adapt and survive. The Mallaghan family decided to transform Carton into a high-class sporting and leisure resort, building a golf course and a hotel. Planning permission was finally granted in 1991, but development was tightly bound by restoration requirements.

The Dublin-based firm of Murray O'Laoire Architects was commissioned to undertake a full architectural survey of the house, following which restoration work began on the stonework in 2000. The house is built of large blocks of dark limestone which, on account of the different quarries used, have a mottled appearance. After cleaning, nearly one-third of the stonework had to be repaired, with grafts or new stone, and the ferrous metal cramps were replaced with stainless steel ones. A policy of minimum intervention was adopted, thus rotten timbers were spliced out on many of the 230 windows, and only damaged glass was replaced. At the roof level, however, more than half the balustrading had to be replaced; the decayed leadwork on the roof was renewed, and the cement-based renders on the chimneys were replaced with lime mortar.

The interiors of the house had, with the exception of the ground-floor, lain largely dormant for several decades. The transformation into a luxury hotel offered similar opportunities for high-class restoration. The upper rooms were modernised as bedrooms, and the ground-floor rooms were recovered as public spaces. Much of the original plasterwork, chimneypieces, and carved fittings survive, and the redecoration of these interiors was informed at all times by careful historical analysis, helped by the discovery of an 1818 inventory for each room.[4]

The quality of restoration indoors and outdoors has been of a very high order, and perhaps the most astonishing part of this operation is that it has been privately funded. Carton has received no state aid, nor any funding from Europe. How the Mallaghan family was able to finance this has caused controversy in some quarters, but at the same time has pointed to an interesting state of affairs with regard to country houses in Ireland. It is a truism that for a house and estate to survive it has to be economically sustainable, and in Ireland as in the UK, more and more houses, whether in private or institutional ownership have, in the face of falling returns from such traditional enterprises as farming and forestry, turned to a variety of commercial enterprises in order to generate revenue streams that support restoration and secure future ownership. For the Mallaghan family, who had no wish to occupy Carton themselves as late twentieth-century grandees, their vision was to transform a moribund estate into a centre of activity, to bring it back to life as a place where large numbers of people could visit and pursue recreational activities.

At the heart of this lay the transformation of the house into a hotel, which involved a substantial degree of new-build, and the fashioning of two championship golf courses in the demesne. For many people the words 'golf course', 'hotel' and 'country house' spark an almost irrational (although in many cases sadly justifiable) degree of fear and loathing. At Carton this is not so. Today two-thirds of the demesne is taken up with the O'Meara Course and the links-style Montgomerie Course. These courses did not require extensive excavation and reshaping of the parkland, which had always been characterised by vales and slopes of varying steepness – ideal terrain for golfers. The grassland now divides between fairway and rough, and these wide expanses are punctuated with clumps of mature trees. A huge programme of re-planting has also been undertaken, with 150,000 beech and oak trees planted in a 40-metre band inside the perimeter wall. The courses at Carton have won several prestigious golf awards, but perhaps none more significant than the Federation of European Greenkeepers Association 'Committed to Green' initiative in 2006 in recognition of its successful environmental practices.

The Rye Water to the south of the house, a natural water course re-fashioned in the 1760s, has been dredged and is today stocked with salmon fry; these were hatched at a local school as part of a classroom project before being released into the waters. The parkland habitat supports red deer, otters, badgers, owls, buzzards, kingfishers and night jars; and the quality of the river water has encouraged the presence of lamprey, crayfish and the delightfully named vertigo snail. The success of these projects is an important reminder that the flora and fauna contribute every bit as much to the identity of an estate as do family, architecture and collections.

Visitors today who approach from the Dublin Road to the south of the house follow the original meandering drive for nearly a mile through an enormous expanse of green, before crossing the Rye Water. Carton House sits majestically in the distance. The park was considered to be 'among the finest in

Ireland' by Arthur Young in 1776, and today, save for the odd brightly-dressed golfer, he would have little difficulty in recognising the undulating landscape which he described as 'a vast lawn, which waves over gentle hills'.[5]

More astonishing to Young would be the presence of a new 147-bedroom hotel and leisure centre behind a belt of mature cedar trees to the east of the main house. It is indeed fortuitous that this natural screen existed, and only the closest scrutiny betrays this complex from a distance. On the north side of the house much of this new construction is shielded too, behind a long section of low garden walling.

The main entrance to the hotel on the north side is through a small hexagonal pavilion, leading into an airy, bright lobby with an atrium. The external wall of the great eighteenth-century mansion forms one inner wall of the lobby. Above is a small glass roof, making it abundantly clear that the new building abuts the old; at no point is it possible to confuse the two structures. Just off from the lobby is a sight guaranteed to enrage purists: mounted on a wall is the ceiling rose from one of the original rooms, which was removed when a glass elevator was installed. The lobby is therefore a place where people have to confront the issue of how old buildings are modified to suit modern needs. Elevators are an essential part of large buildings today, particularly hotels, and if they can be fitted with a degree of sympathy with existing schemes they should be accepted. After all it is not hard to find examples of houses that were altered in previous centuries to accommodate new technologies.

The remainder of the hotel follows a long, glazed passage, which offers views onto the gardens to the south. After passing the restaurant, one reaches the new three-storey bedroom wing. The furnishings are all contemporary and the décor makes no attempt to exploit Carton's history; wisely, this function is left for the areas in the original house. This mix of the old and new, the historic and contemporary, produces an identity that is in many ways wholly representative of the new Ireland. The big house, for so long the symbol of a troubled past, is now accepted as a significant part of Ireland's heritage. This balance is perhaps best understood by how Carton appears on the one hand an exclusive resort, and yet it is very inclusive, open to the public, with local people free to wander the grounds and enter the hotel.

This transformation of Carton has cost in the order of €120 million, all of it funded through private enterprise. The most contentious aspect of this has been the 60-acre Leinster Wood housing development with 140 new homes. Stretching for half a mile along the north-east perimeter of the demesne, the houses lie within a belt of mature trees, and cannot be seen from the main house; there are three basic styles, some are detached, and some semi-detached, and the exteriors are partially clad in timber.

People who visit Carton today hold opposing views as to its changed appearance, and there are a good many gainsayers who evince a surprising degree of hostility to this transformation. But what they cannot deny is that within a very short space of time decades of decline have been dramatically reversed. The house and grounds have been restored, and above all the estate is a place that is alive, active, and filled with people enjoying themselves. Those who have strong reservations have to ask themselves how else might this renaissance have been effected? Carton was never going to be rescued by the state, nor by a local authority, nor by some other kind of institution. Even if such a body had acquired the house and estate it is doubtful that they would have had anything like the funds to reverse the decline so comprehensively: more likely a kind of holding operation would have ensued, that insidious state of affairs known as managed decline. It might be argued that for a number of years the Mallaghans were doing little more than this until opportunities allowed them to implement their plan for a commercially viable estate.

But this is, of course, not the end of the story, for Carton has to weather the financial storms precipitated by the banking collapse of 2008; this crisis is every bit as ferocious as that faced by the FitzGeralds in the early twentieth century. However, the difference between Carton in 2013 and Carton in 1913 lies with the depth of commercial expertise that has driven through this enormous recovery project; the FitzGeralds and their advisors lacked the necessary business acumen to overcome the economic complexities of the estate. Thus there is good reason to suppose that Carton will ride out the challenges ahead; if so, this will be due to a mixture of prudent planning, a sound and flexible business model, as well as good fortune (this last signally deserted the FitzGeralds in their time of difficulty). Hotel, golf course, headquarters for the Golfing Union of Ireland, international sports training ground – it is this diversity that should help Carton through difficult times, together with the real estate development in Leinster Wood.

The recovery of Carton has to be applauded as both enlightened and pragmatic. The house and desmesne remain intact, and the family have not closed the gates to the wider public. The Mallaghans may not typify the family Simon Jenkins had in mind when he raised the question 'which lasts longer, a house or a family?' but their presence has undoubtedly secured the future of Carton as a place of significant public value. Country estates have always functioned as places of leisure and work, and today Carton may operate in very different ways to before, but in this era (as in previous times) if estates are not economically sustainable they simply have no future. This story of revival and adaptation has something to teach everybody about how a traditional estate can be made secure and open to all.

NOTES

1   Simon Jenkins, *England's Thousand Best Houses* (London, 2003), p. 536.

2   As so memorably described in the early volumes of his diaries, see James Lees-Milne, *Ancestral Voices 1942–43* (London, 1975); *Prophesying Peace 1944–45* (London, 1977); *Caves of Ice 1946–47* (London, 1983); and *Midway on the Waves 1948–49* (London, 1985).

3   Much of what follows is taken from, Christopher Ridgway, 'Triumph or travesty? Carton House, Co Kildare', *Country Life*, cciii:7 (18 Feb. 2009), pp 42–7.

4   This inventory remains in private possession.

5   Arthur Young, *A Tour in Ireland*, ed. A. W. Hutton (2 vols, London, 1780, 2nd ed.), i, pp 18–9.

Index